PAUL CARDINAL CULLEN
AND THE SHAPING OF
MODERN IRISH CATHOLICISM

By the same author:

The Protestant Crusade in Ireland, 1800-70 (1978)
Souperism: Myth or Reality? (1971)
The Idea of the Victorian Church (1968)

DESMOND BOWEN

PAUL CARDINAL CULLEN AND THE SHAPING OF MODERN IRISH CATHOLICISM

GILL AND MACMILLAN

WILFRID LAURIER UNIVERSITY PRESS

8806

First published 1983 by
Gill and Macmillan Ltd
Goldenbridge
Dublin 8
with associated companies in
Auckland, Dallas, Delhi, Hong Kong,
Johannesburg, Lagos, London, Manzini,
Melbourne, Nairobi, New York, Singapore,
Tokyo, Washington

© Desmond Bowen 1983

7171 0889 9

Published in Canada by Wilfrid Laurier University Press
Waterloo, Ontario, Canada, N2L 3C5

ISBN (WLUP) 0-88920-136-6

Canadian Cataloguing in Publication Data

Bowen, Desmond, 1921-
    Paul, Cardinal, Cullen and the shaping of modern Irish Catholicism.

Bibliography: p. 300
Includes index.
ISBN 0-88920-136-6

1. Cullen, Paul, 1803-1878.   2. Cardinals — Ireland — Biography.   3. Catholic
Church — Ireland — History — 19th century.   I. Title.

BX4705.C84B68   282'.092'4   C83-098677-4

Origination by Print Prep Limited, Dublin
Printed in Great Britain by
Biddles Ltd., Guildford and King's Lynn

Contents

Contents, continued

Preface

Paul Cullen (1803-78) was the most important figure in Irish history between the death of Daniel O'Connell and the coming to power of Charles Stewart Parnell. Yet this powerful churchman, who was so influential in the shaping of Irish affairs, has never been honoured with a major biography. Nor has he, generally, been well treated by historians. The brilliant scholar, 'the Eagle of the Schools' in Rome whose intelligence was never underestimated by contemporaries, has been dismissed as an industrious mediocrity'. (Akenson, *Educ. Exper.*, 254) The tough-minded indefatigable political tactician has been interpreted as a world-denying spiritual leader who shrank from the 'gross world of politics'. (Lyons, *Ireland*, 108) The Counter-Reformation zealot for whom the Council of Trent was still a living reality has been considered as a Catholic prelate for whom, at times, 'Protestantism raised no difficulty'. (Steele, *Cullen*, 259) The most devoted of papal servants has been accused of 'preferring the . . . principles of Irish nationalism to the opinions of his friend Pius IX'. (McCaffrey, *Poets, Priests*, 453) On the other hand, the stubborn opponent whom Lord Clarendon called 'the bitter and uncompromising enemy of the English government in Ireland' (Bodl., C143: 4 June 1866) has been viewed by generations of nationalist historians as a 'Castle Catholic'.

Most of the distortions in the various scholarly portraits of Cullen reflect the domination of Irish historical writing by those who serve in one form or another the nationalist canon of history. Even the shrewd and knowledgeable Professor Emmet Larkin in his *Making of the Roman Catholic Church in Ireland, 1850-1860* has seemed hesitant to identify Cullen's Irish mission in other than traditional nationalist terms. The passionate Ultramontanist who came to Ireland as papal delegate at mid-century and became the first Irish cardinal in 1866 has been viewed chiefly as the prelate who enabled the 'emergent modern Irish Church' to be 'consolidated' by his encouraging the priests to establish order among themselves and thus to increase 'their own political power and influence'. (Larkin, *Making*, 488-9)

This study argues that the best assessment of Cullen was that presented by most of his contemporaries, who were far removed ideologically from the concerns of Irish nationalism. Monsignor George Talbot, who was chamberlain and intimate of Pope Pius IX when Cullen was created cardinal, described him as 'a thorough Roman in every sense of the word', and in the eyes of most Protestants, as the obituary assessments at the end of this work reveal, Cullen was an 'Ultramontane of the most uncompromising type', 'a Roman of the Romans'. In Paul Cullen's total oblation to the militant mission of the popes that he served lies the secret to the mind and accomplishments of this most reserved and complex of men. Whatever the contribution made by Cullen to the development of Irish nationalism, it was incidental to what he sought to accomplish, for there is much truth in the judgment that this man who put his stamp so indelibly on the Irish Catholic Church had 'no political theories, only religious and ecclesiastical ones'. (Norman, *Cath. Ch.*, 10)

This study of the mind of Paul Cullen is essentially an exercise in intellectual and ecclesiastical history rather than a biography in the ordinary sense. It was written consequent to research in the archives of the Irish College and Propaganda Fide in Rome, where I had sought to establish the extent of Rome's concern over the Protestant proselytising campaign in the south and west of Ireland in the immediate post-famine period. This was the time that Cullen came to Ireland to revive the divided and disheartened Catholic Church which seemed unable to resist the Protestant threat to the religious faith and traditional way of life of Ireland's majority people. As I read thousands of letters in Cullen's vast correspondence I found myself fascinated not only by the man himself but also by the problem he faced – the bringing of the Ultramontane expression of the Roman Catholic faith to Irish Catholics who were far from enthusiastic in their welcoming of it. What follows is an appreciation of both Paul Cullen as a churchman and the system of thought that gave him, in the words of his enemy Charles Gavan Duffy, his 'decisive will and . . . overwhelming sense of authority'. (Duffy, *Life*, II, 36)

It is probable that one of the reasons why a full-scale study of Paul Cullen has not appeared is that a biography of the man, in the ordinary sense, would be difficult to produce. Throughout his life Cullen was close, guarded, and remote, a man who revealed almost nothing of himself even to those who considered themselves his intimates. Laurence Forde, Cullen's devoted secretary who administered many of the Dublin archdiocesan affairs for him, complained to Dom Bernard Smith, one of Cullen's friends, that 'Neither for purposes of counsel or co-operation will he avail himself of the services of others.' (BS: 17 Feb. 1858 or 1859) Cullen's intensely private nature was commented on by many of his contemporaries, and it is unlikely that even his nephew Patrick Francis Moran, his theological confidant Edmund O'Reilly, or his disciple Tobias Kirby knew much about him in human terms. Paul Cullen from an early age deliberately hid himself behind an ecclesiastical and religious *persona*, and it is impossible to identify him in any way apart from the role he committed himself to playing in the Church.

Even in his service to the Church Cullen is a complex individual. In the refectory of the Irish College in Rome hangs one of his portraits, showing him in full cardinal's regalia, gazing forward with strange eyes which seem to be focusing not so much on differing objects as on differing distances. The artist caught something of the essential Cullen in this portrayal, for if ever an ecclesiastic approached the world and its problems with almost schizophrenic detachment, it was Cullen. However much his one eye might watch immediate developments with canny shrewdness, the other never lost its focus on a more distant perspective which assured him of final victory. It is this duality of vision, combined with his secretive nature, that makes Cullen so difficult to understand. What he reveals of himself in pastorals and correspondence, and in his political manoeuvrings in

Rome and in Ireland, indicates that he was a cautious, suspicious and usually shrewd product of the Roman school of diplomacy. At the same time his writings and actions reveal the fervent and stubborn faith that inspired his passionate concern to bring enlightenment to the misguided and abysmally ignorant Catholics of Ireland by leading them to accept what should be an essential tenet of their belief — the infallible authority of the Supreme Pontiff. The essence of Paul Cullen is that he served the Ultramontane authority of the papacy of his age with the fervour of a Charles Borromeo or a Peter Canisius of the Counter-Reformation era. The real mystery of Paul Cullen lies not so much in the complexity and deviousness of mind that his ecclesiastical and political enemies so often referred to, but in his essential and abiding simplicity of faith. This was the source of his great strength.

The study divides naturally into two almost identical periods of time. The first is the twenty-eight years that Cullen was in Rome as seminarian, professor, Rector of the Irish College and Roman agent of the Irish hierarchy. This was the period when the papacy under Pius VII, Leo XII, Pius VIII, Gregory XVI and Pius IX developed its Ultramontane ideology. It was also the age when Daniel O'Connell's movements of constitutional protest began to change the political aspirations of Irish Catholics. During this Roman period Cullen began to find an accommodation between the demands of Rome's new triumphal conservatism and Catholic Ireland's burgeoning religious nationalism. By the time he came to Ireland at mid-century he was well prepared to carry out the Ultramontane mission which had been delegated to him.

The second part of the study records the progress of Cullen's exercise in ecclesiastical and cultural imperialism in Ireland, an exercise which was so successful that Francis Mahony, the 'Father Prout' of English journalistic fame, could speak of the 'Cullenisation' of Catholic Ireland. It is an account of how this single-minded prelate who never doubted or developed the Ultramontane expression of the faith which he had embraced in his youth put a stamp on Irish Catholicism which has never been lost. When a churchman like Cullen with spiritual zeal and great fixity of aim has reasonable health, a relatively long life, and works in a time of radical social change he can accomplish much — even the 'Cullenisation' of Catholic Ireland.

Cullen's influence in Irish Catholicism has been much modified by historical events since his day, of course, or this study might never have appeared. In his day a maverick Protestant scholar like William Maziere Brady could be admitted to work in Roman archives, but only on the assumptions that his research would be used in the cause of Catholic polemics and that there was a good likelihood of his conversion to the true faith. Since that time the spirit of ecumenism has ensured that the Protestant heretic of Cullen's age would be recognised as one of the 'separated brethren'. It is only because of this development in charity that I was able to work for four successive summers in Roman archives under no sense of obligation but to seek to understand and appreciate Paul Cullen and his mission in terms of historical truth.

The work that follows is largely based on the letters and correspondence of Paul Cullen. I am very grateful for the help given to me when I was examining this material by Monsignor Eamon Marron, the Rector of the Irish College, Rome, the Rev. John Silke, his very conscientious archivist, and my fellow-researcher, the Rev. Pádraig Ó Tuarisg of St Jarlath's College, Tuam. I am also appreciative of the kindness of the superiors of the monastery of St Paul's Without the Walls, Rome, who not only allowed me to use their archives, but followed the example of the Irish College authorities, and those of Propaganda Fide, in allowing my wife to work with me as a research assistant. For all the help given to me in the latter institution I am also grateful. My thanks are also extended to the librarians of the British Museum (now the British Library), the Public Record Offices in Dublin and Belfast, the National Library in Dublin, and the several university libraries where I have worked. I must express my deep sense of obligation to the Social Science and Humanities Research Council of Canada for providing research assistance for the production of this work.

Finally my gratitude is extended to my wife and fellow-scholar, Jean, who patiently laboured with me throughout those hot Roman summer days in our shaded room in the Irish College, laboriously deciphering the vagaries of nineteenth-century handwriting about long-forgotten theological disputes, while outside our window happy seminarians enjoyed the garden swimming pool.

Desmond Bowen,
Institute of Irish Studies,
Queen's University, Belfast.
1982

ACKNOWLEDGMENT

This book has been published with the help of a grant from the Social Science and Humanities Research Council of Canada.

I
The Collegian

1. *The Cullens of Prospect*

The two great recurrent issues of contention between Ireland's warring Catholic and Protestant peoples have been those of land and religion. During the early years of the eighteenth century in particular the majority people deeply resented the confiscations which had followed the Williamite and earlier wars and had placed ancestral lands in the hands of those who supported the Protestant Established Church. The penal laws provided an incentive for Catholics to abjure their church and become part of the establishment, and social and ecclesiastical rivalry was sharp in the south-eastern counties of Leinster. After the waning of the Jacobite cause in the 1760s, however, Protestant toleration of their Catholic neighbours increased. The penal laws were increasingly ignored, and many Protestants helped their Catholic neighbours to buy land. In the rich lands of the wide lowland extending from Athy to Graiguenamanagh, along the banks of the River Barrow, more and more Catholics were becoming 'strong farmers' with rising expectations of emancipation from their position of social subservience.

One of these strong Catholic farmers was Hugh Cullen, descendant of a family which had been strongly Jacobite in sympathy. Born about 1760 near Leighlinbridge, Co. Carlow, he married the daughter of another rising farmer, Mary Maher, and she became the mother of ten children. By a previous marriage Hugh Cullen had had six children. Shortly before the rising of 1798 he bought a property of more than seventy-six acres called Prospect in the parish of Narraghmore, a little to the north of the Quaker settlement at Ballitore. His brother Michael became the parish priest the year after Prospect was purchased. Mary Cullen's brother James was parish priest of nearby Carlow-Graigue. In spite of the rising of '98, the Cullen/Maher extended family flourished as its members became extensive land-owners in Counties Carlow, Kildare and Meath, as were their relatives the Morans, the Brennans and the Lalors. One member of the latter family farmed over a thousand acres.

As the power of families like the Cullens and Mahers increased a new kind of economic and political rivalry began between the emergent Catholic yeoman class that they represented and their well-off Protestant neighbours. (Cullen, *Cult. Basis*, 13-15) The Fenian John Devoy in his *Recollections of an Irish Rebel* stated that the Cullen clan had the reputation of being the 'chief land-grabbers' in Counties Carlow and Kildare and Queen's County. With many of their neighbours the Cullen offspring also began to move into business, and two of Hugh's sons, Michael and Thomas, prospered in the cattle trade, becoming wealthy and socially prominent Liverpool merchants. The Cullens and Mahers made sure that their numerous offspring were well educated — Hugh had forty-five grandchildren, and his brother Garrett had forty — and many of them entered the religious life to make them 'truly a Levitical family'. (PM, I, 339) Three members of this extended family (Patrick Francis Moran, who became Cardinal Archbishop of Sydney; Michael Verdon, who became Bishop of Dunedin in New Zealand; and Paul Cullen, who became Archbishop of Armagh and Ireland's first cardinal) were all distinguished ecclesiastics. The latter prelate was to have an influence in the development of the Roman Catholic Church in Ireland, and in the shaping of Irish society, that would be difficult to overestimate.

Paul Cullen was born at Prospect on 29 April 1803, just three months before the Protestant rebel Robert Emmet launched his sad rising. Like other members of his family, Cullen would have shown little sympathy for the nationalism that lingered in the area around his birthplace long after the Emmet fiasco and was to persuade Daniel O'Connell to hold one of his monster meetings near Prospect at Mullaghmast. During '98 his father, Hugh, was imprisoned for a time and returned home to discover his fine seven-hundred-acre farm destroyed by either the Orange Tyrone militia or the local Catholic yeomanry. His younger brother Paul and two other relatives had been shot at Leighlinbridge. Mary Leadbeater, in her account of the intervention of the Ballitore Quakers on behalf of their Catholic neighbours, records how Hugh's life was spared when one of the Quakers persuaded the Protestant Archbishop of Cashel and the government that Hugh's large family was remarkable for its peacefulness and that Hugh Cullen himself was loyal to the crown.*

His loyalty would not have been unusual. The whole of the Narraghmore parish experienced shocking outrages committed by the insurgents. The parish clerk was murdered, and so was a Catholic priest who denounced the United Irish movement from the pulpit. In spite of the Quaker testimony about Hugh Cullen's loyalty, however, oral tradition in the family ensured that he was pictured as both a deserter from the yeomanry and a leader of the '98 rising. Yet this 'ardent patriot', pardoned by the usually vindictive government of the time through the intervention of Protestant neighbours, did, once he had regained his fortune, entertain 'the greatest hatred of all these secret combinations having for their end an appeal to arms for the attainment of political goals'. (PM, I, 346) This would be an understandable sentiment, for, as was indicated in one report on unrest in Ireland sent to Rome, influential Catholics had little sympathy for the 'misguided zealots' of the age. (PFS, XVII, 94: 29 Dec. 1791) From the end of the eighteenth century, as these men rebuilt their prosperous farms and grazing lands, they went out of their way to assure the authorities that they wanted to promote social tranquillity as men of good sense and moderation. Their expectations were rising, and what they desired more than anything else was to preserve in peace their successful economic and social competition with the Protestant landed gentry.

The Quaker action which had saved Hugh Cullen's life was not forgotten, and the family developed a friendship

---

* For intercession of influential people on Hugh Cullen's behalf see SPO, 620/41/83. Of two other Cullens in the Rebellion Papers, one was a rebel priest and one an informer.

with members of the Ballitore colony. Young Paul Cullen was sent to the Quaker school with other members of his family and remained there for four years. The education in this Protestant school, where Edmund Burke had received the rudiments of his training, was considered to be the best available in the community. Eight other members of the wealthy Cullen/Maher families attended it.

When Cullen was thirteen years old he entered Carlow College as a boarder. Five years after the opening of the college in 1793 a bloody battle had taken place in Carlow as part of the '98 rising. Some of the insurgents had escaped government troops by fleeing through the college grounds, and during the early years of the nineteenth century visitors like the Comte de Montalembert commented on the nationalist sentiments expressed by members of the college. These feelings were kept in check, however, by the president of the college, Andrew Fitzgerald, OP, whose training in continental seminaries had instilled in him a strong respect for constitutional authority.

Cullen's natural gifts were recognised by the professors in the college, two of whom, William Clowry and Edward Nolan, were his kinsmen. The latter was to succeed the celebrated James Doyle as Bishop of Kildare and Leighlin in 1834. Two other influential members of the staff with whom Cullen established good relations were William Kinsella, who became Bishop of Ossory in the year of Catholic Emancipation, and Michael Slattery, a graduate of Trinity College, Dublin, who in 1833 became President of Maynooth and then Archbishop of Cashel. Slattery was always a loyal supporter of Cullen. The most important member of the college in Cullen's time was James Doyle, who was consecrated Bishop of Kildare and Leighlin in 1819.

Doyle, who came from the same conservative farming stock as Cullen, had as a boy witnessed the carnage of the battle of New Ross during '98, and had as a result never lost his abiding horror of revolutionary violence. He had no use for secret societies, nor for any kind of sectarianism, and urged Catholics to have love even for Orangemen. Because he had Protestant relatives he had no great fear of those who supported Ireland's minority religion and culture, and in 1824 he seriously proposed a union of the Roman Catholic Church with the Church of Ireland. On the other hand, he strongly supported the anti-tithe campaign, and as a result of his example the otherwise peaceable Carlow College president, Andrew Fitzgerald, was imprisoned in 1832 for refusing to pay tithes.

One can only conjecture what impression James Doyle made upon Cullen directly, but James Maher, uncle and godfather of Cullen, who was vicar-general to the bishop in his last years, did influence his nephew, sharing with him often what was a strongly biased version of Doyle's theological and ecclesiological ideas. Maher was only ten years older than his nephew and preceded him as a student to both Carlow College and Rome. After his return to Ireland he continued to keep Cullen abreast of Irish affairs. Maher unfortunately had none of Doyle's ecumenical sympathies and throughout his life was considered a strong nationalist priest, 'without discretion, and full of ill-directed, ill-digested zeal'. (C: 29 Apr. 1834) It was Maher's unpopularity with so many of the clergy which kept Cullen from being appointed coadjutor bishop with right of succession to Doyle. Cullen has left no record of what he thought of Doyle apart from a reference to his gratitude for having known 'the good works of so great a man'. (Fitzpatrick, *Doyle*, II, 145)

2. *The Propaganda College Years*
On the recommendation of James Maher, Cullen's family decided that he should follow his strong-minded uncle to Rome. Maher was just completing his theological studies when Cullen arrived in Rome early in 1821 to enter Propaganda College. In his earliest correspondence with his family Cullen referred occasionally to Irish affairs: in one letter to his father he spoke warmly of the visit of George IV to Ireland:

> I am sure his majesty was more delighted with the reception amongst the Irish than he was troubled for the death of his queen. The distressed state of the country which you mentioned in your letter must have excited his compassion, and I hope it will induce him to redress all the grievances of the Catholics and grant them Emancipation.
>
> (PM, I, 90)

In the following spring he praised English benevolence during the famine winter of 1821-22 and hoped that 'the sons of Erin' would 'not forget their benefactors, but will continually show themselves attached and grateful to the English crown'. (PM, I, 105)

As might be expected, however, Cullen soon forgot about the affairs of home because of the exciting atmosphere of the Rome he encountered during the last two years of the pontificate of Pius VII. The city had become the centre of romantic attraction to European conservatives. Pius was revered as the pope who had stood up to Napoleon, and in conservative eyes he became a symbol of all that was worth preserving in the uneasy new world of the early nineteenth century. The Congress of Vienna had restored the states of the Church, and they were being reorganised by the able papal Secretary of State, Cardinal Ercole Consalvi. The pope also was making valuable additions to the Vatican Library and establishing new chairs in the Roman College. Scholars were flocking to the Eternal City, filling its colleges, its libraries, its galleries and museums. European royalty and aristocracy came to visit, especially during the great religious holidays.

The young man from rural Leinster was fascinated by the vibrant intellectual and political life of the city and by its great baroque churches filled with the spirit of the Counter-Reformation. During the Holy Week and Corpus Christi observances of 1821 Cullen was transported by the grandeur of the occasions. He rejoiced in the 'richness of the dress worn by His Holiness and bodyguard, richer than any sovereign's guard in Europe'. (PM, I, 87) Two years later when Pius VII appeared on a gallery in front of St Peter's on Easter Sunday to give one of his final blessings to the huge throng, Cullen marvelled at the sight of 6000 German troops kneeling in reverence alongside Roman soldiers. The pope truly was the universal pontiff, his authority reverenced by an enthusiastic multitude who came to partake in the ever-increasing displays of triumphalism. When Pius died in 1823, to be succeeded by Leo XII, Cullen was so carried away by his description of the coronation of the new pope, in a letter to his sister Margaret, that he felt it necessary to apologise for his enthusiasm: 'These circumstances will be little interesting to you.' (PM, I, 123)

The 'circumstances' were certainly interesting to the young seminarian, however, and they were to give him a system of religious and ecclesiastical beliefs that were to remain with him all his life. The new pope worked closely with reactionary curial officials, the *zelanti*, to undo liberal policies initiated by Cardinal Consalvi. It was Leo XII who nurtured in the government of Rome and the papal states the autocratic spirit that ensured the domination of society by the nobility and the clergy, the tightening of press censorship, the taking of property from the Jews and their confinement to the ghetto. In his first encyclical, *Ubi primum*, he warned the bishops against both crypto-Jacobin ideas which could lead to religious indifference or atheism, and Bible societies which threatened the peace of mind of the faithful. Leo XII was a thorough-going conservative, religiously, ecclesiastically and politically, and all he pronounced and did was approved by Cullen.

In every possible way Leo XII proclaimed the *magisterium* of the Holy See with great confidence. He moved from the Quirinal to take up residence in the Vatican, and from there he directed a triumphal rebuilding of papal Rome. The Vatican Library was rebuilt, and excavations were continued at the Forum, the Palatine Hill and the Coliseum. Gardens were improved throughout the city, and a world-wide appeal for the rebuilding of St Paul's Without the Walls, recently destroyed by fire, brought much wealth to the papal coffers. When the first jubilee since 1775 was proclaimed in 1825 Leo described it as an affirmation of the revival of the one true faith in Rome, in Italy and throughout the world. Among the pilgrims who came to the Eternal City were King Francis I of Naples, the Infante of Spain and the Queen-dowager of Sardinia. Leo had already sent forces to Ravenna to crush the Carbonari, the liberal revolutionaries who sought Italian unity, and in the year of the jubilee he proclaimed a bull denouncing all such secret societies, including the Freemasons.

Although he was still a student, Cullen seems to have caught the attention of some members of the curia almost immediately, for he told his family proudly how he was invited to take a minor part in the pope's first mass after his coronation. Recognising the power of his intelligence, the Vatican authorities suggested that he keep them informed about church affairs in Ireland. He had some of the pastorals of James Doyle translated into Italian for their benefit, and he also arranged for James Maher to keep him well supplied with Irish publications of a similar nature. He especially requested Doyle's *Letters on the State of Ireland*, in which a warning was made that the continuation of social injustice would eventually lead to another rising of the oppressed people.

It seems clear that Cullen maintained that horror of revolution on which he had been nurtured in his home. In 1826 he wrote Maher to describe the public execution of two Carbonari, one of whom was an ecclesiastic, and how they died 'in the most frightful manner possible'. He was not describing their physical sufferings before their beheading, but their attempt to preach from the scaffold 'all the sophisms which have ever been argued by the late atheists and deists of France'. Cullen was clearly shocked by this display of spiritual intransigence, and he told his uncle that the 'height of impiety' was reached when the comrades of these Carbonari 'ruffians' covered their graves with garlands of flowers in memory of these 'immortal heroes'. (PM, I, 13)

Although the political excitement in Ireland was now great, owing to the rapid progress of the campaign for Catholic Emancipation, Cullen's focus of interest was still the Roman ecclesiastical world. James Maher tried to keep him up to date with Irish affairs, but when Cullen wrote on 17 January 1828 to his brother Thomas in Liverpool it was to exult over conversions of Englishmen who had come to the Eternal City. These men had been influenced by the new breed of Ultramontane priests who were coming out of the Roman colleges to 'show the Protestants what a difference there is between our Faith and theirs, and thus become the instrument of their conversion'. Nowhere now were to be found 'Bible-men or other saints of that description to disturb the people's minds or to persecute them for their religious opinions'. (PM, I, 138) Cullen's chief concern at this time was that a similar religious dispensation could be established in Ireland, where the Protestant 'Second Reformation' successes had caught Roman attention.

On the very eve of Catholic Emancipation Cullen turned his full attention from Roman to Irish affairs — at the suggestion of Leo XII himself. By the time that Cullen defended his doctoral dissertation, which covered an immense field of theology and ecclesiastical history (Cullen, *Disput.*) the brilliance of this 'Eagle of the Schools' was widely recognised in Rome. The public defence of his 224 theses was attended by Leo XII, the Cardinal Prefect of Propaganda, the future Gregory XVI, and nine other cardinals. Among the students who attended was Vincenzo Pecci, who was destined to become Pope Leo XIII in 1878, the year of Cullen's death. The defence was masterly, and Cullen proudly told his father that 'Your son was the first among Irishmen who attempted to show his skill in theology in the presence of the Vicar of Christ.'

When the pope congratulated Cullen on his performance — to the utter amazement of the young seminarian who was still in minor orders — the pontiff immediately drew him into his confidence about Irish affairs. He told Cullen that the British government was trying to 'treat of a concord' with the Vatican, but that he was refusing to consider any agreement until the government agreed to Catholic Emancipation. When he reported this exchange to his father on 25 January 1829 Cullen admitted that he had 'been almost reduced to doubt what I heard with my own ears'. His ears had not deceived him, however. From this time forward Cullen was regularly informed about Irish affairs by those who advised the pope on these matters, and his own counsel was frequently sought. In his turn Cullen began a study in depth of Irish developments of which he then knew comparatively little.

His naivety about what was going on in Ireland is revealed at the end of the long letter to his father in which he gave an account of his academic triumph and his unexpected receiving of papal diplomatic confidences. He reported comparative peace in Italy, and then said:

No talk of war except . . . the little that is reported of our Irish agitators to whom I heartily wish success. I hope Edward, William, James, Garrett shall be one day stout agitators also, but so as at the same time to be desirous to maintain and obey the laws of the land. (PM, I, 142)

If he had known the Carbonari form of agitation that the Catholic Emancipation campaign tolerated at its height, he would not have been so naive in his wish that his young relatives would join in the prevailing social unrest. In 1829, as throughout the rest of his life, Cullen was governed by an abiding aversion to revolution or anything that seemed to approach it. His conservative sensibilities, typical of the Irish Catholic strong-farmer class, had been strongly reinforced by Roman anxiety over liberalism in all its forms. Although he was to admire much in O'Connell's type of agitation, he was never fully at ease with its Irish practitioners.

There is some confusion over the date of Cullen's ordination, which was either in 1829 or 1830. Almost immediately, however, he was appointed to the chairs of Greek and Oriental Languages in the College of Propaganda. During this period Europe was rocked by the revolutions of 1830, and once more Cullen told his family of his fear of liberalism and the savagery it could unleash:

> As yet everything is quiet in Italy but . . . a little spark would be capable of exciting a great incendium and the first to suffer would be the ecclesiastics, as there is a party in Italy united with the French liberals, whose only aim is to put an end to all sorts of religion and above all things to put down the Catholics and trample on them. . . . As for me, I am very little afraid of finding myself in the midst of tumults and danger, but I would be sorry such things should occur on account of the ruin which they occasion to religion. (PM, I, 163)

Five months later, in March 1831, Cullen was telling his brother Thomas about the hatred for the papacy shown by the revolutionaries in the north of Italy, who were kept from pressing their cause only by the power of Austria:

> The persons who have declared themselves against the Pope are not numerous: they are in about the same proportion to the entire population as the Orangemen in Ireland, but as they are wicked desperate fellows and many of them good soldiers who served under Bonaparte, they have succeeded in getting the upper hand and suppressing the sentiments of the people. (PM, I, 174)

He ended this report on the violence in Italy with the hope that O'Connell would not drive his agitation too far, as 'anything should be preferred to a civil war'.

The agitation in Lombardy spilled over into the papal states as the revolutionaries tried to take advantage of a succession problem in papal government. Cullen's friend and patron Leo XII died in 1829, and his successor Pius VIII held the throne of Peter for only eighteen months. Although he continued some of his predecessor's conservative policies, issuing encyclicals condemning secret societies, Freemasonry and religious indifference, he was liberal enough to ease some of the harsher aspects of papal government in the states of the Church. Cullen rejoiced that Catholic Emancipation in Britain and Ireland was carried at this time, but in general, like most Roman conservatives, he was worried by the conciliatory moves of Pius and was doubtful whether they would do anything to postpone the threatened revolution. Cullen was not surprised when the death of Pius encouraged a major rising in the papal states which was only put down by an army of 20,000 Austrians.

Cullen had no worries about the conservatism of the successor of Pius VIII. This was his old friend and patron, Cardinal Bartolomeo Cappellari, who as Prefect of Propaganda had made Cullen Professor of Scripture in Propaganda College. The new pope took the title Gregory XVI. An extremely ascetic individual, he belonged to the Camaldolese order and was responsible for the revival of traditional Augustinian and Thomistic theology in the Roman schools. He was considered by everyone to be an unqualified Ultramontanist from the time he published in 1799 his often reprinted *Triumph of the Holy See and the Church against the Assaults of Innovators*.

For ten years before his elevation to the papal throne Gregory had worked in the Congregation for the Propaganda of the Faith, serving for the last five years as Cardinal Prefect. Included in the countries whose churches were under the authority of Propaganda were Britain and Ireland, and Gregory had often consulted Cullen about Irish affairs. It was partly on the latter's advice that new regulations to govern episcopal nominations in Ireland were issued in 1829. Cullen told his uncle James Maher that before his election he had 'a thousand reasons' to be grateful to the new pope, and that Gregory's kindness to him showed no sign of diminishing since his elevation. Unlike his predecessor, who 'was always expressing fears and doubts about the Irish Church', Gregory XVI had persuaded Cullen that he had not only a great knowledge of Irish affairs but also 'a great affection for Ireland'. (PM, I, 183)

The friendship of Gregory XVI encouraged Cullen to display more openly his political conservatism. In letter after letter to his family he expressed his growing antagonism to liberalism in every form, and his abiding fear of social and political violence. He was aghast that in some towns in the papal states men were hanged for their loyalty to the pope, and he blamed the outrages on the international dissidence of the age: 'The French liberals, or at least that part of them which is favourable to Jacobinism is at the bottom of all this.' (PM, I, 186) He assured his parents that if the worst happened and the pope's person was seized in a general uprising, he would be safe himself because he was 'an English subject'. At this time, when revolt was spreading in Bologna and the Romagna, he was eager to return to Ireland, but the illness of the Rector of the Irish College led to Cullen's appointment to that office. He expected to hold the post for only a short time.

Gregory XVI was much less timid than Cullen. He used mercenary troops against the insurgents, and they established a reputation for brutality as they fought alongside the Austrians to halt the spread of the liberal unrest. Although the pope's own life was simple, if not ascetic, he delighted in a great display of papal triumphalism. Papal ceremonies assumed unprecedented magnificence, and audiences were conducted with more than royal protocol. The building programme of Leo XII was continued, more ancient churches and monuments were restored, new palaces were built, and the Vatican was further enriched with valuable collections of art. At the same time the people of Rome were denied street lighting, and the pope refused to allow the coming of the railway to the city. Gregory XVI was a thoroughgoing reactionary, but his policies were implemented only because of the presence of French and Austrian as well as papal troops. When the foreign garrisons were withdrawn in 1838 revolutionary activity became endemic in the papal states and was always a threat in Rome itself.

The first insurgent liberal organisation that the papacy had encountered after the restoration in 1815 was the Carbonari. Its members were divided into cells, controlled by strict discipline from its headquarters at Ascoli, and its campaign was well directed by the time of Gregory XVI. Its hierarchy accepted a strongly anti-religious ideology, developed from Freemasonry and the anti-Roman Jansenism of the late eighteenth century. It had supporters even among papal officials and police, and by the 1830s it was openly declaring that the chief opposition to a movement for Italian nationalism would come from the reactionary papal church.

Even more threatening from the papal standpoint was the Young Italy movement founded by Giuseppe Mazzini in 1831. It was free of the cabalistic rites and organisational weaknesses that had characterised the Carbonari, and it called for a new Italy that was to be unified and republican. Through education the new movement was out to establish among the people ideas of the natural rights of man, liberty, equality, brotherhood, and the need for national identity. It accepted the need for violence to gain its ends. As for religion, Mazzini admitted some reverence for 'the admirable man Jesus', but in no sense did he consider himself or his followers to be sons of the Roman Catholic Church. Rome was the obvious capital of the unified Italy that Mazzini and his followers wanted, and it was accepted that the papacy would not surrender the papal states or the Eternal City without an armed struggle.

Within papal circles there was much discussion of the ideology of the new movement led by Mazzini. The conservatives surrounding Gregory XVI — now including Paul Cullen — were convinced that the essential spirit of Young Italy was that of Freemasonry. Although Mazzini himself was no lover of Masonic ritual, it was nevertheless widely believed that he, together with his lieutenants, Giuseppe Garibaldi and Francesco Crispi, was a militant Mason. Here was to be found the true spirit behind the confused face of Gallicanism, Jansenism and radical liberalism which the movement presented to the world. The real attack was not directed against the temporal power of the papacy but against the revealed truths of Christ's religion, including the sacred authority of the Holy See. The power behind every manifestation of the spirit of Italian nationalism was Freemasonry.

However, not all European Catholics agreed with the Roman conservatives when it came to treating with the spirit of European liberalism. The movement showed no signs of fading away, and in France Felicité de Lamennais, Charles de Montalembert, Henri Lacordaire and others urged the Roman Catholic Church to 'baptise' the ideas which had come out of the French Revolution. They wrote in their journal *L'Avenir* under the motto 'God and Liberty' urging Catholics not to oppose but to promote and give Christian direction to movements which sought to liberate oppressed peoples. They applauded the Catholic liberals of Belgium who won their independence in 1830, and they commiserated with the Catholic Poles who suffered under Tsarist tyranny. Montalembert visited Ireland and rejoiced over the union there of Catholicism with nationalist aspirations. Everywhere the writers in *L'Avenir* saw Europe in the flood-tide of liberal transformation, and they urged the papacy to bless the new political and social dispensation that was coming into being.

Lamennais had high hopes during the pontificate of Leo XII that liberalism might prevail in Rome in spite of the policies urged by *zelanti*. The legacy of Cardinal Consalvi was not forgotten, and Lamennais was kindly received by the pope when he visited Rome in 1824. During the preparation of the jubilee the political content of Lamennais' work was glossed over while appreciation was shown for the Ultramontanism of this champion who opposed religious indifferentism. When he visited Rome again in 1832, however, the revolutions of 1830 had occurred, Gregory XVI was alarmed over the political posturing of bishops in Belgium, Poland and Ireland, and he had now little sympathy for the ideas advanced in *L'Avenir*. Lamennais was treated kindly by Gregory, but in the encyclical *Mirari vos* of 1832 the ideals of liberal Catholicism he had advanced in *L'Avenir* were condemned. Lamennais bowed to the papal judgment externally, but then wrote his famous *Paroles d'un Croyant* which resulted in his leaving the Church. Lacordaire submitted to become a Dominican and to devote himself to re-establishing the order in France. Montalembert remained within the Church, but continued to propagate his liberal Catholic ideas in his historical writings and in the French Chamber of Deputies. After 1832, however, the hope of an Ultramontane/liberal alliance was dead.

3. *Cullen's Ultramontanism*

Cullen was fascinated not only by the ecclesiastical triumphalism of the Rome he came to as a seminarian in 1821, but also by the intellectual excitement in the Eternal City. In 1802 the Vicomte de Chateaubriand had made a brilliant rhetorical defence of Catholic Christianity, arguing that history proved the faith to be the fountainhead of civilisation in Europe. In 1819 Joseph de Maistre abandoned his eighteenth-century rationalist faith to argue in *Du Pape* that the only true basis of society was to be found where the spiritual authority of the papacy was acknowledged. The Roman intellectual world that Cullen knew was filled with Ultramontane scholars from all nations developing their ideological apologetic for papal absolutism. He shared this excitement that permeated most of the Roman colleges, and it was in this Roman crucible that he abandoned whatever liberal tendencies he might have brought with him from Carlow. By the time that Gregory XVI condemned Lamennais and his followers Cullen had committed himself to serve the cause of Ultramontanism without any reservation. What is really unique about the man and his thought is that there was such little theological development in the faith to which he made such a complete oblation in the Rome of his youth. Like so many Ultramontanists of the nineteenth century, Cullen never really understood the radical forces of change at work in secular society. To the end of his life he tended to consider Irish affairs from the standpoint of an émigré Roman curial figure of pre-1848 Rome, never abandoning the Ultramontane vision which had captivated his school of Catholic intellectuals during the pontificates of Leo XII, Gregory XVI and Pius IX. (Costigan, *Rohrbacher*)

On the occasion of Pius VII's triumphant re-entry into Rome in 1814 one of the houses on the Corso displayed an enormous painting on its façade showing the vanquished

Napoleon, completely naked, cringing at the feet of the pope before being dragged off to hell by the devil. Cullen would have found little to criticise essentially in the picture's crude imagery. With his whole being he reverenced Rome as the centre of civilisation, and the occupant of Peter's chair as the bringer of salvation, blessed with the authority to overcome the world of rationalism, naturalism and religious indifference which had been encouraged by the revolutionary liberals led by the French emperor. Allied with them were the demonic forces of Protestantism and Freemasonry, and every other man-made movement which threatened the true church founded by Christ and protected by his vicar upon earth, the Bishop of Rome. Cullen had no difficulty in accepting the belief of the *zelanti* that it was the hand of God that had humbled Napoleon, so that the Roman Church could bring to a sinful and perverse European social order the blessings of Catholic culture.

Cullen accepted the principle of authority presented by the early Lamennais in the first volume of his chief work, *Essai sur l'indifference en matière de religion*, which was published shortly before Cullen arrived in Rome. The pope was the Lord's Anointed, the revealer of the divine will for man. His power had to be absolute, for he was the trustee in moral matters of the entire human race. Without the pope there was no Church; without the Church there was no Christianity; and without Christianity there was no religion in society. Without religion everything decays, and an atheistic society is doomed. Only the true Church of Rome, led by the Supreme Pontiff, can save mankind from the folly and evil of serving either a heretical and false religion or a deified state.

It was typical of him that, even as a young man, Cullen shared few of his deepest convictions with others. When he wrote to the person who was then closest to him, his uncle and godfather, James Maher, he talked at length about matters like the health of members of the curia, new discoveries in the Vatican Library, or the pope's gift of the ancient Umbrian College to the Irish. Maher in one letter finally burst out and said: 'You never tell us in any of your letters what you are doing, or what is being done at Rome.' (C: 29 Apr. 1834) Even when he explained to Maher why it was impossible for him to accept the chair of theology at Carlow College that Bishop James Doyle had offered him he did so in the careful language of the natural diplomat. Whatever the changes that took place in Cullen's mind during these formative Roman years, he kept them very much to himself, but it is clear that from the time that the Roman authorities began to consult him about Irish affairs he was very much a conservative Ultramontanist.

His brother Thomas (who respectfully addressed him as 'My dear Doctor') and other members of the Cullen family were encouraged to keep him abreast of Irish affairs. In the post-Emancipation years, as the Cullens and their relatives became very wealthy, extending their landholdings in several counties, they shared the usual political and social prejudices of the rising Catholic strong-farmer class. In Rome their brilliant Paul, of whom they were so proud, said nothing in his correspondence with them to indicate that he did not share their sensibilities. He read eagerly the family's accounts of James Maher's role in the political and social agitation as the 'tithe war' began, and he noted their appreciation of the pro-Catholic attitudes of the Lord Lieutenant, Lord Mulgrave, and the declining political fortunes of the Protestant Beresfords. Yet his replies to them were rather formal.

One cousin, Anne Maher, who was sub-prioress of the Dominican convent at Cabra, wrote to him often about convent affairs, pressing him for concessions which he might win for her tiny community, 'knowing your influence to be so great in Rome'. (C: 28 May 1831) Cullen bore with this presumptuous woman who insisted upon writing to him as 'My dearest Cousin' and pestered him for some ten years, but generally he kept other members of his family at a reserved distance. In particular he kept aloof from James Maher, who was eager to draw him into the innumerable disputes which concerned him. Maher told him in detail about the jealousies among the Kildare and Leighlin clergy that had kept both himself and Cullen from succeeding James Doyle as bishop of that diocese, though Doyle had wanted Cullen as his coadjutor. Nor did he open himself to Maher when some authorities proposed that Cullen be made President of Maynooth and, a short time later, Coadjutor Bishop of Charleston. This caution on his part was a reflection of his sharing in Rome's suspicion of the agitating Irish clergy who had done so much to bring about Catholic Emancipation and were now encouraging the tithe war. Although he was never to lose the prejudices of the wealthy Catholic farming class from which he came, and always resented the Protestant landowners who were their social and economic rivals, his ultimate loyalty was always to Rome and the Ultramontane cause that he so totally embraced. Cullen was not always convinced that his agitating relatives' promotion of Catholic nationalism served the cause of the Universal Church.

From the time that Cullen began to serve the Holy See by making sure that the cardinals who advised the pontiff were aware of developments in Ireland, he made use of the new 'family' with which he had now identified himself. This was the growing number of young clerics who had, like himself, been nurtured in Rome's Ultramontane atmosphere and who had then returned to serve in Propaganda's direction of the Irish mission. One of these was John McCann, who had studied in Rome and had returned to Ireland to become one of the founders of the Congregation of the Mission, the Vincentian order. McCann was sufficiently close to Cullen to be one of the few correspondents who ever addressed him in familiar terms. Other Roman student contemporaries with whom Cullen kept contact and with whom he discussed Irish affairs were Bernard Smith and Laurence Forde. The former became Vice-Rector of the Irish College after leaving Propaganda, and Forde in later years became Cullen's secretary and almost his confidant. A natural open relationship, even with as long-standing and devoted a friend as Laurence Force, was impossible for Cullen, however. In a gossipy letter to Bernard Smith in later years Forde referred critically to Cullen's intense reserve, his 'over-caution, timidity, apprehension of committing himself'. This made the papal delegate a remote individual who seemed to regard the Irish bishops with 'distrust and suspicion'. Forde believed this to be a real 'defect in governing talent' on the part of Cullen, for it resulted in the Irish bishops keeping 'aloof' from him. (BS: 17 Feb. 1858 or 1859) This reserve was never lost, even when Cullen communicated with his disciple Tobias Kirby or with his nephew

Patrick Francis Moran, who tried to model his life on that of his famous uncle.

Cullen was probably always a reserved individual by nature, but from the age of fourteen he had resided in boarding schools which prepared him for acceptance of the dedicated loneliness, in human terms, which is the lot of the Roman Catholic priest. However difficult a conditioning this was when he was at Carlow College, Cullen lost any natural resentment of his vocational demands when he arrived in Rome. In the heady triumphalist atmosphere of the Rome of Leo XII and Gregory XVI he found identity as an Ultramontanist – an identity he was never to lose. As much as was humanly possible Paul Cullen gave himself totally in service to the Holy See; he endeavoured to live only in terms of this oblation.

In this sense, from the period of his ordination or perhaps from the time of his arrival in Rome as a student, Cullen was religiously a simple man. He was a man under authority: his mind, his heart, his very soul belonged to his superiors, the Cardinal Prefect of Propaganda, the Cardinal Secretary of State, and the Supreme Pontiff. Fortunately for him, he never had the trial of serving under an ecclesiastical superior who did not share his passionate sense of mission, and it was probably as well for his peace of mind that when he did return to his native land it was as Primate of the Irish Church. Throughout Cullen's life his situation was such that he had the luxury of living a dream, a kind of 'realised eschatology'. Wherever he was there was the authority of Peter, and to the extension of this *magisterium* he was committed every moment of his adult life.

Such dedication made many of his actions seem mysterious to his contemporaries, as we shall see. Even Laurence Forde could not fathom what seemed to be his 'rule of thumb' direction of the Dublin archdiocese, which was essentially an often naive application of Ultramontane principle in an ecclesiastical world that was unused to it. His enemies often accused him of Machiavellian manoeuvrings, but Cullen's actions were always understandable, and even predictable, if once you understood the premise upon which they were built. The Vicar of Christ upon earth was directing the universal strategy of the Church Militant in its ceaseless battle with the principalities and powers of a sinful, hostile world. To Cullen in Ireland had been delegated the authority to direct the papal *kulturkampf*. In his mission Cullen deferred to Rome's suggestions, cautions, monitions or directions. With the Irish bishops whom he was trying to bring over to the papal cause he was an authoritarian individual, distant and distrustful, a man they could respect or even fear, but not a man who won their hearts. They seldom understood what he was about, probably because they could not really believe that behind his apparently mysterious machinations was the essential simplicity of his dedication to the Ultramontane movement. It is interesting that the critics who best understood Paul Cullen, as his obituaries reveal, were the heretical Protestants with whom he had battled so long and so well.

When Cullen arrived in Ireland to stem the Protestant advance promoted by the English Evangelicals of the Irish Church Missions they recognised in the indefatigable papal delegate a zealot whose religious dedication was equal to their own. His passion was that of a Francis de Sales, and his goal the essential one of the Counter-Reformation of an earlier age. Cullen's intent was to advance the universal authority of the Supreme Pontiff, to the greater glory of God. Considerations of Irish nationalism, the economic and social well-being of the Irish people, or petty secular political issues were all of secondary importance to this most relentless of Ultramontanists. Whatever he did during his Irish mission reflected service to this cause that completely absorbed him — the advancing of papal authority in any issue, at any time and in any place. Once he had acted Cullen cared nothing for the judgment of his Catholic nationalist critics, the secular authorities, or his Protestant opponents. All that mattered to him was the approval of the Holy Father, the Vicar of Christ upon earth.

4. *The Irish College, Rome*
In February 1832 Paul Cullen informed his family that they should not expect him to return to Ireland for some time. Christopher Boylan, Rector of the Irish College, had been taken ill and was returning to Ireland. When Boylan died shortly after his arrival Cullen was appointed rector in his place.

The Irish College, Rome, was a Counter-Reformation creation of Cardinal Ludovico Ludovisi, nephew of Gregory XV, who had established the Congregation of Propaganda during the early years of the Thirty Years' War. The original suggestion for the college had come from a scholarly Franciscan, Luke Wadding, who had pleaded for a separate establishment for the six young Irishmen in Rome who were studying for the secular priesthood but did not fit in easily with other students. Wadding became the first rector, and the college opened under Franciscan authority in 1628.

Wadding had been President of the Irish College in Salamanca and was also the founder of a college for Irish Franciscans in Rome; he hoped that the two Irish colleges would become centres of Franciscan scholarship. Urban VIII, who succeeded Gregory XV, was a political pope, however, who was more interested in his project of re-establishing the Roman Catholic Church in England with the help of Queen Henrietta Maria. He encouraged Ludovisi to turn the Irish College into a training-ground for young Irishmen who would return to their native country as Counter-Reformation agents. He appointed the cardinal 'protector of Ireland', and when Ludovisi died his will provided that direction of the college should be given over to the Jesuits. This was duly carried out, and from 1635 for 137 years the eight students a year in the college were prepared by the Jesuits for work in Ireland. Each of them had to take an oath that they would return to serve in the Irish mission, a hazardous task. One of the most famous of the alumni, Oliver Plunkett, was martyred in 1681.

During the Napoleonic occupation of Rome the college was turned into a barracks. In 1826, however, Michael Blake, the last student left in the Ludovisian foundation, returned to Rome to reopen the college. Blake's health declined in Rome, and he was replaced after two years by Christopher Boylan, and on Boylan's death in June 1832 Paul Cullen was appointed the third rector of the new Irish College, which had been given a new site in the Piazza S. Lucia by Leo XII.

Cullen had every intention of restoring to the Irish College its Counter-Reformation ethos, a task warmly approved by Gregory XVI, who, following the example of Leo XII, provided badly needed encouragement for the new institution.

In 1833 the students numbered only forty-two, but Cullen's friend John McCann agreed to use the Vincentian house at 34 Usher's Quay in Dublin as an agency to recruit for the Irish College in Rome. He strongly approved of the Ultramontane discipline which Cullen was imposing and which was giving the college a distinctive character compared with that of other Irish seminaries:

> I am fully persuaded of its great utility not only with respect to the religion of this country but with respect to religion in general as it directly tends to the preservation of that strict union with the Holy See which is the peculiar characteristic of the true Catholic Church. (C: 6 Mar. 1833)

Although Cullen was still a comparatively young man, the Irish hierarchy soon realised how much he was appreciated in Rome. Both directly and through the agency established by McCann the bishops began to give their support to the reorganised college and to treat Cullen with considerable deference. On 8 October 1833 Bishop William Higgins of Ardagh wrote to him to say:

> Though the diocese of Ardagh has more than a sufficient number of priests at present, and there is scarcely a prospect of any immediate vacancy, still I have ventured to send eleven young men to your college. Perhaps my anxiety for the prosperity of that establishment has caused me to over-step the bounds of prudent administration but I hope I have so managed matters that the result must be useful to Religion. By looking over the condition on which these candidates have been allowed to enter the college you will feel quite secure as to their solvency and good conduct. (C)

Cullen's prestige was such, and the help given by the bishops so considerable, that by the summer of 1835 Archbishop Daniel Murray of Dublin was able to announce that the Irish College in Rome was full.

To build up the college so quickly was a considerable accomplishment, and it was clearly the result of Cullen's dedication and the power of his personality. In 1834 he visited Ireland to promote the college, his first visit in fourteen years, leaving the control of it in the hands of his vice-rector,

Michael O'Connor, who was destined to become Bishop of Pittsburg in 1843. (CA, 1834/5) No sooner had Cullen departed, however, than discipline broke down almost totally. Edmund O'Reilly, a senior student who was to succeed O'Connor as vice-rector, wrote to Cullen about the anarchy and begged him to return to put affairs in order. It was at this time that Cullen declined appointment as Coadjutor Bishop of Charleston and, on the suggestion of Propaganda, hurried back to Rome to resume his administration.

His firm hand and sense of authority was certainly needed among the Irish students. The college had first come into being in the seventeenth century because the Irish could not fit in with other Roman students, and their behaviour had hardly improved by the time the institution was re-established. Cullen's predecessor, Christopher Boylan, had complained in 1830 about the reluctance of Propaganda to receive Irish students because of their unruly disposition. He said they were almost always 'outrageous Gallicans almost before they realised the meaning of the term'. (BV: 7 Oct. 1830) It is difficult to know in what sense Boylan used the term 'Gallican', but without doubt he was referring to the seemingly inbred resistance to any kind of authority which the Irish students brought with them. What was needed to control them, as Edmund O'Reilly pointed out in his excited letter of 2 December 1834, was the kind of charisma and firm control of administration that Cullen possessed and Michael O'Connor did not. (C)

It was probably the great need for firm discipline in the Irish College which kept Cullen there during the early years of the 1830s. John McCann told him in April 1835 that he was being groomed to take charge of the seminary in Carlow (C), but Cullen and Propaganda both knew where he was most needed at that time. If Ireland was to be brought into the Ultramontane camp, then the beginning of the movement had to be in Rome. It was to be the graduates of the Irish College in Rome that were to lead in the reshaping of the Catholic Church in Ireland, whose present unsatisfactory character was all too clearly revealed by the unpromising Gallican students who came to Cullen. Not only were they generally unruly, but they were unprepossessing in other ways.

In 1833 Thomas Kelly, the Primate, had actually apologised to Cullen for sending him students whom Cullen considered to be 'stupid'.

Cullen's task was not an easy one. It was expensive for Irish students to go to Rome, many of them did not easily adjust to climatic change, and life in the college was austere. Tobias Kirby, an Ultramontane rigorist, was appointed vice-rector in 1836, and soon criticism of the Irish College in Rome included his puritanical discipline as well as the physical failings of the building that the students had to inhabit. By the summer of 1836 Cullen was able to purchase a retreat house at Tivoli in which the Irish students could escape the heat of the Roman summer. Then Gregory XVI, who as Cardinal Prefect of Propaganda had always supported Cullen, showed that his patronage was to continue now that he was pope. He presented the Irish with a new college building, together with the church of St Agatha in the Via Mazzarino. From this time the fortunes of the college seemed assured. In 1839 John McCann wrote to Cullen to say that as he had not heard from him for six months he presumed the college was now firmly established and his role as its Irish agent was no longer needed.

Not all the bishops were as inclined to support the Irish College as William Higgins had been when he sent his group of young men there. Higgins had been trained in the Eternal City himself and valued the experience of studying in the very centre of Catholic Christianity. On the other hand, Bartholomew Crotty, Bishop of Cloyne and Ross, who had served as President of the Irish College in Lisbon and then as President of Maynooth, had doubts about the value of Irish students going so far afield for their training. Crotty was careful to assure Cullen of his Ultramontane sympathy: 'I would wish to see the bonds of union drawn still closer between our Irish Church and the Holy See.' (C: 17 Oct. 1838) At the same time he told Cullen that he believed a Roman education was too expensive for any but postgraduate students, and he reported that most Cloyne and Ross students who went there fell ill on their return to Ireland. Many students were unhappy with the rigorism of the Cullen/Kirby adminis-tration and wrote home to their diocesan bishops about their dislike of this intensely Ultramontane institution. John Cantwell, Bishop of Meath, defended Cullen against these detractors, but others spread rumours about how unwholesome a place was the Irish College in Rome.

Cullen knew how many enemies the college had in Ireland because of the Ultramontane theology that it was imparting. Michael Blake, who had reopened the college in 1836 and had afterwards returned to Ireland to become Bishop of Dromore, wrote to him on 1 February 1839 to reassure him that 'in spite of your opponents who send calumnious letters', the bishops as a whole continued to have confidence in his administration. (C) However, Cullen was so worried by the growing antagonism that he made another journey to Ireland in the summer of 1840 to see if he could set the suspicions of the Irish bishops to rest. At the same time he took the opportunity of studying the National System of schooling in order to keep Propaganda fully informed about possible dangers in such state-sponsored education.

Cullen knew that the complaints about the college were not a reflection of his direct administration, as he was usually busy acting as intermediary between the Irish bishops and the officials at Propaganda and he left much of the day-to-day running of affairs in the hands of Tobias Kirby. The latter had been in Rome since 1827 and had won attention by writing a remarkable dissertation on *The Right of Appeal to the Holy See*. He was a devotee of St Ignatius Loyola, wrote meditations on the saint's reverence for Rome, and was a thoroughgoing Ultramontanist. He returned to Ireland only twice during his long life and was unappreciative of the spirit of independence which the Irish often brought with them when they came to Rome. Those who withstood his rigorist rule were labelled as 'Gallicans' and soon found they were not welcome in the college. Those who remained were usually conformists to Kirby's regime, like the members of 'the fourth Camerata' who wrote to Cullen on 29 July 1840 to assure their rector that they were all studying hard during his absence. Speaking of themselves and the other students, they reported: 'In recreation we all speak Italian ... becoming each day more obedient, docile and punctual to all the rules.' (C)

Unfortunately for Kirby and his Ultramontane supporters, many of the Irish students in the college were not really becoming more obedient, let alone docile. Some of them kept their Gallican ideas in spite of Kirby's inquisition. Daniel McGettigan, who was to become Primate of the Irish Church in later years, was one of the Irish College alumni who came out of the college a strong Gallican in the view of Bernard Smith, then a student. Smith added to the letter of 'the fourth Camerata' a condemnation of McGettigan's 'Gallican principles, for a Gallican he is to the very core'. Not all the graduates who emerged from the college were to be as strong-minded as Daniel McGettigan, who was about to be appointed a professor in Paris, but there were enough of them to ensure that Kirby's iron rule was often questioned. During his time in Ireland Cullen received letter after letter from Kirby telling of student unrest, financial problems, and his own ill-health, which may have been a reflection of his state of tension.

Finally one of the inner group of Ultramontane students, Edward Norris, wrote to Cullen to report that Kirby was on the verge of a total breakdown. Cullen then returned, and Kirby went to Ireland for a rest. Cullen, however, found matters in such bad shape that after a year of herculean labour he too became ill. It was at this time that he produced a pamphlet promoting the Irish College, sending copies of it to the bishops. (CA, 1841/2) In the summer of 1842, with Kirby in charge once more, Cullen returned to Ireland to recuperate, only to be told of the renewal of trouble among the students.

Again the trouble was Kirby's harsh rule, and complaints continued to come to Cullen throughout the 1840s. Students from Waterford seemed to cause much of the trouble, and the brother of one of them wrote angrily to Cullen about Kirby denying mail privileges to dissidents for up to three months at a time. In 1844 Edmund O'Reilly, then a Professor of Theology at Maynooth, wrote to Cullen as a friend, urging him to curb the harsh discipline which Kirby insisted upon. It 'exacerbated the minds of the students' and 'engendered bitter feeling':

> If I had been under such a man, it is possible either he or I would have had to quit. . . . He is a very good man, but he

is a bad manager of his fellow men. He has zeal . . . and piety, but he has not tact. O'Connor, I suspect, had more and still he nearly blew up the house. For God's sake, if Kirby is to remain with you, leave no power in his hands but do everything as much as you can yourself. Notwithstanding, remember me most kindly to Kirby, whom I really like very much. (C: 11 Oct. 1844)

Cullen was as close to Edmund O'Reilly as he was to any man, and would have paid attention to what he said. All the evidence was before him that something had to be done to ameliorate Kirby's rule, but by this time Cullen was under so much pressure in his work as diplomat and as Roman agent for the Irish bishops that he was obliged to allow Kirby to continue the day-to-day running of the college. He was especially concerned when Kirby tried to make up for his lack of knowledge about Irish affairs by a rather extreme commitment to the O'Connellite cause during the Repeal campaign. In January 1845 William Walshe, then Bishop of Halifax, who had been a Propaganda student with Cullen, wrote to say that Dublin rumour had it that in the Irish College in Rome any student who tried to avoid novenas for O'Connell and Repeal 'had no chance of his life with some of his superiors'. (C: 29 Jan. 1845) The only real solution to the problem Cullen knew — for he was loyal to Kirby and would not dismiss him — was a softening of attitude on the part of the puritanical vice-rector.

This began to take place from late in 1847 when, after a series of crises, Kirby's brother wrote telling him that ex-students spoke of the Tivoli vacation house as a 'penitentiary', that Duffy's *Catholic Magazine* had an unfriendly article on the Irish College in Rome, and that a shake-up in administration was imminent:

It causes me much pain from time to time to hear how your college has fallen in the public estimation and more painful again that the students seem not to be sorry when they can get out of it. I am told that the management of it is going into other hands. (K: 19 Dec. 1847)

This was very disturbing to Kirby, a native of Waterford, because some of the college dissidents came from his area,

and it now seemed that Kirby's family were also involved in
the criticism of his regime. In any case from this time forward
there was sufficient change in Kirby's rule for Cullen to feel
confident, at the time of his final departure for Ireland, that
he could persuade Rome to allow Kirby, who was completely
devoted to him, to succeed him as rector.

In spite of the many criticisms of the rigorist discipline in
the college, and the bad press it received in Ireland, its student
numbers remained high. The *Irish Catholic Directory* of 1845
reported that it held between fifty and sixty students. No
record is available of the turnover among them, but it is likely
that those who could not abide the college's Ultramontane
theology and intense discipline soon left. By a process of
natural selection those who remained were men like Edmund
O'Reilly or Bernard Smith who shared the passionate beliefs
and the vision of Cullen. Many of them were remarkable men
who contributed much to the extension of the Roman
Catholic Church in their generation. In 1843 a cousin of
Cullen's, Father John Doyle, sent to the college a nephew,
James Quinn, who in later years became Bishop of Brisbane.
His brother Matthew, who had followed him to the college,
became Bishop of Bathurst. Another alumnus, James Murray,
who briefly acted as Cullen's secretary, became Bishop of
Maitland. All these men were able and pious and utterly
devoted to Cullen, and they put a very Ultramontane stamp
on the church that emerged in Australia, a process which was
completed by Patrick Francis Moran, Cullen's nephew.
Moran became successively Vice-Rector of the Irish College,
a professor in Propaganda, secretary to his uncle, Bishop of
Ossory, Archbishop of Sydney and, in 1885, a cardinal.

When Cullen went to Ireland at mid-century he left the
actual governing of the Irish College in Rome to the dour and
puritanical Tobias Kirby. Yet until his death twenty-eight
years later his presence and even his authority were recognised
by succeeding generations of students. Like the influence of
Thomas Arnold which lingered in Rugby School long after
his departure, Cullen's spirit of total dedication to the
Counter-Reformation mission survived in the institution he
had nurtured for so long. When the students of the Irish
College left Rome to serve in the Irish or some other mission,

they were dedicated to oppose every evil which threatened the life of the Church and the authority of the universal ordinary — indifferentism, liberalism, Gallicanism, Protestantism and infidelity. Their Roman 'formation' had fully prepared them to follow Cullen in his total oblation to the Vicar of Christ upon earth, and to share in his resolve to extend papal authority in the Irish Catholic Church or wherever else they might be directed to serve.

II

Gallicanism and the Irish Church

1. *The Nature of Irish Gallicanism*

Whenever Irish bishops had to appeal to Rome in some ecclesiastical or religious cause they had the problem of catching curial attention to ensure that there would be an expeditious handling of their problem. Many of them were unfamiliar with either Italian or working Latin, lacked the sophistication to prepare briefs in diplomatic language, and were only too aware that when they approached the centre of the Catholic faith they did so from an area that Rome considered to be remote and primitive. It was not unknown for Propaganda to send letters to Lublin instead of Dublin and to confuse places like Killala and Killaloe.

The natural answer for this problem was for the Irish supplicant to make use of some agent who knew his way around in the complex bureaucracy of papal Rome. The post in any generation was not an official one, the person chosen being simply someone who had access to avenues of power. In the eighteenth century, when the Irish bishops were trained on the continent and had more sophistication than some of their nineteenth-century counterparts, they often made use of the papal nuncio in Brussels, sending him their petitions in French to be passed on to Rome. In the years following the reopening of the Irish College in Rome an attempt was made to use the rector as the agent for the Irish hierarchy.

Shortly after Cullen was appointed rector he received a letter from Michael Blake, then convalescent in Dublin, who told him that Archbishop Daniel Murray of Dublin was using his influence to have Cullen recognised as agent for the Irish hierarchy. Following the death of Christopher Boylan, Murray wrote to Cullen to inform him that his 'agency' was assured. Cullen welcomed this because his appointment as the paid representative of individual bishops would bring him income beyond that which he received as Rector of the Irish College. Early in August 1832 Thomas Kelly, who had just become Archbishop of Armagh following the death of Patrick Curtis, requested Cullen to act as his agent in Rome. Other bishops followed the example of Kelly, though some were initially reluctant to make use of Cullen's offices. John Ryan, who became Bishop of Limerick in 1828, did not officially appoint Cullen as his agent until 1847.

As late as 1822 Rome was grumbling over the lobbying in Irish ecclesiastical affairs carried out by 'agents'. (PFS, XXIII, 699) The appointment of Paul Cullen by his fellow-countrymen, however, was a different matter. Now Propaganda and the other Roman departments would be approached by someone whom the Roman officials trusted implicitly. In any negotiation on behalf of the Irish bishops, Rome knew that Cullen's first concern would be to further the authority of the Holy See.

In many ways Cullen's role as Roman agent for the Irish hierarchy was more important than his being Rector of the Irish College. He was a natural diplomat, deeply interested in the larger issues of the ecclesiastical world in which he lived, and it was for this reason he delegated so much of the actual running of the college to Kirby. It is probable also that he did not enjoy ordinary administration, for in later years he left the day-to-day management of the Dublin archdiocese largely in the hands of his very able secretary, Laurence Forde, while he concerned himself with national affairs.

At first he was diffident about his new role, for he was barely thirty years old and had a shrewd idea of how difficult the job of Roman agent was to be. When Oliver Kelly, the pious and able Archbishop of Tuam, requested Cullen's services he elicited from him fulsome thanks:

I have now to express my most heartfelt thanks to your Grace for your kindness towards me in the honour, by appointing me your agent, and by concurring so liberally with the other bishops towards my support — I shall never forget so particular an honour and I shall endeavour on every occasion to show my attachment and obedient submission to the Irish hierarchy. (C: 24 Oct. 1832)

Cullen's diffidence was never such, however, that when he talked of obedient submission he considered that service to the Irish hierarchy would lead him to oppose his higher loyalty to Rome. Nor was his pledge entirely ingenuous; Cullen had every intention of using his influence with the Irish bishops to ensure that the Irish College would never lack for students.

Almost immediately Cullen's work as agent brought him in contact with Irish bishops who were only too willing to use Roman authority to serve their own ends, but were almost totally lacking in the spirit of submission to the Holy See demanded by the Roman Ultramontanists. On first encounter Cullen could identify some of them as old-fashioned Gallicans, prelates who were quite content with a 'throne and altar' alliance in Catholic Ireland, even though the crown was worn by a heretic. Another group was more difficult to assess because although its leaders talked readily about their loyalty to the Holy See, yet at the same time they resented any kind of Roman direction. As time went on Cullen began to view these prelates as representatives of a new mutation that was taking place in traditional Gallicanism. They wanted the Church to be free to identify with the new spirit of liberalism and nationalism that was sweeping Europe and that in Ireland manifested itself in O'Connell's Repeal movement. The last thing these Repeal bishops of Ireland wanted were papal admonitions about the 'priest in politics'.

Cullen was firmly opposed to the conciliatory views of the old-fashioned Gallicans, who sought to avoid confrontation with the secular power over such issues as a government veto over episcopal appointments and the payment of state pensions to the clergy to free them from dependence upon their flocks. In an *ad hoc* meeting in 1799 ten senior bishops, led by the Primate and Archbishop John Troy of Dublin, had agreed to a government proposal for both a royal veto on episcopal appointments and an 'independent provision' for the Catholic clergy. Troy, who was a personal friend of the Duke of Wellington, acted as the spokesman for this group. In February 1799 he wrote to Propaganda to explain what had happened. Troy apologised for putting the pope in 'a delicate situation', but explained that after the excesses of '98 the bishops were not in a position to stand up to the government: 'We would be branded as rebels. This is a fact. If we agreed to it without reference to Rome we would be branded as schismatics. We are between Scylla and Charibidis.' (PFS, XVII, 129-30)

Nothing came from this introduction of the Irish prelates to the government's plan to regulate their church, but the issue was raised again in 1805 and in 1808. The bishops kept Propaganda informed about what was happening as the government pressed its case. On 8 September 1808 they reported how the government cited the Canadian precedent by which 'the Bishop of Quebec was not allowed to choose his coadjutor until the latter was approved by the civil government'. (PFS, XVIII, 550-2) In a letter to Rome on 27 February 1810 they told of further attempts to satisfy the government by offering to take a simple oath of allegiance and to give assurance that neither they nor the papacy had any intention of interfering in temporal affairs. (PFS, XVIII, 557)

There was nothing strange in the Irish bishops acting so submissively, for by tradition Troy, Curtis and most of the Irish bishops of their generation were Gallican. They had been educated in continental Gallican seminaries, and had no desire to engage in any struggle between church and state. This was revealed very clearly by them in their dealings with one of the proto-Ultramontanists of the age, John Milner, who was Vicar Apostolic for the Midlands in England from 1803.

Milner, who had trained at Douai, was distressed over the lay domination of the Catholic Church in England, where Charles Butler, the first Catholic barrister since the time of James II, was secretary of the Catholic Committee and an unofficial agent of the crown. The only opposition to the domination of the Church by these Catholic laymen of great privilege that Milner found was among the Irish Catholic poor who had been settling in the Midlands in great numbers during the 1790s. Milner developed a great sympathy for the immigrant Irish and brought in a number of Irish priests to help them settle in their new urban environment. As Milner's association with the Irish developed he was asked by the Irish hierarchy to act as their agent in England.

To the great embarrassment of John Troy and the other Irish bishops, Milner began to attribute to them the same distaste for the interference by the crown in church affairs that he found among the Irish poor in England. He also suggested that Rome would have been as impatient with the Irish bishops as the Irish people would have been if the bishops had given their approval to the veto and pensioning schemes of the government: 'Rome is jealous of any intercourse between the Irish prelates and the government, suspecting that the former may be bribed by the latter, and influenced to consent to a concordat and other innovations.' (DAA: 16 July 1807)

Soon Milner was inferring in his correspondence with Troy that the Irish bishops had stood up to the government, and for ideological reasons rather than sheer expediency. Among them he saw a love of Rome and papal authority that was not to be found in the English Catholic community, which seemed to welcome government intervention in religious affairs. Troy was very distressed by this suggestion. He wrote to the Vicar Apostolic of the London District, William Poynter, on 16 November 1810 to protest at the 'insinuation' that the Irish hierarchy was promoting a pro-Roman expression of the faith. (DAA) Troy's protestations did not deter Milner. By January 1813 he was professing near fealty to the Irish hierarchy, telling Troy that Irish Catholics in England generally 'look up to the prelates of Ireland . . . for the rule of their belief and conduct'. (DAA)

Unfortunately for Milner, John Troy and the other Irish bishops had considerable reverence for the crown and were strong Gallicans. At the height of the Whiteboy terror in the Dublin archdiocese Troy had issued a pastoral quoting Bossuet's belief that 'the royal character is holy and sacred even in infidel princes'. He had also in this pastoral denied the popularity of any idea of papal infallibility among his generation of Irish clergy, and even went so far as to make light of the much-hated penal laws:

The magistrates in most places, imitating the tenderness and affection of the king towards all his good subjects, frequently connived at the exercise of our religious rites, and enforced the laws against the harmless ministers of religion with reluctance; but unhappily, neither they, nor his majesty could prevent the cruel operation of laws respecting the property of Catholics.

(PFS, XVII, 17: 10 Apr. 1793)

Troy and the other Irish bishops had to shift their ground, however, when Ireland was convulsed by the uproar over the Quarantotti Rescript. While Pope Pius VII was a prisoner of Napoleon at Fontainebleau Monsignor Quarantotti, Vice-Prefect of Propaganda, using the 'full pontifical powers' granted to him, had indicated to the English hierarchy that Rome favoured the idea of a royal veto. O'Connell, then struggling to establish his political authority, seized upon the issue, and soon Troy and the other bishops found themselves accused of being 'vile slaves of the clerks of the Castle'. In the face of this clamour, Daniel Murray was obliged to accompany Milner to Rome in 1814 to register the protest of the Irish hierarchy to the ideas of the veto and of pensioning the clergy. Milner was so sure that the mild-mannered Murray was in agreement with his sentiments that he wrote to him to urge that 'The whole strength of the prelates, not only of England but also of Ireland must be united in subordination to the Holy See for the safety and common cause.' (DAA: 18 Jan. 1815)

But Murray had been nurtured in the Gallican atmosphere of eighteenth-century Salamanca, and neither he nor any of the other Irish bishops shared Milner's pro-papal enthusiasm. By 1819, when Cullen was in his last year at Carlow College, Milner was telling Murray that John Troy was avoiding him and that other Irish bishops never replied to his letters. No one seemed upset by the Gallican ideas of those who would 'Protestantise our holy church', and his own controversial works exalting the authority of Rome were generally ignored. (DAA: 26 Mar. 1819) Murray was not surprised over Milner's complaints, but he did his best to console him and remained Milner's friend until his death in 1826.

Murray was coadjutor to Troy from 1809 and succeeded him as Archbishop of Dublin in 1823. During 1812 and 1813 he also acted as President of Maynooth when émigré French

professors were openly propagating the Gallican doctrines of
the Sorbonne, and he knew how strongly Gallican in a
traditional sense most of the Irish bishops and clergy were.
He also knew, however, that a new nationalist spirit had
begun to influence the thinking of some of the clergy, particularly at Maynooth, and he was uneasy over this new
development, which increased significantly under his successor
at Maynooth, Bartholomew Crotty.

Crotty should have been as Gallican in his sentiments as
Daniel Murray, for he had been President of the Irish College
in Lisbon and had met and become a friend of Lord Wellesley
during the Peninsular War. When he gave evidence before
parliamentary commissioners inquiring into Maynooth affairs
in 1826 any defender of papal authority like Milner would
have considered his careful presentation to be strongly
Gallican. When, however, the campaign for Catholic Emancipation entered a more intense phase some members of the
government began to have doubts about his loyalty to the
establishment. The *Quarterly Review* of May 1828 questioned
the motives not only of the pro-Emancipation Maynooth
students but also of their mentors. When Crotty eventually
left Maynooth to succeed Michael Collins as Bishop of Cloyne
and Ross in 1833 objections to his appointment were raised
in Rome by Sir John Hippisley, who represented British
interests in the Eternal City.

The British authorities were worried about Crotty's display of a new kind of Gallican spirit, concerned with serving
the temporal ambitions of Irish nationalism rather than those
of the state. When the British pressed their case against
Crotty's appointment Cullen was brought into the affair, as
Rome believed that this was an attempt by the state to
implement the veto over episcopal appointments which it had
long sought. Neither Propaganda nor Cullen appear to have
shown any concern over Crotty's nationalism. Cullen sought
the advice of the Primate, Archbishop Kelly, and received
from him an assurance that the Irish bishops were now firmly
opposed to the idea of a veto, although the government still
very much wanted it:

> The news you gave me of the attempted interference in
> the appointment of Doctor Crotty by the ministry here is

a proof of their hankering after the old veto which, if it were ever conceded to them, would upset Religion in Ireland. We have, however, strong hopes that the Holy See will never allow such applications to interfere with the appointment of the Irish prelates. (C: 6 Nov. 1833)

Cullen had also to maintain vigilance on another route by which the British might attempt to exercise influence in Rome — that of the unofficial diplomatic mission to the pontiff himself. When the Marquis of Anglesey, a former viceroy of Ireland, visited the pope in the spring of 1834 Cullen was very alarmed by the apparently favourable impression that had been made upon Gregory XVI. He told John MacHale, then Bishop of Killala, of his suspicions of this representative of the British establishment who was praising the conduct of the Irish bishops:

Anglesea [*sic*] is still in Rome; and it is supposed that he is endeavouring to induce the British government to send an ambassador to Rome, and the Pope a nuncio to England. I suppose nothing of the kind will be done; and so much the better for Ireland, as an English ambassador would lose no occasion of interfering in Irish ecclesiastical affairs. The consequences that would follow are well known.
(PM, I, 209: 6 Mar. 1834)

Until his departure from Rome to Ireland at mid-century Cullen often concerned himself about this threat to establish diplomatic relations between Britain and the Holy See, and mention of it occurs many times in his correspondence.

Even more threatening than a diplomatic link which might isolate the Irish hierarchy from direct access to Roman authorities was the continuing pressure to have the veto on episcopal appointments established and the priests pensioned. Although Archbishop Kelly had assured him in 1833 that the bishops did not want the veto, Cullen always suspected that Daniel Murray and the others who were Gallican in their ecclesiastical opinions would not object to pensioning of the clergy. As late as 1845 he wrote to Kirby to say:

I have heard that Dr Murray and others have declared openly in Dublin that such a measure would be most desirable.

The great probability is that before this time twelve month
the clergy will be pensioned. The great mass of the people
and the great majority of priests and bishops will be dis-
satisfied, but with the aid of a few prelates the measure
will be carried. After that other measures will be adopted
to keep the clergy in order. God alone can put a stop to
those proceedings. We may hope that He will do something.
We can hope very little in the proceedings of bishops.

Cullen concluded this letter by wondering if the few bishops
who supported the traditional Gallicanism of Daniel Murray
really understood to what degree pensioning would deliver
the Church into the hands of the government: 'What a change
can be wrought by bows and scrapes and £300 or £350 per
annum.' (K: 3 Aug. 1845)

Long before he came to Ireland, however, Cullen had discovered the power of the bold new Gallican spirit among the
clergy. Its most noticeable manifestation was in the authority
assumed by those claiming to represent popular opinions
against bishops whose appointment by Rome was believed to
have been engineered by the government. An example of this
was provided by a bitter quarrel between Bishop William
Abraham of Waterford and the Franciscans in that town.
Abraham was unpopular with the local nationalists, who
considered him an old-fashioned Gallican, opposed to the
nationalist ambitions of the people, and a pawn of the
government. As the popular criticism of him increased and
was encouraged by the friars, Abraham and his vicar-general,
Dominic O'Brien, wrote Cullen letter after letter in 1835 and
1836 seeking help from Rome.

Ostensibly the quarrel was over the demand of the Franciscans that they be allowed to build a new chapel in a town
which already possessed four, one of them being of a considerable size. Generally the secular priests supported the
bishop, who wanted to deny the friars their chapel. On one
level it seemed to be a quarrel over clerical income, but deeper
prejudices were involved, and these led to the use of desperate
tactics. The Franciscans encouraged considerable intimidation
of Abraham and his supporters, made use of their own intermediaries to plead their case in Rome, and forced Cullen to
defend the cause of Abraham and O'Brien in the tribunals of

Propaganda. Abraham saw the friars identifying themselves with local political passions, and told Cullen that if Rome did not support him there would be a scandalous schism in Waterford, pitting 'altar against altar'. In his distress the bishop indicated that he looked for assistance from Rome, not from the state, in this quarrel: 'At all events the Holy See will always find me a dutiful subject.' (C: 23 Apr. 1836)

By the time that Abraham died in January 1837 Cullen was well aware of the confusion of ecclesiastical and political concerns in the Waterford diocese. He was also aware of how much influence he could bring to bear on the situation, to ensure the gratitude of even such a Gallican as William Abraham. This authority was recognised by bishops other than Abraham, and Michael Slattery, the Archbishop of Cashel, wrote to Cullen as soon as manoeuvring for a successor to Abraham began.

Slattery reminded Cullen of the events of the previous election following the death of Bishop Patrick Kelly in 1829. At that time the man voted *dignissimus* on the *terna* was Nicholas Foran, the very popular Parish Priest of Dungarvan. William Abraham had been the second choice, but to the 'great astonishment of everyone, bishops, priests and laity' he had been appointed bishop instead of Foran. Why had this occurred?

> The general, nay the universal impression in the minds of persons not only in Waterford but throughout the entire country is that it occurred in consequence of the interference of the British government with the court of Rome, at the instance of the Beresford family, a name hostile to the interests of Ireland and of Catholicity and odious beyond measure to the people.

Because of this appointment, occurring at the time when tension was high following the Catholic Emancipation struggle, Rome's action 'was productive of very great injury to the character and influence of poor Dr Abraham'. Slattery then went on to say that with Cullen as Roman agent he felt sure that the proper authorities in Rome would be made aware of what might result if Foran was passed over yet again:

> I take this means of stating it to you in order that if any

attempt at intrigue should be made you will be enabled
to avail yourself of this information and to assure the
authorities at Rome that if by any means, no matter what
they may be, Dr Foran should be again set aside in opposition to the unanimous recommendation of the prelates
and clergy, and of the people, it will be ascribed to undue
interposition and intrigue, and the influence of the Holy
See will be lessened to a degree that will be prejudicial to
the interests of religion. (C: 27 Feb. 1837)

Cullen received several other letters supporting the opinion
of Slattery. Then came the dismaying news that the ecclesiastical storm that was building up in Waterford had been
brought to the attention of the viceroy. Daniel Murray wrote
to Cullen on 8 April 1837 to assure him that he was not
about to add to his difficulties by entering the dispute. Confident in the pope's ability to handle the problem, Murray
had no intention of doing anything to complicate 'the mode
in which He wishes to receive information on such occasions'.
(C) On 15 May he wrote to Cullen again, however, to say that
the viceroy had sent for him and had given him an assurance
that no government interference in the choice of a bishop for
Waterford was planned:

He got instructions immediately sent from and through
the Foreign Office to the person who transacts business
for our government at Rome not upon any account to
interfere, but should anyone there ask him about the
character of Dr Foran to say that this government knew
nothing of him but what was highly favourable. (C)

Archbishop Slattery also assured Cullen that there was no
evidence of government interference in the election. (CA,
1837/9)

By this time Cullen was well briefed on the situation in
the Waterford diocese, and he knew that an authority, rival
to that of both Rome and the secular government, had to
be recognised in Irish ecclesiastical affairs. This was the
power of the popular mind, excited by the tithe war and the
O'Connellite movement and vehement in its insistence that
episcopal appointees be free of any suggestion of government
veto. As much as the traditional Gallicanism, which the

government was trying to maintain through its pressure for the veto and pensioning, the will of the people in both ecclesiastical and political affairs confronted Cullen with a formidable challenge in whatever he did.

The more Cullen acknowledged to himself the existence of this authority of the people in both religious and ecclesiastical affairs, the more he began to perceive it as a new kind of Gallicanism whereby the prejudices of local custom and tradition tried to persuade the Church to recognise a kind of national Catholicism in Ireland. When George Browne, the Bishop of Galway, wrote to Cullen in 1832 about a case *solicitatio in tribunali* concerning a Dominican penitent and a lady of high position who wished to avoid public scandal, the Roman agent was warned to be aware of local sensibilities. (C: 30 July 1832) Similarly, when Bishop John Ryan of Limerick urged in 1839 that the vacant parish of St Michael in the city be granted to him to provide mensal income, Cullen was careful to consider the political and social position of the bishop in the city. When in 1845 Bishop John MacLaughlin of Derry cut his own throat and tried to kill his sister in a fit of madness, Cullen arranged for Edward Maginn to act as coadjutor and administrator only after a careful consideration of how much such an ultra-nationalist would reflect local political prejudices, and how amenable he would be to Roman guidance.

Cullen's recognition of how many of the Irish bishops and clergy were becoming new Gallicans, eager to appease popular local political movements and prejudices, stood him in good stead. As more and more bishops and priests from all parts of the country used him as their agent in Rome his authority grew both in the Eternal City and in Ireland. He became increasingly efficient in presenting Irish causes in Roman tribunals, and in getting desired results for the plaintiffs. Many of the more highly politicised Irish bishops tried to make use of him, and brought not only their political concerns to his notice, but often their personal quarrels, including vicious exercises in character assassination. In handling such delicate matters Cullen displayed considerable caution and shrewdness, while at the same time he was able to build up a considerable personal dossier on the political proclivities and other habits of the Irish bishops and clergy. With this detailed knowledge of personal foibles, and of Irish politics and how much they influenced the priests, Cullen found that he was treated with considerable awe and even trepidation by the time he came to Ireland on his mission. Bishops and priests alike expected an inquisitorial inspection of their areas of jurisdiction, about which Cullen knew so much. As we shall see, their fears and expectations were justified.

As a confirmed Ultramontanist Cullen was always an opponent of the traditional form of Gallicanism, such as that tolerated by Daniel Murray, who sought wherever possible to seek accommodation with the state in ecclesiastical matters. It took him some time, however, to identify the new Gallicanism that was appearing among the Irish prelates and priests who were becoming excessively involved in the turbulent politics of their age. This involvement was one of degree, but in the years before his departure for Ireland Cullen was beginning to see clearly how dangerous to the authority of the Holy See this new Gallicanism could become.

When William Kinsella, the Bishop of Ossory, died in December 1845 two candidates on the *terna* received almost the same votes. One was Edward Walsh, a parish priest of no great distinction; the other was John O'Hanlon, a fiercely nationalist Maynooth professor. During the early weeks of 1846 Cullen was deluged by mail from nationalist bishops supporting O'Hanlon and denigrating Walsh. William Higgins, the O'Connellite Bishop of Ardagh, dismissed Walsh as a Gallican who would be a government pawn and thus a 'national calamity':

> For my part I do not know Mr Walsh except by report but I have been informed that he cannot address even his own humble flock in becoming and dignified language; that he is remarkably vulgar in his pronunciation; that he is sixty years of age; that he is a Tory in inclination; that if appointed there is reason to believe he would be in favour of the infamous Bequests Act, and even for the College Act.

Higgins concluded this letter by assuring Cullen that if O'Hanlon was appointed 'all the gold in the power of Britain would not be able to tarnish any of his excellent eccles- iastical qualities'. (C: 6 Apr. 1846) Father T. Green, the curate of Athy, had earlier assured Cullen that Walsh had the support of the parish priests only because he was ex- pected to be lax in his discipline, while O'Hanlon as a vigorous and progressive man would enforce the letter of the canon law in the diocese. (C: 20 Jan. 1846)

O'Hanlon was passed over for this appointment, probably because Cullen was convinced that his strong identification of Catholicism with the turbulent nationalism of the time would pose more of a threat to the extension of Roman authority in Ireland than the state-serving policies of Daniel Murray and the older parish priests. The latter represented the temperament of the *ancien régime*, and Rome knew that it lacked the vitality to oppose the burgeoning power of Ultramontanism. The new Gallicanism, on the other hand, identified itself only too easily with secular liberalism and threatened to resurrect in Ireland the dream of Lamennais — the Catholic Church allied with, or even led by, the spirit of revolutionary nationalism. This to Paul Cullen was anathema.

2. *The Divided Episcopate*

As Cullen handled the voluminous correspondence that came to him as Roman agent, enlarging and extending his knowledge of how the Irish Church was governed, diocese by diocese, he began to identify the bishops as either tradi- tional or new Gallicans. Although some of them from time to time made affirmations of Ultramontane loyalty, Cullen never accepted any of them as other than prelates who served Irish interests whatever the wishes of Rome might be. In fact, Cullen shared the apprehensions of Propaganda over what was happening in the Irish episcopate during the years of O'Connellite agitation. The traditional Gallicans, scorn- fully dismissed as 'hacks of the Castle' by their critics, appeared to the Roman authorities to be too amenable to government meddling in church affairs. The new Gallicans, on the other hand, caught up in the nationalist passions of the time, which included violent attacks on the 'Castle bishops',

presented Rome with the disturbing problem of the Irish
'priest in politics'. They showed little interest in the cautions
of Propaganda about the divisions they were causing in the
Church and the dangerous course they were following in
serving revolutionary liberal political causes.

Three great issues divided the bishops during the years
that Cullen acted as their agent in Rome. These were the
problems associated with deciding what should be the proper
Catholic response to government legislation establishing
the National System of primary education, the reforming of
charity laws in the Charitable Bequests Act, and the setting
up of the non-denominational Queen's Colleges. During the
uproar occasioned by these acts of parliament Cullen was
deluged by letters from the new Gallicans, or nationalist
bishops, bitterly attacking the 'Castle bishops', whom Cullen
heard from much less. In fact, what Cullen knew about the
pro-government bishops came largely from their nationalist
enemies.

The most scorned of these men was the Primate, William
Crolly, who had become Archbishop of Armagh in April
1835. Born near Downpatrick in 1780 to an old Anglo-Irish
family, Crolly had been raised in the 'Black North', where
Catholics were an oppressed minority. His critics pointed
out that he had studied under a Unitarian master as a boy
and had narrowly escaped death at the hands of dragoons
during '98, and claimed he was conditioned to give in to
Protestant bullying. They also pointed out that during his
time at Maynooth French was the language used at table,
that the Gallican theology of the Sorbonne was dominant
in the college, and that Crolly himself had acted as assistant
to Dr Anglade, one of Maynooth's most influential émigré
professors. Crolly was regularly castigated as a Gallican and
a Jansenist.

In his correspondence Cullen used the labels Gallican and
Jansenist as almost interchangeable terms. The French
Jansenists of the eighteenth century had largely abandoned
their early theological speculations, and from the standpoint of Rome their concerns were increasingly political.
Like the Gallicans, they believed that bishops should have
immediate jurisdiction independent of the papacy, that

spiritual authority rested with the whole body of the faithful and not merely with the hierarchy, and that temporal governments should have complete authority in their own domain. A short time before Cullen went to Rome a former Roman College student, Scipione de Ricci, who had become the Jansenist Bishop of Pistoia, had actually tried to establish a schismatical church. Cullen was nurtured on the evils of Jansenism and Gallicanism and their probable alliance with the liberalism of the Carbonari, as well as with the occult power of Freemasonry. The more Cullen was told about Crolly the more convinced he became that he was ideologically a fully committed Gallican — a sworn enemy of everything that Cullen held dear.

This was hardly fair to Crolly, who, as we shall see later, was an exemplary parish priest in the large parish of Belfast, to which he had been appointed in 1812. During his time in Belfast as parish priest, and then as Bishop of Down and Connor from 1825, Crolly had to face problems which Cullen in far-away Rome could not appreciate. Cullen heard of his fraternisation with Protestants, and even his attendance at heretical services of worship, which brought Crolly a rebuke from Propaganda. Yet he never understood the special situation with which Crolly had to deal as, with other Belfast Catholics, he tried to curb sectarian tensions for the sake of law, order and good government. Crolly knew that not all Protestants were unfeeling Orange monsters, but his attempts at reconciliation brought him the reputation of being a 'Castle bishop' when he was still in the see of Down and Connor. When he was translated to Armagh in 1835, shortly after Cullen became Roman agent, the charges against him mounted almost to a crescendo.

The attack was led by John MacHale, the strongly nationalist Archbishop of Tuam, who was furious that Crolly as Primate would be the recipient of so much communication from Rome dealing with the explosive issues of the time: the National System of Education, the Charitable Bequests Act, and the Queen's Colleges.

The nationalists believed that Crolly's privileged position was exploited the government as a means of controlling the Catholic Church, and Cullen shared their suspicions.

He could in no way accept Crolly's argument that there was value in the 'liberal and impartial system of National Education which has been proposed by our paternal government' (C: 4 Feb. 1839) or that the schools could help to ease sectarian animosities. Cullen in Rome viewed the British administration in Ireland as a sinister heretical authority which encouraged Gallicanism in the Irish Catholic Church. Crolly, on the other hand, like Murray in Dublin, or Cornelius Denvir, who had succeeded him as Bishop of Down and Connor, met daily with Protestants who were men of reason and moderation and who willingly sought to help Ireland's Catholic people for the sake of good civil government.

Cullen was in Ireland in the summer of 1845 when the nationalist churchmen were denouncing the new Queen's Colleges as an attempt by the government to advance heretical Sassenach culture. He wrote to Kirby in Rome to describe the tension among Irish Catholics in just such terms:

> The colleges will be resisted by the majority of the bishops. The Primate is not to be relied much on in these matters — it is a pity that Rome makes him the organ of her communications — were it not for him Dr Murray would be easily managed. Dr Denvir is almost dead from terror. Many priests are looking for places at the new colleges — the people will make an example of them if they be appointed. (K: 23 July 1845)

In another letter to Kirby two days later Cullen further denounced Crolly for persuading Irish bishops to serve as commissioners on the Charitable Bequests Board, which had been established to protect charities from mismanagement. This to Cullen was a most deplorable exercise in Gallicanism:

> I wish poor Dr Murray could be got out of the commission — it is Dr Crolly who is holding him on — I wish His Grace of Armagh were after getting a lecture from higher quarters — it would do him good. The next step the government will take is to pension the clergy. Lord Brougham has stated repeatedly in the House of Lords that an Irish bishop (I suspect it was Dr Crolly but I have no solid proof) stated to a noble lord that if a bill for pensioning

the clergy were once passed the priests would flock like rooks to the Castle to take the money — I believe some would do so, but the great majority would not.

(NK: 25 July 1845)

Cullen's opinion about Crolly was probably shaped by his nationalist uncle, James Maher, who savagely and repeatedly attacked the Primate, as well as from his own reading of the Irish situation on the eve of the famine. He knew that the National System and the Queen's Colleges were a matter of satisfaction to the Gallicans, and that few of them would be dismayed by the reappearance of the idea of the veto and pensioning of the clergy. He also recognised that in order to withstand the alliance of these traditional Gallicans with the establishment, the Ultramontanists would have to take the desperate gamble of aligning themselves with the new Gallicans, the prelates like John MacHale who sought to build up a sectarian Catholic/nationalist front. As Cullen told Kirby:

> The priests are generally right, but some hungry dogs are looking for places and pensions. . . . I hope the people are so good that much mischief cannot be done. There is no people like the Irish. . . . (NK: 29 Sept. 1845)

Cullen was never a willing ally of 'the people'. He fretted over his association with the MacHaleites, which threatened to bring him a loss of authority in Rome, but to him the times were desperate, and to do battle with Archbishop Crolly and the traditional Gallicans he was willing to make such a tactical move. This was the time when in Belfast and Dublin, Galway and Cork, more and more clergy were showing support for the new colleges. In January 1847 Cullen was even informed that Bishop John Murphy of Cork was tolerating priests writing in the *Cork Examiner* on behalf of the new colleges.

To Cullen, and to many other Roman authorities, the chief villain in this nurturing of the spirit of old-fashioned Gallicanism remained the Primate, William Crolly. The pressure put upon Crolly by the nationalist bishops to oppose the Queen's Colleges was immense, and in the autumn of 1848 Maginn of Derry and Cantwell of Meath assured

Archbishop Slattery that Crolly had agreed to support the condemnation. (CA, 1848/165/169) Cullen looked for little to come from this rumoured 'conversion', however, for he believed Crolly to be a convinced Gallican. Cullen had no doubt that if only an Ultramontanist was Archbishop of Armagh, the situation in Ireland would have been significantly different. It is probable that when John Cantwell wrote to Cullen on 7 April 1849 to report the death of Crolly, Cullen breathed a fervent 'amen' to the Bishop of Meath's prayer at the end of his report of this 'melancholy event': 'May God forgive him and have mercy on his soul.' (C) In a departure from custom, no obituary for the deceased Primate was published in the *Irish Catholic Directory*.

Cullen's relationship with Daniel Murray, the pious and able Archbishop of Dublin, was quite different from the cold reserve with which he treated Crolly. Like most priests of his generation, Murray was a traditional Gallican, as was his close friend Oliver Kelly, who preceded John MacHale as Archbishop of Tuam. Yet his simple goodness of character persuaded Cullen that though the old archbishop might be mistaken in his policies, there was little chance of his being used by the government. In all Murray did he acted upon principle, and he displayed a spirit of sturdy independence when pressure was put upon him by the administrations in Rome and in London. Cullen always had a deep respect for Daniel Murray.

Murray returned from Salamanca, where he had been Rector of the Irish College, when the French Revolution broke out. He was a curate in Arklow in '98 and nearly lost his life in the rising. This gave him the intense horror of revolution which he shared with William Crolly and James Doyle, both of whom had witnessed the carnage of '98 at first hand. He had briefly acted as President of Maynooth when he was coadjutor bishop in Dublin, and he had been a reluctant member of the delegation which went to Rome in 1814 to express the popular opposition to the veto. In 1825, two years after he took over as Archbishop of Dublin, Murray gave evidence before the parliamentary commissioners looking into state of Ireland, and displayed a spirit of conciliation towards Protestants that not all his clerical brethren appreciated. (PP, VIII, 228)

This conciliatory attitude stood him in good stead when he served alongside Richard Whately, the Protestant Archbishop of Dublin, as one of the commissioners of education. In spite of the fact that he served on such a government body, and at times openly commended the faithful to read Bossuet's exposition of the Christian faith (McGhee, *Murray*, 17), he was cordially received when he visited Rome in 1835 and 1836. He met Cullen at this time who described Murray, then sixty-eight years old, as 'one of the most amiable and excellent men I ever recollect to have met with'. (PM, I, 222)

Strain in the relationship between Cullen and Murray first arose in 1838 over the National System of elementary education which had been set up by the government in 1831. It was a great boon to the poor, and it was soon considered that the education provided for the peasantry was of a higher standard in Ireland than in any other European country. The Catholic hierarchy had no direct control over the schools, however; furthermore, Catholics and non-Catholics received instruction in secular subjects together, and many Catholics were disturbed that religious instruction was confined to that provided at set times by priests appointed for that purpose. In the spring of 1838 John MacHale protested to Rome about the schools, and Murray immediately wrote to Cullen to indicate how misguided MacHale was.

Murray told Cullen that to reject state assistance in providing education for the poor who so desperately needed it was folly. To talk of Catholics receiving a separate grant from the administration for denominational schools was 'so utterly visionary that no rational person could entertain it for a moment'. (C: 28 Apr. 1838) He then passed on to deal with MacHale's charges one by one. He said that the religious instruction of pupils in the training establishment in Dublin, 'exactly opposite our church in Marlborough St', was carefully watched by the Pro-Cathedral curate, John Miley, 'so favourably known at Rome', and 'it is not likely that any abuse could escape his vigilance'. As for the scripture lessons used in the schools, which MacHale decried, Murray observed:

The translation does not favour any error, and the notes contain no doctrine contrary to our faith. This is all we could expect in a book which Protestants as well as Catholics might be supposed to use. (C: 17 Dec. 1838)

Murray also encouraged his staff to write to Cullen on the subject. Archdeacon John Hamilton in two long letters discussed every objection raised by MacHale and told Cullen that no one in Dublin could understand what he was objecting to. In MacHale's territory the people were overwhelmingly Catholic, and where the schools were allowed to operate they were in effect denominational. Murray himself picked up this theme, pointing out that in most parts of the country the government was offering what was in effect a state-aided denominational school system:

Considering a fair sample of the proportion of Catholic teachers to Protestant teachers throughout the country, is it not clear that the Catholics have almost the whole education of the poor population of the country under their control? That is so true that the bigoted Protestants are moving heaven and earth to get rid of the system, and no bigoted landlord will give a foot of ground for the erection of a national school. (C: 21 Mar. 1839)

A worrying factor to Murray was that at the same time as he was trying to control MacHale's agitation over the schools he had also to correspond with Rome over MacHale's war with his suffragan bishop, Francis O'Finan of Killala. As this scandalous strife went on, information which Murray considered to be privileged was leaked to the Roman authorities and became the subject of gossip. He feared that MacHale might attempt a similar trial of the National System by public opinion in both Rome and Ireland. Already it was rumoured that Cullen was on MacHale's side in the dispute. Murray told Cullen on 4 April that if the controversy became public he would defend himself by showing how totally irrational the criticisms of the National System really were:

I may as well mention on this occasion that if the objections now before the Sacred Congregation which were

made to our National System of Education and the Scripture
Lessons should come in any shape before the public I hold
myself at full liberty to publish my answers to them; that
all the world may be enabled to judge how far those
objections appear to have been dictated by a love of truth,
and whether or not they bear any indication of a design to
deceive the Holy See. (C: 4 Apr. 1839)

Two weeks later he told Cullen that if there was Roman interference, against all reason and against the advice of the majority
of the bishops, to withdraw Catholic support from the schools
and thus to place state-funded education exclusively in the
hands of Protestants, who were 'the greatest enemies of our
religion', he would have no choice but to retire from the
Board of National Education so that 'the government may
find some abler and more fortunate person to supply my
place'. (C)

Cullen's replies to Murray did not reassure him. Murray
knew from those who agreed with him in Rome that Tobias
Kirby had worked himself up into a state of near hysteria
over this Gallican educational system. Murray deplored this
extreme reaction and told Cullen that he would be wise to
ignore Kirby's 'severe reprobation' of the system 'of the
working of which he appears to be supremely ignorant'. As
for MacHale's machinations, he knew about them from no
less a source than the Lord Lieutenant, Lord Ebrington, 'a
thinking and benevolent man who has not the least tincture
of religious bigotry', who was popular among the Catholics
on his Waterford estates. He had informed Murray that it
was believed in Rome that

Dr Higgins was the bearer of a verbal assurance to Dr
MacHale from Propaganda that the Sacred Congregation
disapproved the system of National Education altogether,
disapproved the books used for Catholic instruction, and
would immediately direct me to retire from the Board.

This was reported to be what was happening, in spite of the
fact that Lord Ebrington assured Murray that Irish Catholics
'can have no hope of public aid for education on terms more
favourable than those on which the National System is
conducted'. Murray was appalled by this report. He bluntly
told Cullen what would happen if it was true:

It would delight our enemies; it would degrade our hierarchy; it would leave a soreness in the Irish heart which
would be likely to break out into more violent discontent
against the Holy See than ever that which was manifested
when there was question of the Veto. The bigots would
not fail to avail themselves of this occasion to brand us as
patrons of ignorance under the tyrannical influence of a
foreign power. (C: 12 July 1839)

In the face of Murray's convictions, Rome hesitated to act
against what was considered to be Ireland's Gallican educational establishment, and MacHale found himself disappointed
in his expectations. He had hoped that some of the bishops
who criticised the National System might have been called to
Rome to present their case. Instead the pope suggested that
Murray and MacHale send well-informed priests. Murray sent
as his deputies Dr John Ennis, Parish Priest of Booterstown,
and William Meagher, Parish Priest of Rathmines, who arrived
in Rome to defend the schools in November 1839. MacHale
and Higgins, to their great embarrassment, had a hard job to
find scholarly ecclesiastics in their camp who spoke French
and Italian and 'enjoy our full confidence'. Eventually they
settled upon Martin Loftus, Parish Priest of Tuam. Rome did
not make up its mind about the Irish school system, however,
until Cullen himself, at the suggestion of Propaganda, visited
several schools in the summer of 1840 when he was in Ireland.
He submitted a long report on 13 September 1840. Because
there were so few Protestants in Ireland 'mixed teaching is
not so disastrous as it would appear':

> In practice it seems that the teaching in the schools is
> being carried out sufficiently well. Almost all the teachers
> are Catholic and the children generally are Catholic. The
> catechism adopted in Ireland contains a very good exposi-
> tion of the Catholic doctrine and is being taught in all the
> schools. To all outward appearances the system appears
> very satisfactory . . . therefore it would seem that it would
> be very dangerous to condemn it. (PM, I, 232)

The end of all this was that a rescript of January 1841 left
to the 'prudent discretion and religious conscience' of each

bishop the final decision as to whether the system would be tolerated in his diocese.

The unfortunate result of this controversy over the National System, and Cullen's willingness to be so influenced by Kirby and other MacHaleites, was that Archbishop Murray now held him in some suspicion. Early in 1840 he told Cullen bluntly that nine of the ten bishops who were dividing the Irish Church by supporting MacHale were outright hypocrites, choosing to 'allow this heretical plant to shoot up high and thrive under their eyes in every part of their respective dioceses'. (C: 28 Feb. 1840) In Murray's opinion, the image of the Church was being seriously damaged by such conduct on the part of the bishops:

> This apparent double-dealing of so many of our prelates, who denounce in word what they encourage in practice has exceedingly scandalised the intelligent portion of the Catholic body and lowered in the minds of Protestants, to a most humiliating degree, the character of our prelacy. To the government their proceedings appear to be utterly factious not having seemingly any real principle of religion to rest upon. (C: 12 July 1839)

In their exchanges Cullen's regard for the saintly Murray is obvious, and the latter clearly felt kindly towards the zealous, yet still politically immature, Roman agent. Murray often inquired about Cullen's ill-health, his recurrent headaches as well as his 'perpetual anxiety and mental labour'. At the same time his paternal interest in the younger man included a clear warning, which he had voiced earlier, that Cullen's tactics had convinced churchmen and others in Ireland that he was now a committed MacHaleite. This, Murry said, was 'galling intelligence' for the 'great majority of the Irish prelates':

> I lately saw a letter addressed to the government by one of their diplomatic agents in Italy (a Protestant) which stated that nothing could be decided on the education question until the arrival of Dr MacHale's deputy; but that in reality he did not want one; for that all thro' he had a most efficient one in the President of the Irish College.
>
> (C: 28 Feb. 1840)

Cullen at this time still considered MacHale to be sufficiently anti-Gallican for him to be used in the struggle to extend Roman authority in Ireland. In 1841 he warned MacHale not to refer to National Education in his Lenten pastoral. Rather he should show his countrymen that he 'attended literally to the instructions from Rome', and thus persuade them 'to take a right view of the national system'. (PM, I, 236: 15 Feb. 1841) At the same time he must have given some anxious thought to the problem of how MacHale could ever be curbed or directed in his wilfulness. By the end of the year Murray was reporting that only MacHale himself now remained in opposition to the schools: 'His opposition goes, it is said, to the extent of refusing sacraments to those who send their children to national schools.' (C: 20 Nov. 1841) Soon Cullen was to find to his great cost that his covert encouragement of MacHale was to result in a severe estrangement from Murray and the other 'Castle bishops'. It was also almost to cost him his credibility and authority in Rome.

The greatest crisis of Cullen's Roman career came in 1844 when he launched an ill-considered attack on the Charitable Bequests Bill, legislation brought before parliament which sought to regulate charitable legacies. Sir Robert Peel wished to set up a body consisting of Irish judges and commissioners to control charitable bequests in Ireland. The thirteen commissioners, five of them Catholics, were to be appointed and dismissed by the crown, and questions of Catholic charities would be referred to a committee composed only of Catholics. (7 & 8 Vict., c. 97) To Cullen and many other Catholics this was a clear exercise in old-fashioned Gallicanism. They feared that by appointing Gallican churchmen as commissioners the government might convert many of the charities of the Catholic Church in Ireland to purposes very different from those intended by their testators.

In actual fact the legislation, though imperfect from the Catholic viewpoint, was not the sinister measure its critics believed it to be. But MacHale immediately opposed it, and in England the columns of Frederick Lucas's *Tablet* were filled with protests against the bill. O'Connell also decided to take political advantage of the clerical outcry and went along with what became almost hysterical denunciation of this new example of government interference in ecclesiastical affairs. On 11 September 1844 Cullen wrote to MacHale to add his willing support to the protest movement:

I was delighted to see your Grace declare such decided war against the new 'Charity Bill'. It is a most abominable insult to Catholics to pretend that it is a great boon. God grant that no bishop will accept office in the Commission! O'Connell's opinion must have great weight. . . . I hope the opposition will be so strenuous that the government will not be able to advance a step. . . . If all our bishops were united, who could resist our just claims? (PM, I, 251)

This ecclesiastical furor came at the time when the crisis over Repeal had just reached its peak, when Rome was filled with rumours about an English ambassador being appointed to the Holy See 'to intrigue in Irish affairs', and when the division between the supporters of Murray and MacHale was deepening. The former heard of Cullen and Kirby swinging their support to MacHale, while Kirby's statements about the legislation (which he had never seen) were fully in keeping with his exercise in obscurantism over the National System. On 7 September, therefore, Murray sent his own analysis of the bill to Cullen in the hope that he and Kirby might be persuaded that it was not as dangerous as they thought.

Murray pointed out, first of all, how much better the proposed legislation was compared with the existing 'wholly Protestant and bigoted Board of Charitable Bequests'. The new body would not have the power to alter the application of Catholic bequests as the old board had: 'When there is a doubt concerning the intended application the decision is to be left wholly to the Catholic members, a majority of whom will, if they choose, be bishops.' (C) As far as Murray could see from a lengthy and critical assessment of the bill, though it had its faults, it appeared to be a genuine attempt by the government to satisfy Catholic sensibilities. Improvements to the measure were promised if the bishops requested them; and in fact modifications to satisfy them were carried out in 1867 and 1871. (30 & 31 Vict., c. 53; 34 & 35 Vict., c. 102)

By this time, however, Kirby in Rome and the MacHaleites in Ireland were in full cry, stigmatising the bill as 'a penal law of the old leaven'. Murray told Cullen on 1 October 1844 that he hoped the detractors of the bill would at least read it before launching their assaults: 'Whether good or bad let it be judged on its own merits or demerits and not on any misrepresentation of it.' He especially poured his scorn on those who wrote so savagely in the newspapers or signed petitions against legislation in misguided zeal:

> The undersigned without offering the slightest reason to support their opinion declare their conviction of what numbers of intelligent Catholics utterly disbelieve, namely that this Act if carried into operation will finally lead to the subjection of the Catholic Church in Ireland to the Temporal Power. (C)

When even O'Connell admitted that the new statute could be used for good by Irish Catholics, since it gave them benefits denied to Protestants in England and, contrary to the arguments of its detractors, posed no particular threat to the religious orders, Murray wondered why there should be so much obscurantist opposition.

It was now that Cullen made his very serious error in judgment, which almost cost him his authority in Rome. He committed himself to the MacHaleite agitation. In a letter to MacHale on 3 October 1844 he promised to present the views of those who opposed the bill to the pope, and suggested the issue be debated at the next full meeting of the Irish bishops:

> There are some canons and decrees of the Council of Trent that appear to excommunicate persons assuming the functions now to be attributed to the Commissioners. It would be well that Catholics should be made aware of such decrees being in existence. (PM, I, 252)

Influenced by Kirby's polemics and the diatribes of the MacHaleites, who were deluging him with their propaganda, he allowed his own ideological convictions to overrule his usual discretion. He cast aside his characteristic prudence and came out clearly on the side of MacHale and his 'orthodox party' who were heaping opprobrium on the unfortunate Archbishops Crolly and Murray and on Cornelius Denvir of Down and Connor, who had agreed to serve on the Charitable

Bequests Board. Through his zealous opposition to what he perceived to be the advance of traditional Gallicanism in the Irish Church, Cullen was directly contributing to division among the prelates.

Murray could see that Cullen was putting himself into a very dangerous position. Several times he had warned the Roman agent about becoming identified as the servant of the MacHaleites, and on 5 October he expressed his understanding of how difficult it was for Cullen in Rome to understand the truth of what was happening in Ireland:

> I am hardly surprised at learning that the new Charitable Bequests Act has found no favour at Rome. Indeed from the statements that were made of it in the public papers the thing could not be otherwise; for whether good or bad it has not had fair play. How much humbled I was to have a long letter from our friend Dr Kirby thundering with all his might against a clause which is not in the act at all. (C)

Patiently he tried to assure Cullen about the good intentions of the government, telling him that the Lord Lieutenant himself had given an assurance that 'three bishops and two laymen having the confidence of the bishops' should be appointed 'to take charge in the new board'. But Crolly's counsel fell on deaf ears: Cullen was now fully committed to the cause of those opposed to the bill.

What followed taught Cullen a lesson he was never to forget. From this time forward he was never again to put his trust in MacHale and his nationalist Catholic party. A meeting of the Irish bishops in December 1844 degenerated into acrimonious division between the MacHaleites and those who were willing to consider rationally the possible benefits of the bill. This occurred when the British government, through its agents in Rome, was trying to persuade the papacy that some sort of concordat had to be arranged in Ireland, where the populace, following the 'Repeal year' of 1843, was still seriously disturbed. The government argued that something had to be done to curb the political passions aroused by agitating priests. Now MacHale, supported by Cullen, had given the British government another example to be used in presenting its case in Rome. When even bishops were at one

another's throats over a measure as comparatively innocuous
as the Charitable Bequests Bill, what hope was there for peace
in the land unless the secular authorities and Rome worked
together to bring discipline to the Irish Catholic Church?

Following the disastrous meeting of the bishops Cullen
was in full retreat. He begged MacHale to stop writing in
public against the Bequests legislation, which finally became
law in December 1844, and on 28 January 1845 he urged:
'For heaven's sake exert all your powerful energies to restore
peace in the Church.' (PM, I, 257) The pope was far from
pleased with the role that Cullen had played, and in Ireland
there was a groundswell of sympathetic support for Murray,
Crolly and Denvir and a widespread reaction against the
bigots of the 'orthodox party' who had so shockingly censured
them.

One of those who wrote to Cullen to console him over his
diplomatic blunder was his old friend from Propaganda
College days, William Walshe, Bishop of Halifax, then on a
visit to Ireland. He told Cullen:

> I confess my heart bleeds for Dr Murray. . . . The opponents
> of the Bequests Act — if ever so sound in principle — have
> carried on the war against it in so furious, so uncharitable,
> so unnatural a manner that the consequent evils are in
> my opinion ten times more disastrous to religion than any
> mischief this unfortunate bill itself could produce.
>
> (C: 18 Jan. 1845)

In reply, Cullen confessed to his old friend what a terrible
blunder his joining the MacHaleites had been. He was sick
at heart for having 'taken any part at all in the actual proceedings':

> I hope you will have the goodness to say a word to Dr
> Murray. I treated him very badly. . . . There is no man for
> whom I entertain greater veneration or more profound
> respect. The late proceedings in Dublin have taught me a
> terrible lesson. What disrespect for the Pope and for epis-
> copal authority. . . . (DAA: 10 Feb. 1845)

By this time Cullen was so broken that he was on the verge
of total collapse. When Bishop Cantwell of Meath tried to
continue to put pressure on him Cullen replied unhappily:

I cannot do much in the matter. I am not at all well, and besides I was wrong in taking any part in the proceedings publicly.... God grant that nothing bad may occur in Ireland. Things are gone to a terrible state. Every effort should be made to preserve or restore union. For God's sake, exert yourself! It is bad to push things to extremes. I fear it is not wise to introduce censures in such cases.

(PM, I, 258: 8 Feb. 1845)

For the time being Cantwell and the other MacHaleites decided to leave Cullen alone because of his 'great alarm' and his 'terror'. It was clear to them that the English had won their way over the Charitable Bequests Act, with the most significant engagement taking place in Rome. Cullen, as MacHale's Roman advocate, was a casualty of the struggle and no longer of use to them — at least in this battle. Both Cantwell and Higgins advised MacHale of this, and also mentioned the alarm of the pope and Propaganda over the state of the now radically divided Irish Church. Cullen, in an effort to recuperate, spent the summer in Ireland and wrote Kirby long letters about attempts he was making to foster reconciliation among the quarrelling prelates.

When the Queen's Colleges in Belfast, Cork and Galway were established by the government in 1845 Cullen once more found himself at odds with Murray over the issue of 'godless education'. The latter tried in a long series of letters during 1845 and 1846 to assure Cullen that the government was trying to be perfectly fair to the Catholics in setting up the colleges. Kirby, in contrast, tried to influence Cullen against the colleges and did much to persuade him against Murray's argument that the new bodies were a better alternative than Trinity College, which was now attracting the grandchildren of O'Connell and other young men from Catholic families.

Murray also pointed out that when the colleges were established some Catholic priests were bound to make use of them or to seek posts within them. Would it not therefore be wise, he suggested, to let the Church have some say about how the colleges developed? Shortly after he informed Cullen that he had declined a seat in the Privy Council Murray wrote:

The new colleges would seem to be not what we would wish if we had the power to do better, but at least a step in advance in our favour, affording considerable protection to our youth against the greater dangers of Trinity College and those other Protestant universities where our physicians and surgeons and many of our lawyers finish their education.
(DAA: 14 Nov. 1846)

By this time Cullen had recovered his diplomatic poise and could thus appreciate Murray's gentlemanly behaviour, even in opposition, and he never displayed towards the saintly Archbishop of Dublin the cold front he presented to Crolly. At the height of the famine Cullen listened to Murray's expression of gratitude that so much aid from England was pouring into the country, and in his reply he merely remarked:

It would be well, I dare say, to write a line to thank His Holiness — a thousand dollars from him is more than a hundred thousand from the Queen of England.
(DAA: 30 Jan. 1847)

He also avoided comment when Murray, after praising the aid sent by Cardinal Fransoni to help the poor, uncharacteristically lashed out at the MacHaleites, who persisted with their never-ending intrigues even in the midst of this great catastrophe:

Our angry politics and particularly the sums of money sent by priests from the most distressed districts of the country to Conciliation Hall have done much to impede the current of charity which was coming from England to our relief.
(DAA: 8 Apr. 1848)

Cullen's caution with Murray after the 1844 crisis reflected his desire to avoid confrontation politically, but at the same time it indicated his deep respect for the well-loved archbishop. He agreed with Michael Slattery, the Archbishop of Cashel, who observed to him that it was sad to be placed 'in circumstances where I must differ in opinion with so excellent a prelate'. (C: 2 Aug. 1846) But although Cullen respected Murray, he never lost his conviction that the Archbishop of Dublin, in his seventy-ninth year in 1846, was being misled by the government. Nor was Murray the only prominent churchman to be thus influenced: for example, Michael Blake, Bishop of Dromore and former Rector of the Irish College in Rome, could give Cullen cogent reasons why the Queen's Colleges should be accepted:

> Situated . . . as we are, and seeing so great a leaning on the part of the middle classes towards the government offer, I would recommend that we should take advantage of the great ardour with which our rulers endeavour to conciliate His Holiness. They have already made some concessions, and perhaps they may be induced to make more.
>
> (C: 19 July 1848)

Cullen was well aware of these pragmatic arguments for the 'godless colleges', but he remained unconvinced by them.

Cullen's passionate Ultramontanism governed his response to the National System, the Charitable Bequests Act and the Queen's Colleges, making it inevitable that that response was largely ideological. The Irish agent in Rome saw his greatest enemy as heresy, whether advanced directly through tactics such as trying to establish a British representative in Rome who could coerce the pope, or indirectly through Gallican control of Irish institutions made use of by Catholics. It was because of this ideological commitment that his tendency was to listen too often to the savage criticism of the 'Castle bishops' made by the followers of MacHale, the self-styled 'orthodox party'.

One of the sensible voices that Cullen might have heeded on the educational issue was that of James Browne, Bishop of Kilmore, whose diocese was filled with estates controlled by Orange landlords. An intelligent man who had been a professor and a dean at Maynooth, he avoided politics and devoted himself to building churches, convents and promoting Catholic education. In 1839 he urged Cullen to be cautious of letters of advice sent to him from a country 'filled with Catholic polemical writers on the watch for not merely palpable errors but even any word that may be suspected or tortured into an heterodox meaning'. A strong supporter of Murray, Browne assured Cullen that no comparison could be made between the Prussian system of education and the National System of Ireland. (C: 14 Mar. 1839) In the same year he reinforced Murray's correspondence with the Roman agent by assuring Cullen that in his diocese he had complete control of Catholic education. Not only could he exclude from the school curriculum any books which he did not approve, but he could dismiss any master he suspected of proselytising. As for the MacHaleites, Browne told Cullen bluntly that the division of the bishops over the education issue played directly into the hands of the Orangemen. (C: 13 Apr. 1839) When the crisis arose over the Charitable Bequests Bill in 1844 it was Browne's opinion that the furor simply represented the wrath of Whig bishops opposing Tory legislation and thus had nothing to do with religion. In fact, some of the bishops, stampeded into opposing the legislation without even reading it, now regretted they had signed the petition. (C: 25 Nov. 1844)

Another strong pastoral bishop who supported Murray yet had the respect of Cullen was Patrick McGettigan, Bishop of Raphoe from 1820. When he died in 1861 Cullen said that the old bishop had found his diocese without a single church when he first worked there, but he had left it 'well provided with churches and religious institutions'. (PM, IV, 93) At the start of the campaign against the National Schools in 1838 McGettigan described to Cullen in detail the situation in Letterkenny, which he said was typical of the state of affairs in his diocese. There the government had never made any attempt to 'tamper or interfere with the faith or morals of the children':

> No Protestant or Presbyterian have attended the large school in this town. I have the appointment of the Master and Mistress, who both are Catholics, and the whole management of the school to myself. (C: 17 Aug. 1838)

Early in 1839, just before he left for Rome to lobby on behalf of those bishops who supported the National System, he again wrote to Cullen to enumerate the benefits of the government-supported schools in his diocese:

> I have narrowly watched the system since its early commencement and some of my priests are patrons of every school in the Diocese of Raphoe. We have the approval of most of the masters and mistresses and in fact the sole

control among them. It would be most lamentable to turn the children now on their own miserable resources and to put them once more into the hands of people whose avowed object was proselytism and the persuasion of the poor children. (C: 30 Jan. 1839)

Cullen, however, by inclination had little interest in arguments about the schools serving the temporal needs of the people, and he had his suspicions of James Browne, who was perhaps too conciliatory towards the Orangemen, and Patrick McGettigan, who was also mild-mannered. Although he approved of them as non-political pastoral bishops, he considered their opinions about education could well reflect an accommodation to Protestant intimidation. His reaction to Browne was to record him as a Gallican supporter of Murray. Towards McGettigan he became increasingly cool because of the systematic campaign of character assassination carried out against him by the MacHaleites. In 1839 Higgins of Ardagh urged Cullen to ensure that McGettigan had 'no opportunity of delivering his sentiments' in Rome. (C: 2 May 1839) By the time that McGettigan agreed to serve as a member of the Charitable Bequests Board in 1846 Cullen was willing to listen to his most violent detractors, such as Edward Maginn, the intensely nationalist Coadjutor Bishop of Derry, who warned Cullen against those who would 'bind our church hand and foot to an heretical state, yea sell it for less than the thirty pieces of silver for which Judas sold his Master'. Referring to 'your friend, the little doctor-Bishop of Raphoe', Maginn urged Cullen to use his Roman influence to have a curb put on McGettigan's activities:

I say it advisedly to you, but in all confidence that the sooner you at Rome can provide him with a prudent coadjutor the better for the interests of religion and the honour of the episcopacy. This is *entre nous* and with all seriousness. His conduct in Synod, merely known to bishops, is not half as injurious as his conversation in Protestant society where he makes no secret of the secrets of his church or his clergy. It is horrible to hear of this revelation, which Protestants, of course, believe though no Catholic would credit them. (C: 3 Dec. 1846)

Another episcopal voice to which he might have paid more attention in the discussion of the National System was that of John Ryan, who had served as a bishop in the Limerick diocese since 1825. Ryan from the beginning of his relationship with Cullen asserted Ultramontane sympathies, telling him in 1832: 'I am fully of the opinion that the jurisdiction of Rome in the country would be much strengthened by practical interference.' (C: 27 Aug. 1832) A year later he went further in his profession of loyalty to Roman authority, and in his demands for its discipline to be imposed on the Irish Church:

> The ordinary efforts hitherto made will not answer the purpose: some effectual means must be adopted or Ireland will be before seven years as much under the domination of Liberalism as France is at the present day. I hope this timely warning will be attended to, and may I request that you will urge it in the proper quarter. (C: 11 Nov. 1833)

Yet Ryan did not appoint Cullen his Roman agent until 1847, and when he referred with distaste to the division the MacHaleites were causing by their rejection of the National System, Cullen became very reserved in his dealings with the Bishop of Limerick. Ryan was one of Maynooth's early graduates, a typical representative of the well-to-do Catholic farming class in Munster, and in Cullen's eyes he belonged to the traditional Irish Gallican camp in spite of his Ultramontane protestations. Cullen was therefore not surprised when Ryan deplored the 'unnecessary alarms' raised by the MacHaleites or when he displayed his satisfaction with Rome's eventual refusal to condemn the National System.

One of the reasons for Cullen's propensity to support the MacHaleites was the simple one that they wrote to him more often and tried to make use of him in a way that the 'Castle bishops' did not. He was constantly bombarded by communications from the zealots of the 'orthodox party', who were willing to spend a proportionately larger amount of time and energy writing to Rome about ecclesiastical and political affairs than were the supporters of William Crolly and Daniel Murray. The very fact that he heard from the 'Castle bishops' relatively infrequently helped to persuade the Roman agent that they were in reality old-fashioned Gallicans. Cullen believed that the 'Castle bishops', to maintain their relationship with the state, regularly turned for help to their friends in the secular administration rather than to the agent of the hierarchy in Rome.

3. *The Nationalist Bishops*
One of the first clerical nationalists with whom Cullen established contact was William Higgins. He was considered to be one of the few intellectuals in the Irish priesthood; he had studied in Paris, Vienna and Rome, and was admitted Doctor of Divinity in 1825. He had met Cullen when the latter was still a student, and their long acquaintance may explain the sometimes hectoring tone which Higgins used with the Irish agent in Rome. A persistent correspondent, he kept Cullen informed about Irish politics, especially the political machinations of Daniel O'Connell. Proudly conscious of his Irish heritage (his ancestry included notable Irish poets, as well as martyrs of '98, and he himself frequently preached in Irish), Higgins was considered to be one of the most outspoken of episcopal nationalists after he became Bishop of Ardagh in the year of Catholic Emancipation. His Repeal ardour was such that he added the prefix 'O' to his name in honour of the Liberator after O'Connell's death in 1847.

The Catholic clergy in Higgins's diocese were renowned for their secular activities in the buying and selling of land, and the Ardagh area was filled with social unrest because of this jobbery. When Higgins wrote to Cullen about trouble in his diocese in 1830, however, it was to discuss the tyranny and oppression of Protestant landlords and the proselytising activities of Power le Poer Trench, the Protestant Archbishop of Tuam. (PFS, XXV, 253: 27 Mar. 1830) From the time the National System of Education was initiated he castigated it in his letters to Cullen as an exercise in 'latitudinarianism', a vast scheme designed to allow 'laymen and heretics' to usurp Catholic episcopal authority. He readily supplied Cullen with detailed criticisms of the system, such as unequal distribution of funds, and of the dangerous opinions of the Protestant Archbishop of Dublin, Richard Whately. When John Patrick Lyons, the Parish Priest of Kilmore Erris, accepted aid for his schools from the Kildare Place Society and gave his support to the National System, Higgins made sure that Cullen knew about his activities, as well as those of others who were too friendly to the secular authority.

By 1839, when the Irish bishops were deeply divided over the question of supporting or opposing the National System, Higgins was supplying Cullen with the names of those who supported Daniel Murray and welcomed the state-aided schools in their dioceses. He told Cullen that Whately's *Lessons on the Truth of Christianity* was a 'vague' book, one that was essentially 'Arian' in its opinion that the Redeemer was 'nothing more than the adopted Son of God'. Now the ideas of heretics like Whately were being 'earnestly recommended by the Board' for use in the National Schools. Worst of all, a minority of Irish Catholics welcomed this development: 'all the bad priests, lukewarm and Castle-hack Catholics as well as the heretical or Votarian liberals'. It was shocking that negligent priests were actually aiding the sinister purpose of the secular power:

> The English government hope to accomplish by this system what fire and sword could not do — the extinction of the Catholic faith in Ireland. (C: 1 Feb. 1839)

Very much a political populist, Higgins warned Cullen about the inadvisability of listening to the pro-establishment viewpoint of some Catholic gentry and aristocrats: 'the Sassanach propensities of our invidious anti-Catholic neighbours':

> Their forefathers preferred the smiles of Henry's court and the plunder of churches and convents to the preservation of the true faith, and their worthy descendants can never forgive the Irish clergy for believing that the countless thousands of virtuous faithful are more to be attended to than the few worthless creatures called aristocrats.
>
> (C: 26 Mar. 1839)

As for Murray and his 'Castle Catholic' supporters, Rome should ignore their blandishments as unrepresentative of the Catholic mind of Ireland. Higgins told Cullen bluntly that 'Dublin is that which most imperfectly represents or expresses the clerical mind or feeling of Ireland.' (C: 6 Dec. 1839)

When the Dublin clerical world had nothing to say about a scandal like the selection of the Grand Master of the Free-masons to hand out prizes at the Dublin Model School, it was clear that it had lost all credibility with the people. The truth was, Higgins told Cullen, that Daniel Murray was toler-ating priests like the infamous Thaddeus O'Malley, an eager polemical writer in Dublin, who propagated the 'foulest Jansenism' and was plainly 'the paid agent of the government for schismatical purposes'. (C: 18 Jan. 1840)

Following Cullen's visit to Ireland in 1840 and his decision to recommend that the National System be tolerated so long as 'safeguards' were built into it, Higgins shifted his attention to other than the educational threat to Irish Catholics. As we shall see shortly, he committed himself so strongly in support of the political movement launched by Daniel O'Connell for Repeal of the Union that he had a severe nervous collapse. By 1844, however, he was once more deluging Cullen with letters about the Charitable Bequests Bill, describing the legislation as a 'golden link between the Castle and some of our brethren'. (C: 2 Oct. 1844) So many Irish Catholics were willing to accept this 'sacriligious spoliation' that he begged Cullen to use all his influence in Rome to protect the faithful against Castle intrigue and Catholic weakness.

After Cullen's loss of favour in Rome over his incautious support of the Charitable Bequests agitation promoted by bishops like Higgins, it might have been expected that the Roman agent would be spared further pressure from the Bishop of Ardagh. When the 'godless colleges' were established in 1845, however, he was once more in full cry, demanding that Archbishop Crolly be brought to heel by Rome and 'either sent from Armagh or made to recant his scandalous errors'. (C: 15 Oct. 1845) By 1849 Higgins was declaring that both Crolly and Murray shared the 'spirit of Jansenism' in Ireland, and neither had any respect for Roman authority: 'The Castle of Dublin and not the Vatican is the object of their confidence and veneration.' (C: 22 Feb. 1849) Any priest who accepted a position in the new colleges was denounced from the altars of Ardagh. When William Kirwan, Parish Priest of Oughterard, who had accepted appointment as President of Queen's College, Galway, was stricken with a fatal illness, Higgins disclosed to Cullen what he thought this visitation signified:

> Kirwan of Galway has had a third attack of paralysis and his life is despaired of. One of his curates, an ardent admirer of the Infidel Colleges, has also been attacked by paralysis, whilst a second curate of his who detests these establishments is quite well! Is it a judgment from God?
>
> (C: 16 Sept. 1849)

It is difficult to assess how much influence Higgins by himself ever had with Cullen in spite of the never-ending flood of letters he sent to the Roman agent. Cullen knew well that in his days at Maynooth as Professor of Dogmatic and Moral Theology, immediately following the era of the French émigré professors, Higgins was considered to be a strong Gallican. He used the Gallican works of Bailly in his classes and bluntly informed the parliamentary commissioners of 1826 that 'Cisalpine doctrine' prevailed in the college. (MacNamee, *Ardagh*, 423) It is probable that Cullen never took seriously Higgins's unceasing animadversions on the need for Roman authority to be exercised in Irish affairs. Rather he watched with considerable concern Higgins's extravagant use of episcopal and clerical authority in the social agitation he promoted, and probably wondered how much of his Gallican outlook he had ever lost.

Higgins's ideas were continually reinforced, however, by other nationalist bishops. One of the most prolific writers to the Roman agent was John Cantwell, Bishop of Meath, who was not only an ally of Higgins but also a close friend of John MacHale and a devoted supporter of O'Connell. Cantwell had been wholly educated at Maynooth, and Cullen seems to have been much more reserved in his correspondence with him than he had been with Higgins over the issue of the National System. When Cullen seemed prepared to support openly the 'orthodox party' during the agitation over the Charitable Bequests Bill, Cantwell opened a full-scale attack on the 'invidious Sassenach plot' promoted by Crolly and Murray as 'paid advocates of the government'. Angrily he told Cullen what this would mean in the diocese of Meath:

> Eight hundred acres confided in and by the clergy of this

diocese for Catholic charity will in the hands of a Protestant board prove a sure and powerful means to colonise this Catholic diocese with Protestants, of the *right sort*, thereby propping up Toryism and propagating error. Yet all this will be carrying into effect the charitable wishes of the dying person's Catholic testator. It is difficult to conceive anything more monstrous than to have Roman Catholic prelates parties to such a sacrilegious confiscation.

(C: 20 Nov. 1844)

As a result of Cullen's encouragement during the Charitable Bequests crisis, communication with the Bishop of Meath increased, and by the time of the 'infidel colleges' uproar Cantwell was thanking Cullen for 'secret messages' sent to him. In return he transmitted to the Roman agent full details of the reaction of the 'horror-struck' people when they realised that some prelates were supporting the colleges. He warned Cullen that such 'an alliance between the successors of the Apostles and the enemies of the Faith' was bringing about 'a want of confidence on the part of the laity towards the prelacy' and the loss of any hope of 'religious peace' in the Irish Catholic Church. In the same letter, marked 'strictly confidential', he reported with approval O'Connell's view that the colleges were set up by the government 'as an effectual means to break up the confederacy between the clergy and the people which must end in decatholicising Ireland'. (C: 19 Dec. 1845)

During the famine Cantwell had little to say to Cullen about the suffering of the people, but his scathing attack on the government over its policies never slackened. In his usual rhetorical vein he told Cullen that every British action in Ireland sought only one end — the elimination of the Catholic faith in Ireland. This was what lay behind the 'nurseries of infidelity and vice' that were called Queen's Colleges. The 'licentious profligacy' within them was attracing every 'loose and disedifying Catholic', and only 'orthodox bishops' like himself, MacHale and Higgins stood ready to resist the advance of heresy:

British power abroad and gold at home are bent on affecting what British cruelty and injustice, assisted by the powers of earth and Hell, has for centuries tried to accomplish.

(C: 31 Jan. 1846)

Two years later he was begging Cullen to ensure that Rome would not inhibit the political activities of the Irish priests, and would leave the Irish Catholic Church 'free to fight her own battles'. The Holy See should ignore the 'foul and fiendish calumny' against the nationalist clergy, who sought only to expose the intention of England to do nothing to help the Irish Catholic people and their church:

> They can command plenty of money to erect infidel colleges, to squander on miscalled and ill-conducted National Schools, and upon the innumerable profligate State officials in the various ramifications of our enormous State patronage, but when there is question of a grant to mitigate the horrors of famine and pestilence the answer is England is in difficulties and the Treasury would not afford such an outlay. (C: 17 Jan. 1848)

In Cantwell's view, the only answer to the 'godless colleges' was for the Church to establish its own alternative Catholic university, dedicated to the memory of the Liberator.

The most eloquent of the nationalist bishops who wrote to Cullen was Edward Maginn, who had been the first student to go to the Irish College in Paris following the French Revolution. He administered the see of Derry for Bishop John MacLaughlin during one of the latter's bouts of madness, and was consecrated coadjutor bishop in January 1846. Skilled as a journalist, Maginn attracted wide attention for his strongly nationalist public letters to Lord Stanley. He procured the escape of Thomas D'Arcy McGee, the Young Irelander, from Ireland, and McGee wrote Maginn's biography after his death from typhus in 1849.

Shortly after his elevation Maginn informed Cullen that 'Dr MacHale is more than a brother — a father to me.' Like the Archbishop of Tuam, he looked upon the Queen's Colleges as 'a government snare to entrap the mind of Ireland and make it indifferent to all religions, or, at least, to estrange it from the faith of our fathers'. (C: 28 Jan. 1846) Not only were the colleges designed to ensure that 'Catholicity and nationality in Ireland shall be forever bound to the chariot wheels of England's domination', but he feared they might prove in the end to be more dangerous to young Irish Catholics than the much-hated Trinity College. In a rhetorical letter to Cullen he described the baneful influence of that institution:

> We have ... never yet known a Catholic youth to have spent any time in Trinity College who did not return home shipwrecked in faith and in morals, wholly profligate. In faith latitudinarian, Protestants, in morals, are no less so. The very best of them would in the eye of our Catholic ethics be considered anything but a safe companion. Laxity in morality has ever been the consequence of laxity in religious belief. ... I doubt whether Paganism in its filthiest *lycées*, where Venus and Bacchus were deified and recommended to the gentle youth as objects worthy of divine worship, exhibits ... anything more detestable than our Dublin, Edinburgh and Oxford stews.
>
> (BV: 16 Aug. 1848)

Not only was Maginn a thoroughgoing bigot in religious matters, but his hatred of everything English knew no bounds. The Earl of Clarendon as Lord Lieutenant was castigated as a 'modern Mountjoy' and condemned, together with the rest of the Whigs, for his 'cold-blooded treachery'. His chief pre-occupation, according to Maginn, was the protection of 'profligate members of every bankrupt Orange family' who loved nothing more than to domineer over a people whose race and creed they hated. When it became clear at the height of the famine that the English were suffering as well as the Irish, Maginn told Cullen:

> It is a satisfaction that we are not suffering alone. The cup of bitterness of which Babylon the great forced us to drink for ages is now being returned to her own lips and she too is drinking of it and if it be not a profanation to say it 'much good may it do her', if not for temporal it might be for her spiritual good, were she forced to drink it to the dregs. (C: 4 Nov. 1847)

Other bishops like Charles MacNally, who was Coadjutor of Clogher from 1843, and John Derry, who was consecrated

Bishop of Clonfert in 1847, joined in the patriotic chorus at times. When they did so, like Higgins, Cantwell and Maginn they made appropriate professions of loyalty to the pope in his difficulties, but the tone of their letters was different from the rhetoric we have just looked at. They did not address the Roman agent as 'My dear good Dr Cullen' as Maginn did; but neither did they ever go so far as to write, as he did in 1848, about the British declaring war on the Irish, 'panting, as in olden times for the blood of the half-starved Celts'. (K: 29 July 1848) They also avoided open division with their fellow-bishops, who, as a majority, did not agree with their passionate nationalism. Maginn, on the other hand, did not hesitate to describe his fellow Ulster bishops as outright slaves of the Castle, hungering for pensions from the government: in his words, they were 'in the market to be sold like bullocks in Smithfield'. (C: 28 Sept. 1848) Division among the bishops was dreaded by Cullen, representative as it was of ecclesiastical intrigue that could not be easily controlled by Rome. At its worst it could degenerate into a kind of Gallicanism resentful of any Roman admonition; and Cullen at times feared he could detect such a spirit in the man who was the acknowledged leader of the 'orthodox party', John MacHale.

4. *The Lion of the West*

During the years that Cullen was serving as agent for the Irish bishops the influence of Maynooth began to be felt in the Irish Church as out of that institution poured eager young curates imbued with the spirit of a Catholic nationalism which, to his eyes, appeared to be suspiciously Gallican in its attitude to Rome. At the heart of this movement was that most irascible of men, John MacHale, whom O'Connell had dubbed 'the Lion of the Tribe of Judah'. Anti-Repealers delighted in calling MacHale 'the Lion of the Tribe of Dan'. Cullen, while he tried through the years to deal patiently with this most difficult of prelates, referred to him as 'the Lion'. There was seldom a time when in some form or another he was not made aware of the Archbishop of Tuam's roaring disapproval of how affairs were developing in Ireland.

Born in 1791 in Mayo, MacHale was a native Irish speaker whose roots were deep in the culture represented by the hedge-school in which he had received his early education. After a brilliant course of studies under émigré French Gallican professors at Maynooth, MacHale succeeded Louis Delahogue as Professor of Dogmatic Theology in 1820. It was at this time that he first came to public notice in his *Letters of Hierophilos*, which criticised the contemporary political establishment in Ireland. The publication won him considerable notoriety in the Catholic community and helped to secure his appointment as coadjutor with right of succession to Peter Waldron, the aged Bishop of Killala in 1825. When Waldron died in 1834 MacHale duly succeeded to the see.

From the time he began to work in Killala MacHale displayed amazing energy in raising funds for the building of a cathedral and other ecclesiastical ventures. He also earned considerable notoriety as a very political prelate during the battle for Catholic Emancipation. At the same time he continued his literary activities, publishing his respectable *Evidences and Doctrines of the Catholic Church* (1828), which was translated into French and German. Public letters to the Prime Minister, Earl Grey, during the famine of 1831 gave him the reputation of being an ecclesiastical tribune of the oppressed people of Connaught. When he supplemented these letters with others to the editor of the *Morning Chronicle* about Ireland's grievances over proselytising by Bible societies, tithes, and Grand Jury jobbery, MacHale had established his reputation in both Ireland and England as a prelate to be reckoned with.

MacHale also caught the attention of authorities in Rome, and when he visited the Holy See in 1832 he was warmly welcomed by Gregory XVI. He was allowed to preach to the English-speaking colony and took the opportunity to acquaint the pope with the failings of the National System of Education and the need to be on guard against government plans to pension the Irish clergy. He also met Lamennais, Lacordaire and Montalembert, who had come to Rome in the vain hope that the pope would give his blessing to their form of liberal Catholicism, which was close to MacHale's own theological position.

On his way to Rome MacHale had heard of Cullen's growing influence. He wrote to him while he was still on his journey, and the two met as soon as MacHale arrived. When MacHale visited Naples during the summer he wrote to Cullen, and the letter indicates that a considerable rapport had been established between them. MacHale chatted about visiting Protestants expressing scepticism over the liquefying of the blood of St Januarius, and other matters. At the same time he expressed his pleasure that Archbishop Murray was willing to support the Irish College and promised that he too would give what aid he could — an offer which Cullen gratefully received. (C: 2 June 1832) After MacHale's return to Ireland correspondence between the two was maintained, the *Freeman's Journal* was sent regularly to the Roman agent, and MacHale assured Cullen of his unyielding opposition to British plans to interrupt 'that confidential intercourse now so happily subsisting between this country and Rome'. (C: 10 Feb. 1834)

When Oliver Kelly, the Archbishop of Tuam, died in Rome in April 1834 and the clergy chose on their *terna* Dean Bernard Burke of Westport, whom MacHale loathed, the latter immediately wrote to Cullen for help in his hoped-for translation to the senior see. He attacked Burke as a non-intellectual and bluntly told his Roman friend that 'The occasion is too serious for any false or affected modesty.' If Burke was appointed by Rome, he would undoubtedly prove to be a dupe of the Whigs, and for such an event to occur when the Irish Church had a patriot like MacHale willing to serve in Tuam was nothing short of a tragedy. (C: 6 June 1834) Cullen's advocacy of MacHale's cause in Rome was certainly needed, for Lord Palmerston, the Foreign Secretary, soon indicated that the government was not happy about the prospect of the Bishop of Killala becoming Archbishop of Tuam.

During the episcopate of Oliver Kelly Tuam was considered to be one of the more peaceful of western dioceses. When he gave evidence before the parliamentary committee of 1825 on the state of Ireland Kelly said there was little anti-Protestant feeling anywhere in his archdiocese. Where anticlericalism did exist it was directed against the priest as much as against the parson. In fact, much appreciation was

shown by local Catholics for Protestant help in building the
new slated churches that were now appearing. The government reckoned that this situation would change, however, if
the fiery MacHale was translated from Killala – and, as
events were to show, it was not wrong in its assumption.

The objections made by the British government were
serious enough for the Cardinal Prefect to consult Daniel
Murray about MacHale's suitability for the see. Murray in
characteristically charitable fashion replied to Propaganda on
30 July 1834 to 'scout the charge' that MacHale might contribute to civil commotion:

> I confess, indeed, Most Eminent Lord, that prelate, other-
> wise most worthy, sometimes uses too sharp a style, as it
> seems to me, when he writes about political matters. It
> must be remembered, nevertheless, that he is surrounded
> by poor persons languishing in want and misery: and if he
> adverts to the cause of this misery more sharply than I
> would wish, I think it should be attributed to his sense of
> duty towards the poor and to a zeal which burns for
> religion, although for a little while perhaps it went beyond
> the limits of prudence as some believed.
>
> (Broderick, *Holy See*, 91)

It is likely that Cullen reinforced Murray's opinion in the
same letter that MacHale was 'learned, pious, eloquent and
deserving well of election', for he had himself told MacHale
of his wish that the latter would be 'numbered among the
worthiest of the long series of Archbishops of Tuam'. (PM, I,
216: 21 June 1834) On 26 August 1834 Gregory XVI
appointed John MacHale as Archbishop of Tuam.

The pope must soon have had second thoughts about the
wisdom of this appointment, for almost immediately MacHale
promoted a scandalous schism among the clergy of the
Killala diocese. During the Emancipation campaign MacHale
had tolerated the Killala clergy engaging in political agitation,
and by the time he left them to go to Tuam they had become,
in the words of Monsignor D'Alton in his *History of the
Archdiocese of Tuam*, 'a factious, disaffected and ignorant
body of priests'. (II, 5) The storm that now broke out in
Killala was occasioned by Rome's appointment to the vacant

see of Francis O'Finan, a native of the diocese who had served the Dominican order in Rome since 1792.

The new bishop, an elderly and unworldly man, immediately infuriated the clergy by appointing as his vicar-general John Patrick Lyons, the Parish Priest of Kilmore Erris. In this remote area Lyons ruled as a reforming landlord, an enlightened patron of education who accepted financial aid from Protestant sources, and a rural patriarch. He was also something of a scholar, and he contributed to the publication of an Irish prayer-book for his people. In his earlier days he had received a doctoral degree for a study of episcopal duties, and soon he was busy advising O'Finan on clerical affairs — especially the task of getting the priests away from the political arena and back to their pastoral duties. When O'Finan tried to implement what Lyons was suggesting there was a violent reaction among the Killala clergy.

MacHale had left Lyons alone in his Erris fastness when he was Bishop of Killala, but he had no use for the new vicar-general, who had at an earlier date been touted as a possible successor to Bishop Waldron. Almost as soon as the storm broke in Killala in 1835 MacHale began an unremitting campaign of character assassination. He left Cullen in no doubt that O'Finan's unfortunate handling of the clergy reflected the sinister influence of Lyons:

> All this proceeds from the erroneous step he took at the outset of committing himself entirely into the hands of a man who has not, as he proved never to have had, a view but of sacrificing even the most holy things to his cupidity whether of avarice or of revenge. (C: 1 Nov. 1835)

One of O'Finan's most unpopular acts was to dismiss the incumbent of Crossmolina, John Barrett, and replace him with a priest named Edward Murray. When Dean Lyons went to Crossmolina to explain the reasons for O'Finan's action he was met by a howling mob and had to be protected by police. Lyons then went to Rome to present O'Finan's case, a move which prompted MacHale to warn Cullen of what might be expected of the 'wicked' and 'treacherous' Lyons when he arrived in the Holy See:

> He is none of your ordinary fellows. There is not perhaps

another in the Church more persevering in his purpose. Fawning on those whom he can flatter, as he is insolent to those whom he can terrify, there is no artifice, however mean, he will not descend to to obtain his ends.

(C: 29 May 1836)

To Rome's horror the Tory *Mayo Constitution* began to write about the Killala struggle, interpreting it as one between conservative parish priests, represented by O'Finan and Lyons, and radical political curates whom MacHale was encouraging against their superiors. On 17 June 1836 the paper spoke of mutiny by 'low-bred curates against the parish priests who are their superiors in birth, Christian conduct and intelligence'. To make matters worse, the trouble in Killala was not an isolated phenomenon: at the very time when the scandal was coming to public notice two curates named Crotty in Birr, King's County, were leading their whole parish into open schism. To try to calm the situation Rome appointed a commission led by the Primate, William Crolly, and Cornelius Denvir of Down and Connor to visit Killala to bring the feuding partners together.

It was at this juncture that Cullen received his first real intimation of how resistant to Roman authority MacHale was to be. On 10 February 1837 Cullen was told rather bluntly by MacHale that 'Roman officials' were not really needed in this instance, and that 'meddling' in the affairs of the Irish Church was not going to help the situation. (C) Something had to be done, however, for O'Finan brought a civil lawsuit against the proprietor of the pro-MacHale *Mayo Telegraph* and Rome was shocked to hear that both Archbishops Crolly and MacHale had been summoned to appear in the civil court. The divisions in Killala had become so desperate that quarrelling factions had disputed the celebration of mass in the chapel at Kincon, with rival priests celebrating at different ends of the building while police with loaded guns kept their congregations apart. One priest even proclaimed that anyone accepting the sacraments from a priest suspended by O'Finan risked eternal damnation. An opponent compared O'Finan to Martin Luther and claimed he had been excommunicated for simony. As for MacHale, he never ceased his attacks on O'Finan, and his letters to Cullen were filled with defamatory indictments of 'the downright fatuity of the unfortunate old man'.

Although O'Finan was suspended after being recalled to Rome, and Thomas Feeny became administrator and eventually Bishop of Killala, the clerical warfare continued. MacHale warned Cullen that several priests now carried pistols, and in March 1839 Cullen was informed that John Barrett, the ousted Parish Priest of Crossmolina had been murdered. MacHale kept up his vendetta with Lyons, telling Cullen in 1842 that Lyons was intent upon mischief when he visited Rome that year: 'Many a less dangerous man has been kept in safe custody in the Castle of S. Angelo.' (C: 24 Apr. 1842) By this time Cullen fully understood how difficult a man MacHale was going to be if Rome ever chose to oppose him in ecclesiastical affairs, and he was hardly surprised when 'the Lion' began to roar over the National System of Education and to wage war with those bishops who did not agree with his point of view.

MacHale urged Cullen in 1840 to ensure that 'the parental protection of Rome' be extended to Irish Catholicism to save the people from the type of state intervention in religious and educational affairs that was to be found in Belgium and Prussia. He also wished the authority of the Holy See to be extended in Ireland to deal with 'Catholics who are for the most part heretics, who care not for His Holiness' authority'. (C: 19 Feb. 1841) After what MacHale had shown of his intransigent spirit in the O'Finan affair, Cullen probably had grave reservations about how seriously such Ultramontane sentiments should be received by Rome, but he knew the charismatic leadership abilities which 'the Lion' possessed, and he wanted to make use of him. Like the Liberator, MacHale understood intuitively, in a way that Cullen never did, Irish nationalist aspirations. Cullen was quite willing to give him his head in criticism of the National System, which might win concessions for greater Catholic control of it, while simultaneously he informed Propaganda that the school system was the best that could be hoped for at that time. He knew from his own visit to the schools in 1840, and from the evidence he received from MacHale's opponents, that the National System, which in effect provided state-subsidised Catholic primary education in most parts of the country, was not to be despised or rejected.

A result of Cullen's qualified encouragement of MacHale's position over the National System was a continuing communication with 'the Lion' and, inevitably, a growing sympathy with the nationalist position. When the Charitable Bequests crisis arose in the autumn of 1844 Cullen congratulated MacHale on his opposition to the legislation. He also expressed his hope that no Catholic bishop would serve on such a state-sponsored body in the event of a decision from Rome that it would not be in the interest of the Church for them to do so. (PM, I, 252)

As soon as MacHale recognised Rome's willingness to treat the crisis ideologically he wrote the pope and the Cardinal Prefect to urge that bishops be forbidden to serve as commissioners under the new act. He also increased his pressure on Cullen. He warned the Irish agent that what the legislation really represented was a resurgence of traditional Irish Gallicanism: the pro-government bishops would act as 'political popes' who wholly rejected papal authority. (C: 26 Nov. 1844) Cullen, as we have seen, overreacted to the hysteria which the MacHaleites had created, and as a result was identified by his critics in both Ireland and Rome as a nationalist party adherent, contributing to the growing dissension in the Irish hierarchy. This uncharacteristic loss of prudence on his part was never to be forgotten. After the intemperance which MacHale had shown in the O'Finan affair and the imbroglio over the Charitable Bequests Act, Cullen resolved that from this time forward he would be wary of any involvement he had with 'the Lion'.

But although Cullen was determined to avoid identification with the MacHaleites, he could not do without them. When the issue of the 'godless colleges' was being debated Crolly and Murray once more emerged as apologists for government policy. Criticism, as was expected, came from MacHale and his followers, and 'the Lion' again launched a torrent of letters to Cullen about the threat to the faithful who would attend the Queen's Colleges. MacHale described Crolly and Murray as 'bought' by the government; they were, he told Cullen, unable to resist this new imposition because they

were 'unfortunately bound up with the government as servants dismissable at its pleasure'. (C: 5 Dec. 1845) Cullen
told MacHale that he was much obliged to him for his correspondence on the colleges, for neither Bishop Murphy of
Cork, nor Kennedy of Killaloe, then in Rome, had anything
to say about the new legislation, and other bishops neglected
to write about it.

Cullen, however, was careful by this time in accepting
anything that MacHale said about his fellow-bishops or other
Irish churchmen. When a Dublin curate, Thaddeus O'Malley,
criticised MacHale's policy of keeping the National Schools
out of his archdiocese the enraged 'Lion' began a vicious
assault on the 'notorious O'Malley'. In a series of letters to
Cullen between 1840 and 1844 O'Malley was variously
described as a priest guilty of 'ecclesiastical insubordination'
and love of the 'patronage of the world' and as 'pregnant
with impiety and schism and so insulting to the Holy See'.
When one of the few priests who openly dared to resist
MacHale in his own domain, Michael Waldron, Parish Priest
of Cong, visited Rome, Cullen was warned about the 'known
cunning of the man', whose journey was patronised by an
Orange landlord. (C: 13 June 1841) This was reminiscent of
the slanders inflicted upon Bishop O'Finan and Dean Lyons
a few years earlier, and it was clear to Cullen that he might
suffer the same fate if he openly crossed this most intransigent
of men.

The truth of this apprehension was borne in upon Cullen
when Father Theobald Mathew, the famous temperance
reformer, incurred the wrath of MacHale. Having launched
his great crusade in 1838, Father Mathew was by 1841 en-
rolling people in his cause by their hundreds of thousands
and was rapidly becoming an Irish folk hero. He had met
Cullen in 1840, and through the intercession of the Roman
agent with the pope and the Superior-General of the Capuchins
he had been released from obedience to his superiors and
appointed Commissary Apostolic of the Irish Province. As
he used his freedom to preach throughout the country he
became a very well-known figure and was widely regarded as
'the moral regenerator of Ireland'. O'Connell tried to win his
support for the Repeal campaign, but Father Mathew showed

little enthusiasm for the suggestion. O'Connell bore this rebuff easily and was in the course of time to make good use of the friar's mass rally techniques. MacHale, however, was less flexible in his attitudes, and Father Mathew's refusal to become involved in secular politics may have marked the beginning of the Archbishop of Tuam's resentment of him.

Father Mathew's social background was different from that of MacHale, he had many Protestant friends, and above all he appealed to the masses whom MacHale wished to use in his exercise in Catholic nationalism. 'The Lion' was a jealous man when anyone challenged his authority in the countryside. In 1841, in a letter thanking Cullen for his help in Rome, Mathew revealed that MacHale had emerged as the 'implacable enemy' of the temperance campaign. He was appalled by the archbishop's 'calumnies' and his direct encouragement of some of his priests to return to the use of alcohol 'when he is perfectly aware that intemperance was the predominant sin of the Irish priesthood'. MacHale had actually denounced Mathew in the mensal chapel of Kilmeena 'in the face of a large and astonished congregation':

> After a long tirade in Irish against the society he said that I was a vagabond Friar, that I went about with a *woman*, that she sold medals for me, charging a shilling for bits of Birmingham pewter which cost only a few pence, and that we spent the money drinking brandy and water, laughing at the poor dupes whom we robbed. (C: 20 Sept. 1841)

Mathew thought that MacHale's hostility might have reflected the friar's friendship with Dean Bernard Burke of Westport, whom the archbishop loathed; but, whatever the reason, it was causing him embarrassment and trouble. He had even been attacked from the altar of Tuam cathedral, and to visit Dean Lyons's remote fastness in Erris he had been obliged to travel by way of Enniskillen and Sligo because MacHale had forbidden him to set foot in the Tuam archdiocese. He assured Cullen that he was totally innocent of the charges that MacHale was making to the great delight of the enemies of the Catholic Church, and that he was 'in hourly terror lest His Grace should attack us in the public papers'. (C: 21 Sept. 1841) He went on to beg Cullen and

Kirby to do all in their power to placate 'the Lion' so that he should stop embarrassing the Church.

Cullen, however, had been receiving reports of Father Mathew's friendship with Protestants, and praise of his work by Lord John Russell had also been noted. In 1843 a MacHaleite priest told Kirby that the Capuchin was saying 'queer things' and had administered 'Holy Communion' in English in Waterford. (K: 30 Aug. 1843) While he deplored this latest exhibition of MacHale's ability to create serious dissension among churchmen, Cullen began to have some qualms about the Capuchin's religious soundness. When he commiserated with Mathew over the 'public opposition' given to him by 'persons high in dignity in Ireland' he also indicated his dismay that some of the Capuchin's sermons revealed a tendency 'to entertain sentiments too liberal towards Protestants in matter of religion'. It was all very well to exercise charity towards Protestants, 'but at the same time we should let them know that there is but one true Church and that they are strayed sheep from the one fold'. If this were not done, 'we might lull them into a false security in their errors and by doing so we would really violate charity'. (PM, II, 11: 11 Oct. 1843)

Certainly MacHale succeeded in sowing enough seeds of doubt in Cullen's and other minds that when Bishop John Murphy of Cork died in 1847 Mathew was passed over for the appointment, although he had headed the *terna*. The Capuchin wrote to Cullen when he heard that the moderate nationalist Michael Slattery, Archbishop of Cashel, had opposed his elevation. He told Cullen he was without personal ambition, but he did fear that the complaints made against him might hurt the temperance movement. From the hints made in letters to Cullen at this time, it is clear that a considerable pressure was put on Rome to elevate Mathew. Cullen's influence in Propaganda was sufficient, however, that the appointment went to William Delany, Parish Priest of Bandon, a man he considered less likely to be open to government influence. Denis Murphy, Parish Priest of Kinsale, who had known Cullen since student days, praised the appointment as 'a striking example of the wisdom of the Sacred College'. He also remarked: 'I dare say a certain Irish ecclesiastic at the head of a college in Rome had a hand in the matter.' (C: 7 Sept. 1847)

Cullen by this time was determined to make sure he could never again be identified with the MacHaleites. 'The Lion' had been savage in his attack on the Capuchin, but his onslaught had been pale compared with the sheer scurrility of Higgins of Ardagh. In a terrible letter marked 'private' Mathew was described as 'a man whose notorious latitudinarianism, lying and hypocrisy, have scandalised his most ardent former admirers'. The Orangemen loved him as 'the hired tool of a heretical government'. He based his sermons on texts taken from a Protestant version of the scriptures and had been known to pray for the departed soul 'of a brutal Protestant bishop'. In return for his beguiling of the people through his crusade he had received an annual royal pension:

> How will we persuade the poor people that a pension can be bad when Dr-Fr Mathew, with the Cork crozier in one hand, receives his government bribe with the other! He will be in all the secrets of the ministry — will be a check and a spy in our deliberations. He will command the treasury to enable him to go to Rome for all ministerial intrigues, and should he be appointed I must look upon the event in conjunction with all my episcopal friends as a national disgrace and a national calamity.
>
> (C: 30 June 1847)

What particularly dismayed Higgins was the Capuchin's intense dislike of O'Connell because the latter had tried to make use of the temperance crusade for political ends. Higgins resented the charismatic quality of the Mathew movement, which seemed to detract from the nationalist cause and the authority of the O'Connellite clergy. He told Cullen that Mathew was a direct threat to the cause of unity among the Catholic clergy: 'He rode rough-shod over all episcopal authority, pitted people against priests, and was well-nigh introducing a schism in Ireland.' Cullen would have heeded this part of Higgins's tirade in particular, for it was reasonable to assume that when Father Mathew had enough personal authority to stand up to O'Connell's beguilements, and MacHale's and Higgins's attempts at ecclesiastical coercion, he might also be a difficult man for Rome to control.

When Father Mathew was passed over for the Cork diocese he ceased to be a real political factor in the Irish Church, but the same could not be said for MacHale, Higgins, Cantwell and their supporters. Their intransigence, even in the face of Roman admonitions, over the National System, the Charitable Bequests crisis and the Queen's Colleges had shown Cullen clearly that the nationalist Catholicism they promoted was in reality a new assertion of Irish Gallicanism. As for MacHale himself, Cullen knew well that the cantankerous behaviour he had displayed during the O'Finan and Father Mathew affairs could as easily be directed against the Irish agent in Rome, or any other Roman authority, if any attempt was made to interfere in Irish affairs without the explicit approval of MacHale himself.

By the time that Cullen was ready to begin his Irish mission he knew how to handle the MacHaleites; he believed it was possible for him to maintain at least communication with, and perhaps even some control over, 'the Lion'. MacHale was always at war — with the British administration, with Crolly, Murray and their followers, and with sturdy individuals like Dean Burke of Westport who had the courage to stand up to him. He often turned to Cullen for help, taking it for granted that the Roman agent, if not fully in the MacHaleite camp, was at least a close sympathiser with the nationalist movement. Cullen, for his part, encouraged MacHale and his followers to be his clients. They provided him with intelligence, his inside knowledge of ecclesiastical affairs that was to be the source of his true authority when he came to Ireland. By mid-century Cullen had a mental dossier on the Irish clergy in every part of the island. As for the MacHaleite bishops, far from Cullen being in their pocket, they were in his, and indebted to him for a multitude of favours he had obtained for them in Rome. The hectoring tone sometimes adopted by people like Higgins when dealing with Cullen was to change to one of almost complete obsequiousness when he arrived in Ireland as Primate and Apostolic Delegate.

III

The Problem of Irish 'Agitazione'

1. *The Irish Priests and Repeal*

When Cullen communicated with either Murray's supporters or MacHale's followers over issues like the National System, the Charitable Bequests Act or the Queen's Colleges, he considered he was dealing with concerns where the Catholic clergy might validly register protest opinion. Matters dealing with education, wills and testaments or universities were traditionally considered to be of legitimate interest to the Universal Church. When the state threatened to encroach upon the Church's authority in these matters it was the duty of the faithful to try to safeguard Catholic interests through every means short of violence which would threaten law and order.

Rome was uneasy, however, when priests became too actively involved in issues like Catholic Emancipation or tithe reform, which certainly affected Catholic society but which could be dealt with by Catholic laymen. Even more disturbing was the involvement of priests in more purely political matters like the Repeal movement. Although the Catholics of Ireland generally identified themselves with the nationalist cause, Rome realised the danger, in terms of a new kind of Gallicanism, if priests served the nascent nation rather than the mission of the Universal Church. So often, it seemed to Rome, the clerical political agitators in Ireland were advancing liberal ideas redolent of those of Felicité de Lamennais or the Belgian Catholics who had allied themselves with secular agitators in the cause of Belgian freedom in 1830. Liberal enthusiasm had led Polish Catholics into the abortive rising of 1831 which resulted in Rome admonishing the Polish bishops to teach submission to the legitimate power of the schismatic Russian Tsar. Rome drew back from urging a union of throne and altar when the secular ruler was not a Catholic, but at the same time it was not prepared to allow priests to promote rebellion by the faithful, regardless of how oppressive their rulers might be.

Cullen and other Roman officials were very uncertain about how they should direct the Irish bishops and priests in the years following Catholic Emancipation. The clergy were euphoric after tasting political power in O'Connell's campaign, and they were in no mood to confine themselves to merely ecclesiastical or religious causes. During the sectarian 'tithe war' of the 1830s the countryside was filled with clerical agitators, and Cullen was ambivalent in his feelings about them. Among them was James Maher, a popular champion of the wealthy Catholic grazier families of Queen's and Carlow counties who were doing little to quell disturbances which were so discomfiting the parsons. One of Cullen's clerical supplicants from Callan, Co. Kilkenny, told him that 'Your uncle, Fr Maher, is a first-rate agitator.' (C: 11 June 1832) When Maher brought considerable notoriety to himself by accusing Lord Beresford of tyranny in his dealings with his tenantry in one parish, and the local parish priest accused Maher of being credulous and bigoted, the Bishop of Charleston, then visiting Carlow College, told Cullen about the affair in great detail — including the anger of the Cullen/Maher family over the incident. (C: 1 May 1835)

What Cullen thought about the agitation of the 1830s can only be conjectured, for although he had instinctive sympathy with the social response of his family to the tithe war, he was immersed in the affairs of papal Rome, which had just experienced revolution in the states of the Church. To Cullen's Roman mind bishops and priests who resisted Roman directives about over-involvement in secular political and social movements were as misguided as the Gallicans or Jansenists of an earlier age. Like any Italian curial figure, he was very alarmed when he was told by reliable churchmen in Ireland of priests exciting mobs to acts of violence as they encouraged *agitazione* for the social cause of changing tithe laws and the political one of repealing the union with Britain.

One of the first to write to him about the unrest in the Irish countryside was his one-time professor at Carlow College, William Kinsella, who had become Bishop of Ossory in the year of Emancipation. He was not much older than Cullen and a friend of his family, and the two men shared the same sentiments on the subject of revolution. Kinsella had been one of the first bishops to ask Cullen to act in Rome on his behalf, and in 1831 he asked for advice about how to handle a Capuchin in Kilkenny who regularly preached at mass on the need for Repeal and 'stigmatised every man who would not join in the mad attempt'. Unfortunately, said Kinsella, the zealous friar was only symptomatic of the very disturbed state of the country:

> This country is in a very disturbed state. The people are beginning to assemble in large crowds of five and ten thousand, armed with large sticks and threatening the Protestant ministers. Such conduct is illegal, and I fear that bloodshed will be the result. It gives me great pain to hear that a Carmelite Friar who lives about ten miles off has been encouraging the mob and has actually accompanied them to the house of a minister. The Protestant Bishop has complained of him to me, and I fear that I must proceed severely against him. (C: 3 Jan. 1831)

The problem with this situation, Cullen soon discovered, was that by no means all the priests were enthusiastic about Repeal, particularly those of the older generation. Not only was there tension between the older continental-trained parish priests and the Maynooth-educated curates, but with the advent of political agitation long-buried feuds between priests and their parishioners began to surface. In the Waterford diocese there was open warfare, as we have seen, between secular priests and friars, and in 1833 Cullen was told of an O'Connellite mob insulting and spitting upon Bishop William Abraham on the streets of the town. (C: 8 June 1833) The friars put great pressure on the clergy of the diocese to declare themselves in favour of Repeal and boasted that such was their influence in Rome that the bishop could count on no support from that quarter.

When Robert Laffan, Archbishop of Cashel, died in 1833 John Ryan, Bishop of Limerick, wrote to Cullen to have his name withdrawn from the *terna* sent to Rome, although several of the clergy had voted for him. The diocese was filled with feuding priests and laity; and as he had once been a parish priest in the Cashel archdiocese, he knew that he would be drawn into this faction-fighting if he was translated. Appointment of a stranger to Cashel was the only answer for this scandal, said Ryan, because only a stranger would have any hopes of transcending the agitation, to bring order among the priests and save the Church from further hurt. Ryan told Cullen that whereas agitation for Catholic Emancipation in Cashel had been 'excusable, perhaps laudable because necessary', the present turbulence over tithes and the O'Connell movement did nothing but seriously divide the Catholic community:

> The clergy of that diocese by their factious efforts to secure a successor favourable to the wishes and interests of their respective parties are divided and torn asunder by dissensions of the most rancorous nature, a state of things dangerous to religion everywhere, but awfully so in an heretical country where fatal advantage may be taken of such unedifying conflicts. (C: 19 Sept. 1833)

Later in the same year Ryan took upon himself to write to Cardinal Thomas Weld, for whom Cullen had great respect owing to his interest in Irish affairs. Ryan sent a copy of this letter to Cullen, and in it he referred to the seriously disturbed state of Ireland, where 'liberalism, which in reality means infidelity and revolution is every day making fearful progress'. He deplored the ease with which agitators and demagogues could flatter and lead astray the Catholic clergy who ignored 'the admirable admonitions issued by the court of Rome'. The result was an Irish priesthood whose 'principles and objects differ in nothing material from those of the Frenchmen of the present day who . . . are no great friends to Religion or her ministers'. (C: 11 Dec. 1833)

As the tithe war dragged on, the situation became increasingly alarming from the Roman viewpoint. When Bishop Patrick MacMahon of Killaloe laid the disturbed parish of Birr under interdict in 1835 Cullen was shocked to be told how the two curates of the parish led almost the whole of the townspeople into secession from the Catholic Church (C: 25 Nov. 1835) The scandal in Killala surfaced when MacHale began to write to Cullen about O'Finan's failings, and it was clear that Roman suggestions for law and order in the Irish Church were everywhere ignored. An insight into how desperate the situation was came to Cullen when he received a letter from Bishop Edward Kernan of Clogher defending his policy of never holding a meeting of the cathedral chapter. He had long been the Parish Priest of Enniskillen, he knew how bullying by chapter members and their incessant fighting had driven his predecessors almost to distraction, and he was determined to forestall the making of clerical cabals in such meetings. He told Cullen how he had defended himself to Cardinal Fransoni of Propaganda:

> I am now forty years on the mission of Ireland, having left the College of Salamanca in the autumn of 1795; and can safely affirm that the Chapter of Clogher and the members of it, or of many of it, has been destructive of the peace and harmony and charity which should have subsisted among us, which cannot be unknown to the Sacred Congregation; the two pious and worthy Bishops O'Reilly and Murphy who preceded me were annoyed to the last moments of their existence. Since I came into the administration of the diocese the peace of God has reigned throughout. (C: 5 Aug. 1835)

Bishop Kernan's peace was to be short-lived, however, for in the summer of 1843 a native of the town of Clogher, Charles MacNally, who had been trained in Maynooth, was appointed coadjutor. He was a strong nationalist and a member of the MacHaleite faction, and his toleration of political action by the priests once more had Clogher in an uproar. Because of this, though MacNally was to prove to be an ecclesiastical triumphalist in his own way and a great builder of churches, Cullen always had reservations about his loyalty to Rome.

It is probable that Cullen's ideas about Irish politics were ambivalent and in a continuing process of development. His natural prudence and reserve, as well as native good sense, kept him from being too much influenced by Tobias Kirby, who, although he had spent almost all his adult years in Rome

and had little first-hand experience of Irish affairs, had
become deeply committed to O'Connell's cause. Similarly, he
was reserved in his relationship with the family hero, James
Maher, when it came to politics — although Maher did manage
to influence him against Crolly and the other 'Castle bishops'.
Cullen lived for almost twenty-nine years in Rome as a zealous
champion of the Ultramontanist cause, and his view of Irish
affairs was very much that of any curial figure of his age.
Inevitably he viewed Irish bishops and priests who resisted
Roman guidance on the problem of the 'priest in politics' as
Gallican or Jansenist in spirit.

Cullen also identified the revolutionary spirit proclaimed
by some Irish churchmen with that which he had encountered
in Rome during his student days and during the attempt at
insurrection just before Gregory XVI became pope. Mazzini
and Garibaldi had been checked in their revolutionary
activities, and both had fled from Italy by 1834. Yet revolutionary unrest was everywhere, and even the repressive rule
of Gregory in the papal states was not able to crush the
continuing agitation. Like other Roman curialists, Cullen
was convinced, as we have seen, that behind the agitation
was the sinister occult power of Freemasonry. Each of the
popes that Cullen faithfully served issued during their pontificates a proscription of what they believed to be a sinister
and dangerous movement. To Rome it was clear that Freemasonry offered liberal Catholics and other misguided souls
a rival naturalistic religion to the true faith, by promoting
religious indifferentism and other errors.

The Grand Lodge of Ireland was the second oldest in
Europe, and Cullen took it for granted that Freemasons were
active in the various nationalist causes which were so often
led by Protestants or liberal Catholics. As we shall see throughout this study, whenever some new development threatened
Rome's authority in Ireland Cullen's instinctive reaction was
to detect behind the occurrence the work of the Freemasons.

The place where Freemasonry was considered to be most
openly at work was Dublin Castle, and Cullen was inclined to
agree with James Maher when he told him that the Protestant
administration 'would rather see the island sink into the
depths of the sea than that poor Catholic Ireland should

enjoy her rights and liberties'. (C: 24 Mar. 1848) Maher also had much to say about pro-Castle priests who neglected their religious duties to concentrate upon collecting dues from the people and who physically assaulted fellow-clergy who did not agree with their activities. Such populist and nationalist sentiments must have appealed to Cullen with his wealthy grazier family background and the rising expectations of his social class. He certainly listened sympathetically when his brother Thomas, the wealthy Liverpool cattle dealer, described the spirit of rebellion among the people:

> In Ireland the hard treatment of the landlords has again driven the poor people to resistance and having no chance to redress by fair means have unfortunately taken to murder some of their oppressors, but as usual it is not from amongst the bad ones they have selected their victims. Mr Scully of Kilfeale, Co. Tipperary, has been shot a few days since. He was a Catholic. . . . This is a sad state of society, but what can the poor people do — they have no redress from the law. (C: 15 Dec. 1842)

Yet Cullen must have been uneasy about such accounts, for division among the priests, or *agitazione* by the people encouraged by their Catholic leaders, was not in the long-range interest of the Universal Church. There was too much chance that, as in Italy, the unrest could be taken over and used by men who were dedicated enemies of the faith.

In 1842 Cullen sent O'Connell information on papal policies in Spain, to be used in a parliamentary speech. This gave the Liberator the opportunity to assure Cullen in a long letter that in no way did he 'wish to have the relation of Ireland with the Holy See relaxed or diminished'. No one was more attached to Rome than he was, and he was 'convinced that the stability of the faith depends on the submission to and union with the Holy See'. It was true that he sought the aid of churchmen to obtain Repeal, but only because it 'would be an event of the most magnificent importance to Catholicity'. Following Repeal no support would be given to the useless Protestant political church. Alienated church lands would be returned to the Catholics, and this new wealth could be used to build seminaries and housing for bishops and priests.

Catholics would at last control education, would bring spiritual solace to those in poorhouses, prisons and hospitals, and would obtain the greatest blessing of all: 'a resident Cardinal of her own at Rome to be entrusted with all communications to the Holy See in due obedience to the Canon Law'. (C: 9 May 1842)

Although these sentiments made a favourable impression upon Cullen, as did a meeting with O'Connell during the summer of 1842, he never displayed towards the political leader the kind of fawning admiration shown by Tobias Kirby. The latter assured him that the pope 'by no means disapproved of the legitimate and peaceful struggles of Mr O'Connell, and the Irish bishops and clergy in the assertion of the rights of their oppressed country by such means'. (C: 16 June 1842) It was the means that bothered Cullen, however, especially the latent violence in the monster meetings of 1843, and the division which was growing among the bishops and clergy. 'Legitimate and peaceful struggle' to promote a Catholic culture in Ireland was one thing, but *agitazione* for a secular political goal, encouraged by bishops and priests of the Church, was another.

In 1843 Daniel Murray warned Cullen about one Repeal priest whose name was on the *terna* for the coadjutorship of Clogher. When the priest presided over a political meeting one of his supporters was murdered by opponents:

> He had been previously warned by the Resident Magistrate that he would be answerable for any blood that this collision of political parties would cause to be spilled. I am grieved that so many of our clergy (aye and of our bishops too) are taking such a prominent part in the political movement that is at present agitating the country. . . . I fear very much that they are not serving the cause of religion.
>
> (C: 25 Apr. 1843)

Cullen agreed with Murray, especially when he received an account of how Bishop Higgins of Ardagh had told Repealers at Mullingar that if meetings were prevented, 'we would retire to our chapels and suspend all other instructions in order to devote all our time to teaching the people to be Repealers'.

(C: 29 May 1843) When Higgins's speech was widely reported, and he knew that Cullen would have heard of it, he hastened to write to Cullen in a tone that was almost threatening:

> Of course the Holy Father will never interfere with the Irish Church in matters of a political nature. . . . Nothing ever occurred so imminently calculated to cause a *most* dangerous misunderstanding between Rome and the Catholics of Ireland as any papal interference with the prelates or priests against the present peaceable struggle for common justice to the poor people of the oppressed country. If His Holiness knew the real state of the case he would sincerely thank us all. (C: 28 July 1843)

Cullen certainly would not have agreed with Higgins's last statement a year later when his loss of caution during the Charitable Bequests crisis enabled his enemies to identify him clearly as a member of the MacHaleite party. It was then clear to the Roman authorities that the Irish clergy were almost out of hand, swept along by the excitement of the 'Repeal year', followed by that over the Charitable Bequests issue. Through the office of Metternich, British pressure in Rome had increased in 1844, and Cullen began to see that his position in official circles was threatened. His worst fears were realised when O'Connell was released from prison in September 1844 and Cardinal Fransoni sent the Rector of the Irish College a terse order that no demonstration was to take place. He also informed Cullen that His Holiness was far from pleased over what was taking place in Ireland.

2. *The Lesson of 1844*

Cullen, as we have seen, was crushed at this time. He had allowed himself to be seen as the Roman agent of the MacHaleites who promoted *agitazione* within the Irish Church. His friend William Walshe, the Bishop of Halifax, counselled contrition for having 'acted imprudently'. 'What can one do,' he asked, 'not only after an error of judgment, but even after a deliberate crime, but humble oneself in God's presence?' The crime was that the MacHaleite uproar had succeeded in dividing not only the Catholic clergy but even the Repeal movement, to O'Connell's great annoyance:

> If left to himself he would have been as neutral on the
> Bequests Bill as he was on the educational question. *On
> dit* that Drs MacHale and Cantwell threatened to with-
> draw from the Repeal movement if O'Connell did not
> agitate the Bequests Bill whilst, on the other hand, Smith
> O'Brien . . . and other Protestants were violently opposed
> to its being mixed up with the national question.
>
> (C: 11 Mar. 1845)

From this time, when he was reduced to a state of nervous
prostration by his diplomatic indiscretion, Cullen resolved
never again to allow himself to become 'vassal of a popular
party' — a phrase he was to use many times in later years.
On 8 February 1845 he told Cantwell that they had all been
wrong in their intemperate zeal and counselled that 'for God's
sake' they should seek to heal wounds that might even cause
a 'rupture with the Holy See'. (PM, I, 258)

Once his health was restored Cullen renewed his relationship with the MacHaleites, but his attitude towards them was
from this time forward much more critical; he was determined
to persuade them to abandon their old ways and return to
their pastoral duties. There was indeed a serious need for this.
When Cullen visited the west of Ireland during the famine he
told Kirby of several parishes abandoned in MacHale's territories because 'no priest can be found to accept them on
account of the dangers of death from starvation or fever'.
(NK: 2 Sept. 1847) He was astonished to hear from Edward
Maginn that MacHale had returned to Cardinal Fransoni
money sent to the starving people of Connaught, saying there
was no need for charity in his province. Maginn also remarked
that when a prelate acted in this manner he 'must have lost
his reason, his veracity, or his religion'. (C: 27 Jan. 1848) As
for Cantwell, Maginn had noted that while the people starved,
this bishop was wealthy enough to offer endowment for the
promised Catholic university. Waspishly Maginn told Cullen:

> His Lordship of Meath has set a brilliant example. He gives,
> as I understand from Dr MacNally, a commodious site, and
> heads the list of the contributions for your new university
> with a donation of ten thousand pounds. Would that the
> Hill of Tara were in his gift. (C: 4 Nov. 1847)

James Maher reinforced what Cullen learned from Maginn about the lack of pastoral responsibility of some of the Irish bishops and priests during the famine when he told his nephew how 'bishops travel about in their carriages, our priests in their gigs as comfortably as in the most abundant of seasons'. (C: 25 July 1847) Cullen might have questioned such censures if they had come from the Murray camp, but by no stretch of the imagination could either Maginn or Maher be interpreted as anything but fervent nationalists. By now Cullen's eyes were opened to the pastoral failings of the Irish clergy, especially those who were apt to neglect their people while at the same time they agitated strongly for political causes. In letters to Archbishop Slattery he indicated how disappointed he was that the bishops had neither ordered public prayers for famine victims nor expressed thanks for Roman aid sent to them. (CA, 1847/13/41)

The problem for Rome, and for Cullen, on the eve of his departure for Ireland was how to persuade the MacHaleites to serve the strategy of the Universal Church rather than narrow nationalist interests. Cardinal Fransoni sent two private paternal letters to Primate Crolly warning him about the dangers which accompanied an over-involvement of bishops and priests in Irish politics, but Cullen knew that the much-hated Archbishop of Armagh had no chance of influencing the MacHaleites. Yet something had to be done. In Rome Lord Minto was representing the British government, pressing for pensioning of the troublesome Irish clergy and, Cullen was sure, giving encouragement to the Italian nationalist insurgents. At this juncture Cullen put aside the resolutions he had made after the crisis of 1844 and wrote to MacHale himself on 28 January 1848 in the hope that 'the Lion' might promote 'legitimate agitation':

> It would be well if John O'Connell or some of the big men would get up a good agitation against Minto for being at the bottom of these calumnies, for interfering in the colleges question and for encouraging the radical party in Switzerland and Italy. Some stir and a good strong one should be made in Ireland in order to put a stop to all the scheming with which they are going on in Italy. (PM, I, 309)

This was another imprudent action by Cullen, prompted by his Ultramontane zeal, one which might have made him as vulnerable as had his similar folly in 1844. Propaganda was then being systematically sent excerpts from Irish newspapers by the British government. (PFS, XXIX, 557-69) The *Freeman's Journal*, the *Dublin Evening Mail* and the *Tipperary Vindicator* reported denunciations from the altar that had led to the assassination of those condemned by the priests, and inflammatory sermons by men like Archdeacon Laffan of Cashel, who spoke of 'the Saxon scoundrel with his belly full of Irish meat'. Propaganda was sufficiently alarmed by these reports of *agitazione* for Cardinal Fransoni, at the express urging of the pope, to write to Archbishop Slattery of Cashel to request a full report on what was actually happening in his part of Ireland.

Slattery replied to Rome in great alarm and in considerable detail. On 28 January 1848, the very day Cullen had written to MacHale about the need for 'good agitation', he sent a copy of his twenty-page letter to Cullen. In it he denied that chapels were used for secular purposes, and tales of the clergy encouraging murder were 'vile, vague and confounded calumnies against us'. What was causing the social unrest was the depopulation of the country by the 'tyranny of the landlords'. Only the clergy defended the people against the 'national bigotry of England'. (C)

Two weeks later Slattery again wrote to Cullen to say that he had discovered that similar letters of inquiry had been sent to Archbishops Crolly and Murray – but none to MacHale, 'though this was not generally known'. Also someone (Slattery thought it was Murray) had leaked Fransoni's letter to the press, and it looked as if the Irish hierarchy faced 'a true bill of indictment, endorsed by Rome itself, against us'. (C: 12 Feb. 1848) He told Cullen that the Fransoni letter was now believed to be from the pope himself, 'his act of condemnation, and censure on Dr MacHale and the great body of the clergy of Ireland'. (C: 22 Feb. 1848) MacHale, to weather the storm, maintained a discreet silence, but Cullen wrote to him urging that he get all the bishops of his province to write to the pope directly 'informing him of the real state of things and protesting against English lies and English interference'.

He also suggested that 'profanation of the churches' should cease. (PM, I, 312: 18 Feb. 1848)

At this point it would seem that Cullen was not only trying to make use of the MacHaleites, even as they were trying to use him, but was also reluctant to give up the confidential relationship he had established with them. Events, however, determined what position he was to take towards the nationalist clergy of Ireland in the future. In July 1848 the abortive Young Ireland rising took place, and Cullen could but agree when Archbishop Murray reminded him that 'Some of our clergy had a large share in promoting among the people that excitement of which the calamity which lately impended over us should have been foreseen as the natural growth.' (BV: 10 Mar. 1849)

Events in Italy also definitely shaped Cullen's thought about *agitazione* from this time forward. Although the Italian nationalists in the papal states urged the pope to aid in driving out the Austrians, Pius IX hesitated and then declined. Rioting broke out in Rome; Prime Minister Rossi was assassinated in November; the pope was besieged by the mob in his palace and was finally obliged to flee in disguise to Gaeta in the kingdom of Naples. Cullen, as a foreigner, was reckoned to have immunity and stayed in Rome as joint Rector of Propaganda College and the Irish College. He saved Propaganda by putting it under the protection of the United States, but during the negotiations he came face to face with the mob. It was an experience he was never to forget. It was during this time of crisis in his life that news came to him of the death of Primate William Crolly.

An insight into how Cullen's thought was being influenced is provided by his correspondence with one of the few ecclesiastics he allowed to approach him in an intimate way. This was Edmund O'Reilly, eight years his junior, who had been a student at the Irish College, Rome. It was O'Reilly who wrote to Cullen on behalf of the student body in 1834 to urge him to return to the college and end the near anarchy under Michael O'Connor's administration: 'I have spoken pretty plainly, but superior as you are of the college, I think it lawful to acquaint you even with suspicions.' (C: 2 Dec.

1834) O'Reilly was the second vice-rector of the college, then went to Maynooth as Professor of Theology in 1838. Cullen was to use him as a theological adviser at the Synod of Thurles. A highly intelligent man, he became a Jesuit in 1851, was appointed Professor of Dogmatic Theology in the new Catholic University, and established a close friendship with John Henry Newman.

While he was at Maynooth O'Reilly worked hard to introduce a Roman spirit and tradition there, and it was during this period that he wrote to Cullen in an almost chastising way over the latter's public alliance with the MacHaleites during the Charitable Bequests crisis. Bluntly he told Cullen on 11 December 1844 that his imprudence had given 'several of your friends considerable pain'. He said the professors at Maynooth knew well the 'factious spirit' of the MacHaleites among them, such as Dr O'Hanlon, and Dr MacNally, now made Bishop of Clogher. They were always intriguing, trying to secure the appointment of members of their party to college posts, and were, on occasion, as 'turbulent' as MacHale himself. He also warned Cullen that Kirby in Rome was allied with the MacHaleites, as his letters ('foolish productions') clearly showed. He was 'exacerbating' the minds of the students, and O'Reilly wondered if it was wise to keep him on as vice-rector.

O'Reilly wrote to Cullen again on 21 January 1845 to tell him of his personal sorrow on discovering that the Irish agent in Rome was being 'charged by some with being a downright party man, I mean a partisan of Dr MacHale'. This was tragic, said O'Reilly, because the MacHaleites, by their alliance with nationalism, were promoting a form of churchmanship that was anathema to any Roman: 'Under the name of refusing to the Pope authority in temporals, the spiritual authority which our faith teaches us to recognise in him will be jeopardised. . . . We are in danger of falling back into Gallicanism.' Cantwell had gone so far as to proclaim, on his own authority, that he would deny the sacraments to anyone who held office under the Charitable Bequests Board. What was going to happen when Dr Murray visited friends in the Meath diocese, as he often did? This kind of scandal was encouraging priests everywhere to 'exculpate the highest authority of the Irish Church'. There was now even talk of a boycott of Maynooth because it received a government grant:

> I have been told that some of the bishops are quite ready at the *least provocation* to withdraw their subjects and get up another college to be maintained by voluntary contributions of the people. The Maynoothians would be looked on as an odious government pack. One great misery of the present state of things is the mixture of religion and politics, not merely a personal coincidence, the same men being priests and politicians, but the same cause being treated as political and religious. (C)

But in spite of the fact that O'Reilly was so candid and outspoken in his approach to Cullen — and we shall see further examples of his frankness of speech later — it seems clear that Cullen knew what he was about when he flirted with the MacHaleites. When he allowed the relationship to get out of hand in 1844, and as a result nearly lost his authority in Rome as the one Irishman the pope and Propaganda could trust to transcend the divisions in the Irish Church, he was filled with 'terror'. Once he re-established his Roman authority, however, he maintained communication with the MacHaleites, regardless of how dangerous the exercise might be. O'Reilly had warned Cullen in his second personal letter that 'Rome requires to act at this moment with consummate *religious policy* to keep things from getting worse.' (C: 21 Jan. 1845) Cullen had resolved through diplomatic finesse to seek for the needed 'consummate' religious policy, and though he was careful not to be used by the MacHaleites again, he was willing to let Cantwell and others, including MacHale himself, think that he might yet be persuaded to help their nationalist cause.

3. *The Armagh Appointment*
While Cullen was immersed in his diplomatic negotiations with the revolutionaries who had taken over control in Rome news came that William Crolly, the Archbishop of Armagh, had been stricken with cholera and had died. In the *terna* established by the election following his death Joseph Dixon,

a Maynooth professor, was *dignissimus*, the fiery nationalist John O'Hanlon, also a Maynooth professor, was *dignior*, and the third name was that of Michael Kiernan, Parish Priest of Dundalk. Immediately intense political manoeuvring began by the 'orthodox party' to have O'Hanlon appointed as Primate in succession to the generally unpopular Crolly.

One of the first letters that Cullen received came from Michael Lennon, Parish Priest of Crossmaglen, writing on behalf of James Maher, who told the Roman agent on 21 June 1849 that only O'Hanlon, who was from outside the diocese, could transcend local differences among the priests which Dixon and Kiernan as local men were bound to encourage. (C) John Cantwell had written also, on 10 May, but his letter was concerned with the possibility that the British government might persuade Rome to appoint neither Dixon nor O'Hanlon but Cullen's friend Edmund O'Reilly of Maynooth. The tone of Cantwell's letter indicates not only his ignorance of how close Cullen and O'Reilly were but also his tacit assumption that the Roman agent would approve of O'Hanlon as Primate — although, he added flatteringly, all 'true friends of Ireland' really wanted one whom he 'will not name' but 'whose appointment they would hail as the special and merciful interposition of Providence'.

Cantwell went on to warn Cullen that the government was doing all in its power to push Edmund O'Reilly into the see of Armagh:

> A more calamitous choice could hardly be made. He is a good man, it is true, but the Castle influence, who have their faction in the college professors, united with that of his relatives and their connections among the hollow and worthless Catholic aristocracy, succeeded in making poor O'Reilly an anti-O'Connell gentleman, an enemy of agitation, an admirer of Whig liberality towards Ireland in Church and State ... the echo and pliant tool of the authorities in Dublin. (C)

After this attack on O'Reilly as an 'Orange Catholic', Cantwell waited until 30 May before writing to Cullen again to urge the appointment of O'Hanlon rather than one 'whose thoughts turn oftener on the Castle than on the Vatican'. (C)

O'Reilly, we should remember, had already had much to say about O'Hanlon during the Charitable Bequests furor, and on 28 May he reminded Cullen further about the man's failings. He began by saying that neither as a student nor as a professor was O'Hanlon 'remarkable for piety'. He celebrated mass infrequently and was never seen at prayer in chapel. His temper was so violent that the professors at dinner no longer talked about either theology or politics lest they bring forth from O'Hanlon an outburst, 'overbearing and offensive in the extreme'. Because of his lying nature and love of intrigue, O'Reilly doubted the sincerity of his much-vaunted attachment to MacHale's party, which was so often delivered in language that 'although not immoral is often coarse and vulgar and unbecoming on the ground of lowness'. O'Reilly realised that Cullen might doubt that O'Hanlon could be 'such a mean person', but he assured his friend that his assessment was based on eleven years' observation. It was simply inconceivable that such a man could become Primate of the Irish Church even though 'this would involve his remaining here, an incubus on the community'. (C) In a further letter of 3 July O'Reilly completed his case against O'Hanlon:

> I do not mean to say that O'Hanlon is an unconscientious man in the sense of either having no conscience, or of going against this conscience deliberately . . . but I consider him a man who would not always consult his conscience first, nor make it his chief guide. (C)

A similar epistle was sent to Archbishop Slattery by O'Reilly. (CA, 1849/37)

It is probable that even in the summer of 1849 Cullen knew there was no likelihood of the Armagh appointment going to either O'Hanlon or O'Reilly. MacHale never joined in the chorus of those supporting the former, and it seems clear that his choice was always Cullen himself. Although the official appointment was not announced until 27 December, when Cullen wrote to MacHale to thank him for his help in obtaining such an honour, many of the nationalists shared in what was an open secret. As early as 5 December Charles MacNally had written to say: 'Your removal to

Ireland may be sooner than you expect.' (C) The letter to MacHale indicates that the appointment was no surprise to Cullen, whose only hesitation about accepting the appointment was the consideration of who would succeed him in Rome. He told MacHale he would insist upon Kirby, whose role as a sturdy opponent of 'godless education' could be counted upon. (PM, I, 330)

Although Daniel Murray's letters to Cullen following his appointment were rather subdued in tone, Michael Slattery, a moderate nationalist, probably expressed the feelings of the majority of churchmen over Cullen's appointment. Slattery was a graduate of Trinity College, Dublin, had been a President of Maynooth, and had taken a moderate line on both the National System and the Charitable Bequests Act; nevertheless, Cullen thought well of him because he firmly opposed the Queen's Colleges as a British attempt to 'Prussianise' Irish higher education. In political matters Slattery stood by O'Connell and had bluntly told Cullen in 1846 that 'The Young Ireland faction . . . are a bad set, in religion they are latitudinarian and in politics revolutionary.' (C: 2 Aug. 1846) He deplored MacHale breaking up unity among the bishops, but he also deplored MacHale being denounced from the altar by one of Murray's supporters in Westland Row, and O'Connell being called a 'humbug' and 'a huge living lie'. (C: 4 Feb. 1849)

In the months before Cullen's appointment Slattery was almost in despair over the state of the Catholic Church in Ireland, which he described to Cullen in the gloomiest terms:

> Never was our church in greater peril when Jansenistical principles and evasions are openly used to make naught of and trample under foot the authority of even the Holy Father's solemn decision. . . . For my part I am afflicted and heartbroken at the prospect before me. The country prostrate at the feet of England, her people starving, her social and political condition at the very lowest ebb, and worse than all, her faithful and hitherto independent church in imminent danger of ruin at the hands of her own anointed ministers. (C: 4 Feb. 1849)

Cullen agreed with Slattery that Jansenism acutely threatened the Irish Church and that some authority had to be brought to bear on bishops and clergy alike in order to put an end to scandals like that of Killaloe, where Patrick Kennedy was openly at war with his priests. (CA, 1849/12)

When Slattery heard of Cullen's appointment he was filled with a deep sense of relief. He told the new archbishop that he had become to disillusioned that he had actually asked Propaganda to relieve him of his post. But now he rejoiced 'for the sake of religion in our poor church over which it convinces me that Providence has yet a watchful eye'. At the same time he suggested a Roman consecration for Cullen, which would 'enable you to enter at once on the duties of your office', as well as saving 'a good deal of trouble'. (C: 9 Jan. 1850) Cullen took to heart this warning, and though Murray had hoped the consecration might have been held in Drogheda, it was carried out in the church of the Irish College on 24 February 1850. It was from Rome that the new Primate addressed his first pastoral letter to the clergy and laity of Armagh.

Cullen did not reach Ireland until early in May. During his last weeks in Rome he arranged for the Cardinal Prefect to write to those bishops whose dioceses contained the Queen's Colleges, warning them that their priests were to have nothing to do with the 'godless' institutions. In April he was made Apostolic Delegate and ordered to convoke a national synod as soon as he arrived in Ireland. Not only was he to strengthen the links between Rome and the Irish Church, but his immediate and pressing task was to bring the bishops together to end the bitter dissension among them.

During this interregnum the Irish newspapers began to write in apprehensive terms about the coming among them of the prelate the pro-government papers called 'an Italian monk', an 'unnaturalised Irishman', an agent of Ultramontane advance. (PFS, XXX, 311ff) Other papers spoke of him less critically, but even in those which supported the MacHaleite cause there appeared to be some reservation over the appointment. Cullen year after year had listened to the complaints and gossip of bishops and priests alike and had patiently helped to bring about many changes in the Irish Church. By 1849 there were few Catholic leaders who were not indebted to him in some regard. He knew much about them, and he had acquired a formidable insight into the problems of Irish ecclesiastical life generally, while even the tensions and scandals which existed on the level of the parish were well known to him. His future colleagues were obliged to recognise in Cullen an authority much greater, and potentially more threatening, than that which he was accorded formally as Primate and Apostolic Delegate. Few Irish Catholics doubted that he would be someone with whom they must reckon.

As for the new Primate, his first task was to find a means to end the strife between the followers of Murray and Mac-Hale that was paralysing the Irish Catholic Church. The achievement of unity to Cullen was, however, but a means to an end, as was the project of bringing the priests out of politics. Cullen was completely an Ultramontanist, and to his mind his Irish mission was but his generation's campaign in the ongoing battle of the Church Militant against the forces of heresy, infidelity and other spiritual wickedness. The pro-government papers were not far wide of the mark when they viewed him as essentially 'an Italian monk' intent upon bringing the Catholics of Ireland under papal direction for the extension of Ultramontane authority.

In terms of mission, Cullen had been shocked by his visit of 1847 and knew what had to be done. He had met the distinguished convert, John Henry Newman, in the same year, and he was passionately interested in the pro-Catholic movement in the Church of England. He was even more concerned about Protestant proselytising in Ireland. Maginn of Derry kept him abreast of Protestant advances in Ulster. On 20 January 1847 Denis Murphy, the Parish Priest of Kinsale, brought him up to date on the work of 'the Exeter Hall fanatics' in West Cork. (C) Mary Collins of the Presentation nuns in Dingle wrote to him on 4 February 1848 to describe aid given to local proselytisers by zealots from the Achill colony. (C) On 16 February 1848 Cornelius Egan, Bishop of Ardfert, apologised in detail for the widespread and successful 'bribery' of converts to Protestantism in his diocese. (C) On 13 June 1848 James Maher reported on a major study of the Protestant proselytising by John Miley, the former Roman student and scholar whose books on the papacy were shortly to win his appointment as Rector of the Irish College in Paris. It seemed clear that in Cork, Dublin, Limerick, Kerry and, above all, Connaught conversions were taking place by the hundreds; and once the division between the bishops was ended the Church was to go to war with the proselytisers. (C)

The problem was how to raise the morale of the bishops who were so divided and disheartened. When Maher wrote to his nephew again on 13 October 1848 his usual ebulliency was gone. The Catholic Church seemed to have lost its spirit in Ireland, as had been demonstrated in the most recent synod:

> The bishops opened their usual synod on Tuesday last, passed a few resolutions and forthwith prepared to return. ... The resolutions passed, but a reference to the state of the poor, to the pensioning of the clergy, or an expression of sympathy for the pope in his present embarrassed circumstances, none of these topics were taken up with heart or spirit or dignity and consequently will be little attended to.

Nor, reported Maher, did the bishops even consider issuing a pastoral to raise the morale of the poor people who were now abandoning the Catholic faith in droves. Especially in Connaught it looked as if nothing could contain the Protestant advance:

> The *Saunders* of yesterday supplies its readers with a report of the Presbyterian congregations in the kingdom of Connaught. They boast of considerable success in the erection of schools and meeting houses. The famine, they assert, has afforded them many opportunities of impressing upon the needs of the poor their views of religion. In truth, proselytism is conducted with spirit and activity. The wickedness and uncharitableness of the proselytisers are generally passed over in silence. (C)

Paul Cullen had no intention of allowing 'wickedness and

uncharitableness' of any sort to be ignored in his native land when he returned there as Primate and Apostolic Delegate. He had spent twenty-nine years absorbing the ethos of Ultramontane Rome, and his brief loss of papal favour in 1844 had been compensated for by his heroic labours during the revolution. His task was clear: to put the Catholic Church in Ireland on a war footing against Protestantism and every other enemy of the Supreme Pontiff. He was only forty-six years of age, his health was reasonably good, and his prestige was high. He knew he had a guarded welcome awaiting him from many bishops and priests, especially the MacHaleites, who were hoping to use him. But Paul Cullen had learned much about the working of the Irish Church, and he was not likely ever to be used again by anyone except his Roman superiors.

IV

The Primate

1. *Homecoming*

Paul Cullen did indeed receive a guarded welcome when he returned to his native land. Early in January 1850 both the *Dublin Evening Post* and the *Freeman's Journal* reported rather tersely on 'very respectable authority' his appointment as the new Archbishop of Armagh. The latter paper on 10 January told its readers that the new Primate was a nephew of James Maher, 'who has done so much for the benefit of the poor of Ireland and whose labours in the cause of his country can never be sufficiently appreciated'. It was not until 14 January that the *Freeman's Journal* reprinted comment from the *Tablet* on the significance of Rome's passing over the nominees on the *terna* to elevate this Roman ecclesiastic who was almost unknown to the great mass of the Catholic population of Ireland. The editorial expected that many people would 'conceive a certain modified regret that the affair has turned out otherwise than they at· first desired'. It went on to point out that Cullen 'for learning has not his superior in the Irish Church', while his 'confidential position' in Rome, especially in Propaganda circles, would be of immense benefit in the future. As to his personal characteristics, though he was 'a man of unbending firmness', his 'character is peculiarly fitted to sooth, to conciliate, to attract'. Although Cullen represented 'the tendency of this time towards practical Ultramontanism, towards throwing the whole power of the Church upon the successor of St Peter', yet Irish Catholics need not fear that other than a sound appointment had been made:

His sentiments on all public questions are well known, and everyone who detests state interference with religion in general and the godless colleges in particular must feel that the new Primate will be a tower of strength to the Church in Ireland.

There was enough resentment over Rome's action in passing over all candidates on the *terna,* however, for the *Tablet* to publish a letter from Monsignor Alessandro Barnabo of Propaganda explaining, if not apologising for, the appointment. This was reproduced in the *Freeman's Journal* of 21 January:

> Our most holy Father, having duly weighed all particulars and having taken into account what ever had been alleged in behalf of the two ecclesiastics who otherwise are excellent both in piety and learning, judged however that another should be chosen in whom are united all the most industrious endowments qualifying him for the right discharge of the office in question.

Barnabo praised Cullen's 'probity and learning', his 'prudence and mildness of character', but the pro-Cullen faction felt it necessary for John Miley, the Rector of the Irish College in Paris, to write to the *Freeman's Journal* on 23 January to assure its readers that Catholic nationalists had nothing to fear from the new Primate whose appointment was being treated with such reserve:

> In his character are blended the accomplishments of the polished gentleman, the learning and piety of the gifted ecclesiastic, and all the public and private virtues that adorn the true patriot.

When the same paper's editors commented on Cullen's first pastoral two days later they apologised that it was so 'un-Irish' in its form and content, but asserted their approval of it for striking 'at the two master vices of the country — division and enmity'.

The Protestant press snidely noted the appointment of a Roman functionary as the new Catholic Primate and Apostolic Delegate, but refrained from major comment. The MacHaleites waited with considerable anticipation for this Roman reinforcement which would help them in their struggle with the 'Castle bishops'. As for Daniel Murray and his followers, they expected Cullen to exercise his legatine authority at their expense as soon as he had settled himself in Armagh in May; and, as events were to show, they were correct in this assumption.

In dealing with the 'division and enmity' among the bishops and priests, Cullen felt best prepared to cope with the old Gallicans led by Murray. Like most curial figures of his generation, he was confident of victory in any contest with representatives of traditional Gallicanism, and he was particularly well informed about the affairs of Daniel Murray. This was so because from the time of the struggle over the Charitable Bequests Bill he had had a spy or agent serving him within the very household of the Archbishop of Dublin. This was Peter Cooper, a curate at Marlborough Street, who was also a canon of the chapter of the Pro-Cathedral.

Cooper had gone to Rome in 1840 to receive a doctoral degree and had there fallen under the spell of Tobias Kirby. He returned to Dublin a convinced Ultramontanist, determined to resist those churchmen who opposed the increase of Roman authority in the Irish Church. In a letter to Cullen in 1844 he 'opened his soul' to the Irish agent in Rome and assured him that many Dublin clergy were as pro-Roman as he was but were 'holding back lest they should give displeasure to the good archbishop'. These clerics did not like Murray's confidant, a meddling ambitious Tory named Anthony Richard Blake, who encouraged the archbishop to defend interdenominational education, yet they hesitated to give their support to the party led by MacHale. Like Cooper, they considered MacHale to be the cause of the 'ill-concealed schism' in the country and heartily disliked his 'haughty, imperious, overbearing' spirit which caused so much 'irritation and rankling'. Their hope was that soon there would be built up an Ultramontane party in Ireland that could withstand the errors of both Murray and MacHale and their followers. (C: 25 Sept. 1844)

Cullen immediately tried to make use of Cooper, urging him to foment opposition to the Charitable Bequests Bill in the Dublin archdiocese, but Cooper at that time shrank from open confrontation with his archbishop. He told Cullen of his hesitation, 'though your wishes and opinion have the greatest weight with me'. (C: 25 Oct. 1844) He did agree,

however, to send Cullen confidential reports on the activities
of those clergy who supported the Queen's Colleges. By early
1846 Cooper was scurrilously attacking as a man and as a
priest J. W. Kirwan, the president of the college in Galway,
who had at one time been a fellow-student of his. As for
the Catholic students who attended the Queen's Colleges,
Cooper's investigations had convinced him that they were as
profligate as those Catholics who had recently fled the
Dublin medical college 'in order to escape prosecution and
shame for an act that would disgrace the infidelity of Paris'.
(C: 12 Jan. 1846) Cooper told Archbishop Slattery of a long
confidential conversation he had with Cullen at Maynooth in
the autumn of 1847 (CA, 1847/90), and throughout 1848
Cullen wrote to Cooper about three times a week as he followed
the Irish discussion of university affairs. (CA, 1848/177)

From this time until Cullen arrived in Ireland Cooper kept
him apprised of everyone in the Murray camp who served the
old Gallican cause, like Myles Murphy, Bishop of Ferns, who
refused to object to interdenominational education. As for
Murray himself, Cullen knew that he saw no need for Rome
to interfere in Irish affairs through the office of an Apostolic
Delegate. In spite of the trouble caused by the MacHaleites,
Murray's sensible and conciliatory policies had wrung much
from the government for the Catholics of Ireland, and there
was no reason why further concessions would not be granted.
Murray had sent Dr Ennis, the Parish Priest of Booterstown,
to Rome to present to the pope a memorial recording what
Murray's 'peaceful persuasion' tactics had accomplished. The
Freeman's Journal had been so impressed by this document
that it summarised its contents on 15 August 1848:

> Every session of every successive parliament has produced
> laws favourable to the increase of Catholicity and decrease
> of Protestantism. Passing over in silence the general eman-
> cipation, let us enumerate alone the religious abolitions,
> the very germs, the roots of the Protestant propaganda
> destroyed; for example, the Charter Schools, and those of
> the Bible; the exclusive nursery of that religion is entirely
> destroyed . . . the military and sailors were all brought up
> in Protestantism . . . and now have their chapels and Roman
> Catholic chaplains with support from the state. It is not

necessary that I should record the destruction of ten dioceses of Protestant bishops, the abolition of all the municipal corporations of Protestants, the refusal of every government to assign and not to allot any part of £100,000 for the education of the poor to the Protestants. . . .

Cullen, however, like most Roman Ultramontanists, was not impressed by what Murray's policies of 'peaceful persuasion' of a heretical government were achieving. The Universal Church was not to be merely tolerated as a religious organisation by a liberal government bowing to the pressures of an age of reform. When the majority people of Ireland were Catholic, then it was just and proper that there should be an ascendancy religious establishment that was Catholic and shepherded by the universal ordinary. Cullen knew from his Roman experience that argument alone would never encourage the British government to reverse traditional policies and to grant Catholics in Ireland the kind of religious settlement which they were due. When the state would not bow to the kind of pressure brought about by those who had protested against the National System of Education, the Charitable Bequests Act or the Queen's Colleges, then a new kind of campaign had to be attempted under direction of the Apostolic Delegate.

Cullen had no intention of allying himself with MacHale when he came to Ireland, in spite of the expectations of some of the nationalist bishops and priests. By the time of the Charitable Bequests agitation MacHale had lost all credibility in Rome, and following the upheavals of 1848 liberal agitation was anathema. At the same time Cullen looked enviously at MacHale's authority among the masses who still granted to him the devotion they had once given to O'Connell. He also remembered the constitutional victories of the Liberator, who had established his authority among the people and then persuaded the government that he could control them only so long as concessions were granted. Neither Murray's policies of conciliation nor MacHale's blind obstructionism were to be pursued by Cullen, but he knew that to persuade the leaders of the two warring clerical factions to follow him in a new struggle with the government he had somehow to bring them together. Once the Church was united again, then the people could perhaps be persuaded to support the Apostolic Delegate as he attempted an O'Connellite campaign for peaceful constitutional change which would advance the interests of the Roman Catholic Church.

This was an age of social reform everywhere in Europe, and Cullen was an astute enough politician to know that history was on his side in his demand that the Protestant ascendancy must go because it did not represent the desires of the majority of the population. He also knew that the Protestants were defensive and anxious, like other privileged minorities throughout Europe, and that advantage could be taken of their depressed state of mind. As early as 26 June 1827 the *Newry Telegraph* had reported Protestant dismay over the success of the Emancipation campaign. A mass meeting of two thousand local Protestants had been held against 'the pretensions of the Roman Catholics', who, led by their priests, had 'the avowed object . . . to exterminate the Protestants from the face of the land'. At the very time of Cullen's coming to Ireland the *Quarterly Review* of December 1849 and March 1850 expressed its alarm over the too conciliatory policies of Lord Clarendon, the viceroy:

> Having for some years past looked at the state and course of government in Ireland with great uneasiness, we now see, with still more alarm, the growing subserviency of the Irish administration to the anti-Protestant and anti-British spirit of the Popish agitators. We have even been occasionally forced to ask ourselves whether Her Majesty's minister had not some occult design of establishing Roman Catholic *ascendancy* in Ireland . . . the overthrow of the great principles of 1688. (*Anti-Prot.*, 2)

Cullen's shrewd assessment of the government's mind, especially its desire to conciliate the new Primate in the hope that he would be as easy to work with as Crolly or Murray, was soon shown to be correct. He was immediately invited to become a member of the Charitable Bequests Board, which he politely declined. Then he was informed of the government's willingness to have Catholic bishops nominated as visitors to the new Queen's Colleges, and to have Catholic deans of residence appointed by local bishops, such arrangements being deemed necessary in view of the large numbers of Catholics who were attending the new institutions. Cullen's response to the government initiative was revealed in a letter written to Kirby soon after he had settled himself in Armagh:

> The government ... has sent to sound me about the colleges. They promise to make great changes, provided the bishops will be very good. I desired them to put their project in writing, but they will not do so. Tell them at Propaganda not to believe them if they make promises. All they want is to impede the bishops from doing anything at the Synod by holding out hopes. (NK: 11 July 1850)

The government and the Protestants, as well as the bishops, priests and laity of the Catholic Church, were soon to find out how resolute Paul Cullen was to be in his Irish mission. The coolness of his reception by most churchmen and the enormity of the task before him in no way daunted him. At least the friendly noises made by the government, however hypocritical they might be, showed that they would be willing to negotiate with the new authority about to establish itself in Ireland, so long as he could force them to take the Apostolic Delegate seriously. The immediate task for Cullen was obviously to clear the Church of its divisions so that it could then put itself on a war footing. This task was begun in 1850 at the Synod of Thurles.

2. *The Synod of Thurles*
Twice in the early years of the century the Holy See had refused approval for national synods, but now with Cullen exercising legatine authority, and with the division between the bishops becoming a public scandal, it was felt that bringing the quarrelsome prelates together had to be risked. To prepare the minds of everyone as to the solemnity of the occasion the meeting was trumpeted as the first held in Ireland since the reign of Henry VIII, and the first exercise of legatine authority since that of Archbishop Rinuccini in the 1640s. Cullen himself, long accustomed to the hot Italian summer, did not take easily to the change of climate, and he later told his friend William Walshe of Halifax that he was so weak during the proceedings that he 'could scarcely walk a

perch'. In spite of that, he was a formidable governing figure throughout the synod, for, as he told Kirby, 'I must be pretty stout, otherwise nothing will be done.' (NK: 2 July 1850)

Michael Slattery, the elderly and infirm Archbishop of Cashel, had impressed Cullen by his negative reaction to a great gathering of priests for the opening of the Cork Queen's College, so it was arranged for the synod to be convened at Thurles in his archdiocese. Cullen's friend Laurence Forde was appointed master of ceremonies, and Peter Cooper was rewarded for his intelligence work by the office of secretary of the synod. The most important person at the synod, however, was Cullen; indeed, it was Cooper's opinion that only the Primate's 'firmness' saved them all from disaster, as many bishops came to Thurles 'with the predetermination to trample (the word is not too strong) on him and his legatine authority'. Murray in particular had been impressed with Cullen's performance: 'His friends knew he had much in him, but no one believed his powers to be so great as they have proved.' (K: 9 Oct. 1850)

Murray may have appreciated Cullen's ability to preside effectively, but in the synod he led a strong resistance to the attempt by the Apostolic Delegate to have the bishops accept without discussion the rescripts of Propaganda sent to them in 1847 and 1848, as well as more recent instructions which condemned the Queen's Colleges. During the synod Cullen told Kirby that Murray and his followers were 'most violent in defence of the colleges' (NK: 31 Aug. 1850), and John Cantwell later characterised the defence of the colleges made by Murray and the twelve bishops who supported him as the display of 'a most factious and disobedient spirit'. (K: 6 Oct. 1850) The argument used by Murray was that the colleges were the only means available to Catholics for higher education, apart from the Protestant Trinity College, and that the rescripts were binding only on those to whom they were addressed. Priests and laymen remained free to do what they liked about the colleges.

The condemnation that Cullen desired was barely carried, by one vote, and Murray and his supporters also opposed as impractical Rome's desire to have a Catholic university established in Ireland. Cullen, however, was very astute in his handling of the synod. He insisted on proper procedures being followed, and through great tact he even persuaded Murray to become a member of the committee to establish the new Catholic university. He also managed to secure the ratification by all the bishops of the synodical address to the clergy and the faithful which concluded the synod on 9 September.* The address stressed that from time immemorial it had been the custom of the Irish Church to refer all questions to the Holy See, a precedent established by St Patrick himself. At the conclusion of the synod, in spite of his physical exhaustion, Cullen felt satisfied. He had had no trouble with the MacHaleites, who had kept a low profile while the Apostolic Delegate dealt with Murray and his Gallican followers. Cullen knew that it might all have been much worse had not his tight procedural control done wonders in damping Irish excitability. As he commented to Bernard Smith, then Vice-Rector of the Irish College in Rome, 'In a synod things are done so orderly that there is not room for much digression and a violent man can be kept in order.' (BS: 18 Oct. 1850)

Cullen soon found, however, that the issues raised in the synod had by no means been finally resolved there. Some 400 Catholics were attending the Queen's Colleges, and Murray and his followers intended that they should be joined by others. While Cullen recuperated from his exhaustion in the comfortable home of his wealthy brother Thomas in Liverpool the dissidents began to rally and prepare a counter-offensive. Bishop Delany of Cork, O'Donnell of Galway, and the two Ulster bishops, Denvir of Down and Connor and Blake of Dromore, all of whom represented areas where Queen's Colleges were established, were particularly upset at the condemnation of the new institutions and were determined to support Murray in his fight.

The synodical address which was presented to the faithful in the columns of the *Freeman's Journal* on 16 September 1850 was modelled in an Ultramontane framework of thought. It had much to say about a world-wide onslaught on the

---

*For the details of Cullen's *tour de force* at the synod see Emmet Larkin, *The Making of the Roman Catholic Church in Ireland, 1850-1860*, Chapel Hill 1980, 27-58.

Catholic faith, spearheaded by attempts to subvert the young
through institutions like the Queen's Colleges. Only a Catholic
university could protect the faithful young people of Ireland
from the evil literature with which the world abounded, or
from the proselytising by Protestants which was the curse of
Ireland. The thirteen bishops who formed Murray's party
were quite willing to question this peculiarly Roman outlook,
however; and Cullen was, moreover, soon to find that the
fourteen bishops who supported the condemnation of the
Queen's Colleges, and the establishment of a Catholic university to take their place, were little more than lukewarm
Ultramontanists.

Murray's counter-offensive began with a petition to the
pope on behalf of those who had protested against the
propositions that had been approved at the synod. This
action was brought to public attention when a National
System commissioner, John Corballis, wrote to the *Dublin
Evening Post*, a Whig and 'Castle Catholic' paper, asking Archbishop Murray whether Catholics should now withdraw from
Trinity College after they had been battling for fifty years to
be admitted. Murray's answer was to reveal the existence of
the minority party petition that had been sent to the pope.
Peter Cooper immediately wrote to Kirby to identify Murray's
ploy as 'a thing *got up* to instruct the people in the way of
disobedience'. (K: 2 Oct. 1850) Kirby then wrote to Michael
Slattery to say that Rome had rebuked Murray and his
followers for publishing the secrets of the synod and opposing
its decrees, but Slattery in reply told Kirby that this had
done little good as no one knew of the Roman admonitions:

> It has been kept a profound secret among themselves and
> seems not to be taken the least notice of by them as far as
> one can judge from their acts. . . . Everything goes on as
> before regarding the colleges. (K: 23 Nov. 1850)

The result of this intransigence was that Cullen's temporary
euphoria following the synod soon disappeared as he found
himself obliged to carry on a campaign to ensure that there
was no wavering among the bishops who supported him.
James Maher tried to help his nephew by lurid descriptions
of what happened to young Catholics who were exposed to

the infidel and Arian opinions fostered in the Queen's Colleges and Trinity College. One lad who attended the latter institution emerged 'a hopeless infidel' dying from dissipation and threatening to shoot any priest who came near his deathbed. (Maher, *Galway*, 37) In spite of the noisy aid offered by the MacHaleites, Cullen's letters to Bernard Smith at this time were almost filled with despair. He doubted if many churchmen were enthusiastic about the proposed Catholic university; little financial support was forthcoming; and Murray's party were adamant in their opposition to the concept:

> The Castle bishops are just as hostile as ever. Not one of them will give their names or contributions and some of them are preaching against the undertaking and turning it into ridicule. (BS: 17 Jan. 1851)

Even the publication of the synod's decrees in May 1851 with full papal sanction did little to ease the situation. The opposition of the Gallican bishops continued, and it was clear that there was little general enthusiasm for a Catholic university, and no waning of Catholic support for the 'godless colleges'. Cullen knew that time was on his side, for Murray was eighty-three, Blake of Dromore was deaf and perhaps senile, Denvir of Down and Connor was not well, and others in the Murray camp were advanced in years; but still Cullen was anxious, telling Kirby that

> The only way to put things right would be to remove one of those bishops, and to put an administrator in his place — one such step would establish things as they ought to be.
> (NK: 1 July 1851)

His anxiety continued throughout the summer of 1851, and to his alarm he realised that the resistance of Murray and his party was hardening. On 15 September he told Smith that unless Rome or the Deity intervened, the Gallicans could yet have their victory:

> They are determined not to yield an inch to the Synod of Thurles, nor to the Pope himself. . . . Is it not an awful thing to have the education of the Irish clergy depending on those men? They can make all Ireland Jansenistical in a dozen years. There is no way of removing them. (BS)

Cullen told Archbishop Slattery that Murray, with his Gallican outlook, would accept the Thurles statutes only if they were not contrary to already existing diocesan ones. (CA, 1851/30: 29 Nov. 1851)

Cullen certainly could not count on Rome helping him by any draconian action in Ireland at this time. The restoration of the Catholic hierarchy in England enraged the Protestants of that country, and their anger became hysterical from the time that Nicholas Wiseman, the new Cardinal Archbishop of Westminster, issued his triumphalist pastoral 'From Out the Flaminian Gate' in October 1850. The 'No Popery' cry led to the passing of Lord John Russell's ill-conceived Ecclesiastical Titles Bill. It also resulted in diplomatic manoeuvring in Rome, where final confirmation of the decrees of Thurles was taking place at the time when in Ireland resentment of the British legislation was at its height. The most Cullen could hope for was a passage of the decrees of the Synod of Thurles without interference by British agents.

Although much abuse came his way during the 'papal aggression' hysteria, Cullen knew that most of it was bluff. He had no intention of easing his campaign against the Gallicans who resisted the reform measures of the synod, nor had he any intention of bowing to the government if an attempt were made to deprive him of his ecclesiastical titles:

> If they prosecute I will not expend a shilling in defending myself. I will tell them what I am and prove that I have a right to my titles, and then let them act as they wish. It is generally known that the threats will never be realised.
>
> (BS: 15 Sept. 1851)

A breathing space was given to him in November 1850 by the death of Patrick Kennedy of Killaloe, one of the fiercest defenders of the Queen's Colleges. Cullen now began a replacement policy which he was to maintain throughout his mission in Ireland. The new bishop appointed through Cullen's influence was a safe man from the Ultramontane standpoint, Daniel Vaughan. With a slightly increased numerical support, Cullen now felt free to begin a diplomatic offensive that would persuade the government that it should pay attention to him as the leader of the majority party in the Roman Catholic camp.

In a long letter to Lord Aberdeen in the late spring of 1851 Cullen indicated to the government that it would be advisable to negotiate with him as well as with the Gallican bishops led by Murray. Although he had deliberately refrained from serving on government commissions, Cullen wanted the state to know that as the chief representative of the papacy in Ireland he represented the real authority of the Church, and that as such he was willing to engage in diplomatic negotiations on behalf of Roman Catholicism. The pretext for writing to Aberdeen was to thank him for presenting in the House of Lords the petition of the Irish bishops against the Ecclesiastical Titles Bill. Cullen included in the letter the pastoral address of the Synod of Thurles, pointing out how the document properly concerned itself with only moral and religious matters such as the condemnation of 'tyranny and oppression on the one side, and every attempt at resistance, violence and revenge on the other'.

Cullen stressed how the Church traditionally stood by that authority which maintained law and order in society. In no way did the Church

> sympathise with those apostles of socialism and infidelity, who in other countries, under the pretence of promoting civil liberty, not only undermined the foundations of every government but artfully assailed the rights of the Apostolic See and sought for the destruction of the Holy Catholic Church.

In no way was the Roman Catholic Church to be considered a body which encouraged the excesses of those who would use the cause of social or political injustice as a means to stir up revolution for their own ends. Cullen particularly drew Aberdeen's attention to the section of the address where the bishops urged 'patience and resignation' among the people:

> . . . to respect the rights of property, to honour the rank and station of the great and powerful, to be grateful for favours received, and to pour forth fervent prayers for their benefactors. (BM, 43247, 190-3)

While he was making these representations to the British authorities Cullen was also maintaining his close scrutiny of the religious and ecclesiastical opinions of the traditional Gallicans led by Murray. The more he studied them the more he realised what a task lay before him if he was to carry out an Ultramontane revolution in Ireland. His growing uneasiness is revealed in a letter written to Bernard Smith in Rome:

> Have you seen the examination of Drs Doyle and Murray before the parliament in March, 1825? I never saw such a quantity of Gallicanism put together. It is astonishing that any church could exist in which such doctrines are held. I dare say a great deal of our misfortunes have arisen from acting on and holding such doctrines. Give a few abstracts from this examinaton to Dr Barnabo. Dr Doyle's ideas were outrageous. I think there is a copy of this examination . . . among my books. Get it and read it.
>
> (BS: 20 Feb. 1852)

As for promoting an Ultramontane revolution, Cullen to his dismay found that though he had faith in the people's reverence for Roman authority, they were not really conscious of what Ultramontanism was. Government members and state officials, whether Catholics or Protestants, displayed a similar ignorance:

> The Catholics and Protestants here are strangely at a loss. They know what Ultramontanism is. They think it is some horrid monster. Scully, the MP for Cork, went down to Maynooth a short time ago and spent a whole day there getting himself instructed on the nature of Ultramontanism. What lessons he received I know not — but I think the people and all the real Catholics here are all Ultramontanes.
>
> (NK: 30 Nov. 1852)

Early in 1852 Cullen was still very much on the defensive against the Gallicans. Murray's popularity was not in question in Dublin, and the Protestant *Dublin Evening Mail* of 2 February excoriated the Apostolic Delegate as a 'bold despot priest', both 'crafty and hypocritical', for his opposition to the Ecclesiastical Titles Bill. Then the long-expected yet sudden death of the aged Daniel Murray occurred, and with his passing the Gallican party, bereft of his wise leadership, began to break up. Cullen was fond of Murray as a person, but to his confidant, William Walshe of Halifax, he admitted that Murray's death was politically advantageous to him:

Dr Murray died. . . . Everyone admired his great virtues, and we are all inclined to forget his faults, which had their origin in the persuasion that others were as honest as himself. His death has been a fatal stroke to all the plans of government. (DAA: 7 Apr. 1852)

Where traditional Gallicanism remained as a force among the bishops and clergy it was to show itself in the future in sturdy resistance by those churchmen who wanted to maintain traditional national customs against the new order that Cullen was bringing from Rome. A strong resistance, for example, was mounted by the Munster bishops to the attempt by Cullen to end the tradition of having 'stations', house masses said by the priests, often in parts of the parish far from the chapel. The Synod of Thurles had decided as a reforming measure to regularise the celebration of the sacraments, and Cullen did not approve of the excesses which sometimes accompanied the hearing of confessions, baptisms, marriages and the celebration of mass in private houses. When the Munster bishops held a week-long provincial synod at Thurles in early September 1853 they decided to keep the custom of the stations, which was of considerable pastoral value in widespread parishes. Appeals were made to Rome over the issue, and finally a limited toleration of the stations was allowed, though only after considerable bitterness which soured relations between Cullen and the Gallican bishops of Munster. On 20 September, when the delegation from Munster was leaving for Rome, Dominic O'Brien, the President of St John's College, Waterford, wrote to his friend of Propaganda days, Tobias Kirby, about the continuance of this Gallican resistance to Cullen's reforming policies:

Two bishops, Dr Delany of Godless College notoriety, and Dr Keane, have been deputed to Rome to have decrees approved by the Holy See, and to rebut some charges said to be made against the Bishops of Ireland, and also to complain of interference on the part of Dr Cullen in dioceses that do not belong to him. The Sacred Congregation should listen to them with great caution. (K)

Although Cullen managed to win over William Keane, Bishop of Ross and then of Cloyne, he never trusted William

Delany of Cork, who outlived him and always supported the
Queen's College in his diocese. Nor was he ever sure of the
complete loyalty of the Munster bishops, to whom traditional
local customs meant so much. Even more disturbing to
Cullen were some members of Daniel Murray's household
who never abandoned their Gallican ideas and were always
ready and willing to criticise the policies of the Apostolic
Delegate. The Dean of Dublin, Walter Meyler, was one of
these Gallicans who carried on an irregular opposition to
Cullen's policies, whenever it was possible, especially in the
matter of education.

The most troublesome of these men to Cullen was an
erratic priest, Thaddeus O'Malley, also a member of Murray's
household, who had visited interdenominational schools on
the continent to gather evidence which had been of use to
Murray, and also to Meyler, who was for a time a member of
the Board of National Education. O'Malley never ceased his
defence of interdenominational education, nor his attacks on
Cullen for his use of legatine authority against the traditional
liberties of the Irish Church:

> With respect to the papal prerogative I will venture to say
> that no one respects it more sincerely than I do when con-
> sidered, as every enlightened Catholic in these countries
> always considers it — that is as limited to its just bounds
> and exercising itself only upon purely religious matters.
>
> (O'Malley, *Education*, 76)

In later years O'Malley advocated a Catholic/Protestant
alliance for Home Rule and directly attacked Cullen for his
alleged belief that 'there is no Ireland but Catholic Ireland —
the Protestants are not Irish at all'. (O'Malley, *Home Rule*,
106) The desire of Cullen, said O'Malley, was for Ireland to
be a 'martyr nation'; the country was bound to suffer through
the demands of the Apostolic Delegate that Ireland contribute
to so great an extent to the vain attempt of the pope to
regain temporal authority in Italy. Such criticisms continued
so persistently from O'Malley and others that in 1858 Cullen,
in a fit of depression, confessed to Kirby that he was seriously
considering resigning his legatine authority since it had
brought him nothing but opprobrium. (NK: 27 June 1858)

3. *Cullen and the Armagh Archdiocese*

Before his appointment as Archbishop of Armagh Cullen had never visited the 'Black North' (as his ecclesiastical correspondents referred to Ulster). When he arrived the pastoral challenges he met put him in a quandary. His training was that of a diplomat and ecclesiastical administrator; his focus of interest was the Universal Church and its Ultramontane mission. Yet in Armagh and Dundalk he found himself obliged to deal as a diocesan bishop with the important yet time-consuming and often wearying problems which beset any prelate responsible for the development of a local church in a relatively remote rural area. To add to his difficulties, Armagh during the eighteenth century had developed a tradition of 'turbulence and sedition'. It was here that the warring Catholic and Protestant peoples were so often to be found at each other's throats. Previous Catholic archbishops had often been non-resident, and neglect of pastoral duties by the priests was not uncommon. (PFS, XII, 68: 30 Oct. 1773; XIII, 97: 25 Apr. 1777) Matters were improving by the time Cullen arrived, but from the standpoint of a zealous Roman reformer the ecclesiastical and religious state of the Armagh archdiocese left much to be desired.

Cullen's predecessor, William Crolly, had come to Armagh as Primate in 1835 and had proved to be a conscientious pastor. Although he was then advanced in years, he lived alternatively in Armagh and Drogheda and tried through exhortation and visitation to encourage reformation among the priests. He laid the foundations of Armagh cathedral, and built a diocesan seminary largely at his own expense. In the mid-1840s he organised the people to defend themselves against Orange rioting, while at the same time trying to conciliate Protestants who were angrily resisting the spread of Catholic culture in the southern part of the archdiocese. He also tried to persuade the government that the new Queen's College for Ulster should be built in Armagh rather than Belfast, arguing that such a rural setting under his immediate jurisdiction would protect young Catholics from the heretical and impious atmosphere of Belfast.

Because of the numerous accusations levelled at William Crolly in the unrelenting campaign waged against him by

Cullen's uncle James Maher, the new Primate expected the worst when he got to Armagh, in terms of neglect of administrative and liturgical affairs. (Crolly, *Life*, cix) First impressions did little to offset Maher's slanders, for Crolly had shown little interest in implementing the kind of Ultramontane religious revolution that Rome was promoting. Cullen's first shock was to discover that though Armagh appeared to be filled with large and respectable houses, the new Primate had no place to live. Crolly had willed a house, purchased by public subscription, to his successor, but the Charitable Bequests Act viewed the gift as null and void as it had been made only the day before his death. By law the house had to go to Crolly's nephew, who was a minor. It took six years of proceedings in the Court of Chancery to straighten out the affair, and during much of his time as Archbishop of Armagh Cullen had to reside in Dundalk.

Administrative chaos also prevailed in the Primate's office. There were no diocesan archives, and Cullen in disgust told Kirby: 'I have not got one scrap of paper to learn even the names of the priests.' (NK: 16 May 1850) There was not a single convent in the town, and one of Cullen's first acts was to persuade Sacred Heart nuns to come to Armagh to found a school for young ladies. As for the priests, he found their standard of religious life primitive, and those who were not apathetic were troublesome. Cullen confided to Kirby that the general tone of religious life was about what he would have expected to find in Oregon or California.

Soon after Cullen's arrival there was a service to commemorate Crolly in Armagh cathedral, and the new Primate was shocked to find how 'un-Roman' was the service in a building which he described as a 'miserable hole'. Cullen and his secretary, Laurence Forde, were aghast at the general air of liturgical casualness displayed by priests gathered about an altar with only one candle on it, while those in the choir were nearly all without soutanes. In disgust Cullen asked Kirby to send him as quickly as possible a 'good surplice as a model for the priests'. (NK: 20 May 1850) He was soon to find, however, that the liturgical failings of Armagh were not unusual. He was particularly offended to find that Daniel Murray's processional cross was of plain wood, without any crucifix upon it, and he began to urge Kirby to press Monsignor Barnabo for help from Propaganda to raise the liturgical level of life in Armagh and in the Church in Ireland generally.

Cullen was filled with chagrin to find that while his own circumstances were so poor, his heretical counterpart, the Primate of the Church of Ireland, Lord John George Beresford, lived in a 'palazzo magnifico', a veritable 'villa Borghese'. Apparently the two Primates never met. Beresford made a courtesy call on Cullen when the latter first arrived, but on being informed that Cullen was 'out' he never repeated the exercise. This was understandable because from the time of his arrival Cullen had harsh words to say about the Church of Ireland, which he described as a body which encouraged religious indifferentism accompanied by a wild revolutionary spirit. Neither the huge amounts of money nor the rivers of blood shed to propagate it could assure its survival. The Established Church was 'now effete and bearing all the marks of the decrepitude of age and of approaching inevitable dissolution'. (*Armagh Letter*, 29-38)

In this same *Letter to the Catholic Clergy of the Archdiocese of Armagh* of 1850 he stressed the role of the Supreme Pontiff as guardian of the faith, insisting that only total submission to the pope would protect the faithful from infidelity and heresy: 'They who resist the prelate of the first see, resist the ordinance of Christ, and unless they repent, will have to undergo the punishment of their contumacy.' These harsh words reflect his experience of how troublesome were the priests of Armagh. In July 1850 he told Kirby that 'Italian bishops who have their curia may go on very smoothly — but here it is quite a different story.' (NK: 1 July 1850) He said that he had to spend hours and days dealing directly with troublemaking and often rebellious priests, curates and laity. In November he told Kirby how only a few months' experience of such work had wearied him:

I have spent the day examining into charges against priests and disputes between curates and parish priests — you may imagine what a pleasant business it is. However, some unfortunate man must do such business.

(NK: 11 Nov. 1850)

The truth was that Cullen resented his rustication in Armagh. He was much more interested in operating as papal delegate in the centres of power than he was in acting as metropolitan in rural Ulster. After two years he told Kirby in a plaintive letter that he was almost bowed down by the need for reform on a parochial level in his 'sadly neglected' archdiocese. He even found his clergy dull and little interested in affairs outside their own rural world. (NK: 9 July 1852) When the Ecclesiastical Titles Bill stirred up controversy and talk of reviving the penal laws, Cullen found there was no excitement among his clergy even though he called a meeting for them to express their support of Cardinal Wiseman. Resignedly he reported to Bernard Smith:

> The No-Popery cry is going down fast. It has not reached us. A few parsons only made a little stir and my Episcopal brother of Armagh gave me a gentle reprimand for assuming his title. Probably you will have seen his letter.
>
> (BS: 17 Jan. 1851)

Cullen even found it difficult to keep abreast of what was happening on the wider scene. He persuaded the bishops to meet to discuss the 'new penal legislation', but the gathering was held in Dublin and Cullen did not feel he was in control of the situation. He told Kirby that what he wanted was presentation of a united front which might draw upon them the ire of the government: 'Perhaps we may be united — if so the persecution will do good.' (NK: 20 Feb. 1851) Little came of this action, however, and Cullen was reduced to reading hungrily the occasional attacks made on him by the government. He proudly informed Kirby:

> Lord John Russell favoured me with several remarks in his late speech. He was particularly offended because I did not consult him as Dr Murray was wont to do. Get the *Times* and read the speech. I will answer his attacks on the Synod of Thurles. (NK: 13 Feb. 1851)

The frustration that Cullen felt at this time shows clearly in his letters to Rome. He was obsessed with the refusal of the 'Castle bishops' to oppose the Queen's Colleges or to give their financial support to the Catholic University, whose establishment Cullen was eagerly planning. He had begun his wooing of John Henry Newman for the new body, and in July 1850 he even invited him over to the 'Black North' to preach a sermon at the dedication of Killeavy church. Yet most meetings to promote the Catholic University were held in Dublin or London, and Cullen felt increasingly confined by the pastoral demands his rural archdiocese was making upon him. His frustration became almost unbearable to him when his own intelligence sources and reports from Propaganda indicated that Protestant proselytisers had begun a major mission with considerable success in the pastorally neglected dioceses in John MacHale's province of Connaught.

Promotion of the Catholic University was now of primary concern to Cullen, and he realised how much Armagh held him back in the spring of 1851 when Murray brought the division between himself and Cullen to public notice. Murray's friend, John Ennis, Parish Priest of Booterstown, published a short letter in the *Freeman's Journal* of 12 March which he had received from the archbishop:

> It was, I am told, announced at some of the altars of this diocese yesterday that I ordered a collection to be made in our churches on next Sunday in aid of the intended Catholic University. I beg to assure you that I have given no order whatever on the subject.

The announcement had been made first by Cullen's agent, Peter Cooper, from the altar of Murray's metropolitan church, and on 14 March Cooper tried to justify himself by attacking Murray in the *Freeman*. The division was at last fully public, a great embarrassment to Cullen. From this time Murray openly refused to aid the Catholic University, continuing his opposition until he died, and in January 1852 he even replied to a personal letter from Pius IX by refusing utterly to repudiate the Queen's Colleges. At this juncture Cullen first received the impression that John MacHale also was not going to be a supporter of the new university.

Opportunity to move from the rural confines of Armagh came to Cullen when Daniel Murray died on 26 February 1852. Now it was possible for him to move to the richest and most influential of the Irish sees, the seat of government, the headquarters of the religious orders, and centre for every important development in society. In Dublin Cullen would know immediately of every important development, and he would be freed from the fatigue of constant travel. It was the natural place from which he could direct his legatine mission, and perhaps also build a model archdiocese on the Ultramontane model — a task that was clearly impossible to achieve in backward and destitute Armagh.

V

The Archbishop of Dublin

1. *The Protestants of Dublin*

As soon as Murray died there was immense political activity in both Rome and Dublin to ensure that Cullen was translated to the capital city. Laurence Forde on 26 February 1852 wrote to his old Irish College classmate Bernard Smith to argue that Armagh should be occupied by 'some person whose *vocation* is not, as Dr Cullen's is, to benefit the *entire* Irish Church'. (BS) The Murray party, of course, opposed his coming, expressing their fear of the 'monkish severity' which the clergy could expect from the papal delegate if he came, but Rome was determined that the translation would take place. To indicate the determination of the Holy See it was 'leaked' in March 1852 that Cullen had been made perpetual Apostolic Delegate, and this good news was hawked about by Peter Cooper. Cooper and the others were also good organisers, while there was no obvious successor to Murray in the Gallican camp; and it was therefore no surprise that in the voting on 2 April Cullen headed the *terna*, Dean Walter Meyler appearing as a poor second. Quickly the cardinals unanimously approved Cullen's translation, and papal approval was obtained by 3 May. Until a successor was appointed he was also to act as administrator of Armagh.

Cullen knew that the state now recognised him as the dominant figure in the Catholic Church in Ireland — but also that he came to Dublin on Protestant sufferance. On 25 November 1851 he had written to Bernard Smith to say that his intelligence reports from Dublin led him to believe that there was actually collusion taking place between the government and the Gallicans to withstand any Ultramontane advance in the country:

I believe there is some deep-laid scheme concocted against the Pope and the Synod of Thurles. What it is, and how it will be carried out, I do not know, but there appears to be great consultations in Dublin. The Vicar General of Cork has just been there. . . . (BS)

Much of the old 'jobbing' spirit of an earlier age prevailed, as in the Dublin Grand Jury system and in the influence of the Castle in all its pride and arrogance in all parts of society, Protestant and Catholic. The papal delegate needed considerable determination and courage if he was to influence the Protestant establishment in Dublin.

Cullen, as we know, had the determination of a zealot, and it was this that gave him the courage to attempt what might well have daunted other men. As soon as he heard of Murray's death he had begun to estimate the strength of his party, and as early as 13 March 1852 he told Bernard Smith: 'Dr Murray's death was fatal to his party. It is down forever.' (BS) This, combined with his shrewd appraisal of the government's histrionic sabre-ratting in the Ecclesiastical Titles Act, gave him initial confidence. By the end of the year he knew that if he did not overplay his hand he would have no immediate trouble from the remnants of Murray's party or from the government, which appeared ready to accommodate him wherever possible. 'Parliament appears well disposed to let us alone,' he told Kirby, 'and we are not likely to ask any favours of them – so we may live in peace.' (NK: 9 Dec. 1852)

At the same time Cullen knew how much he was feared and hated by the Protestants – and by some Catholics. Throughout 1852 the *Dublin Evening Mail* kept reminding its readers of the new resident alien in the city, come 'to exalt the pope's sovereignty in the United Kingdom and to provincialise Ireland so as to make her subordinate to the scheme'. When Cullen placed Ireland under the special patronage of the Blessed Virgin rather than St Patrick the paper crowed that it had 'predicted the downfall of the old national saint'. The legate's authority would bind the Irish people to ignorance and superstitution: 'Absurdities suited to the latitude of Rome and Naples are sadly of place in Ireland.' Cullen was not immune from aspersions of this type, and a letter written to Kirby at this time shows how hurtful he found them. Injudiciously he had stated before one of his critics that he 'hoped Dr Murray had time to make his peace with God', and the press had immediately attacked him for denigrating the memory of his well-loved predecessor. (NK: 18 Mar. 1852)

The result of this initial encounter with that part of the Protestant establishment that took the form of popular opinion was that Cullen became and remained almost paranoiac about any encounters he had with Protestants throughout the rest of his life. He seldom referred to his antipathy except in his correspondence with Kirby, who shared his bigotry and relished receiving Cullen's sneering accounts of Protestant moral failures; for example:

> Lord Palmerston the papers announced to be tried for adultery. He is now in his eightieth year. Sir Robert Peel is to be tried for assaulting some gentleman – such rulers. . . . (K: 3 Nov. 1863)

Such was the strength of this anti-Protestant bias that Cullen believed that any but unavoidable communication with Protestants was not only dangerous but sinful, ecclesiastically if not morally. Any Catholic who was friendly with Protestants was encouraging those heretical enemies of the Holy Father like the Freemasons and the followers of Garibaldi and Mazzini, all of whom the Protestants loved and supported. On one occasion, Cullen confessed to Kirby, he had almost been compromised himself:

> Catholics who mix with Protestants are all hostile to us. In Dr Moran's work which I sent you you will find at page 457 . . . an old canon which prohibits priests to dine with Protestants or to be even in their company. The bishop who made that canon understood Ireland well. . . . As for me, I never dined with a Protestant. Once years ago I went to a Protestant house in the Co. Louth to a *déjeuner* and I was asked to say Grace. I afterward discovered that the gentleman was one of the leading Freemasons.
>
> (K: 28 July 1865)

This bigotry could at times come into conflict with Cullen's better nature. When he visited Arklow in 1866 to consecrate a bell the local Protestant gentry offered him carriages and an ostler and sent fruit for his dinner, and some ladies even decorated the altar with flowers. Cullen recounted this incident to Kirby, commenting on the strangeness of it all: 'Arklow was formerly a most bigotted place. My predecessor Dr Murray had to fly from it at the time of the rebellion to save his life from the Orangemen.' (K: 1 Sept. 1866) He was also disturbed when in the spring of 1868 he was asked to lay the corner-stone of a new Catholic chapel at Enniskerry on a site provided by Lord Powerscourt's mother, but he regained his composure by recalling the past hostility shown by the Powerscourts to the Catholic faith. Cullen seldom enjoyed having the categories of his faith disturbed, even by charitable Protestants.

Because of Cullen's passionate Ultramontanism there was no way that he would ever lessen his unflagging opposition to the enemies of the Holy Father, no matter what blandishments he encountered. He had no doubt that they were religiously in error and spiritually on the road to damnation. When the American evangelists Moodie and Sankey held a number of revival meetings in Ireland Cullen poured his scorn on the foolish Protestants who listened to these 'irreverent ranters', as he called them in a letter to Kirby: 'It is all a farce, yet very wise Protestants attend — poor fools, they are to be pitied.' (NK: 3 Nov. 1874) They were also to be feared because of their heresy. He recounted how a Belfast professor, challenged by a Catholic for blasphemous remarks at dinner, had informed the company that in the enlightened nineteenth century no one any longer believed in 'the farce of Calvary'. 'How fast', observed Cullen, 'Protestantism is going into infidelity, but Protestants or infidels equally hate Catholicity.' (K: 8 Apr. 1875)

As for those Catholics who from the time of Wolfe Tone had dreamed of Protestants and Catholics working together to secure the independence of Ireland from the British crown, Cullen scorned them for their refusal to see that the great evil in Ireland was not the crown but Protestantism with all its heresies. He confided to Kirby his thoughts on this subject in 1875:

Mr Mitchel and Mr Martin, both Protestants and great Young Irelanders, have lately died. Sir John Gray has also departed this life. He did the Catholics great services, but though he did a great deal to pull down the Protestant Church he had the misfortune to die a Protestant.

(NK: 13 Apr. 1875)

How could Protestants be other than sworn enemies of the faith when they were doing all in their power to oppress and cause suffering to the Holy Father by raising funds for Garibaldi, the scourge of the papacy? On an earlier occasion he told Kirby of the Prince of Wales contributing £100 to the war chest of the Italian nationalists, of Lord Courtown taxing his tenants for the same purpose, and of collections made in Irish Protestant churches:

In Armagh the Protestants made a collection for the red shirts and got £47 – in Scotland one old Presbyterian dame gave forty thousand pounds to Young Garibaldians. I have cut out of the Sunday newspapers of today the enclosed scrap which shows what the English ladies are doing for the revolution. It is probable that Providence will scourge them for their iniquities. (K: 29 Nov. 1867)

Cullen's fervent enmity to Protestantism was the basic impetus in his lifelong battle to have the Church placed completely in charge of the education of Catholics at all levels. Behind his efforts was his Ultramontane conviction that in this world a great ideological struggle was being waged between the Roman Catholic Church and the powers of darkness to control the minds of men. Long before he came to Dublin he knew that one of the Protestants he would find himself in conflict with was Richard Whately, the very liberal Protestant Archbishop of Dublin, who, he told Bernard Smith, was 'a most embittered enemy of Catholicity, and he has the management of all the education of Ireland in his hands'. (BS: 23 Jan. 1851) He requested Smith to see if Whately's *Elements of Logic* could not be put on the Index, filled as it was with Lockian materialism. As for Whately's *Evidences of Christianity* and *Scripture Lessons*, which the Protestants wanted National School pupils to study, Cullen believed them to be not only anti-Catholic but filled with 'a very low idea of the dignity of Jesus Christ'. (*Letters*, I, 109)

This was the kind of teaching that Cullen believed was to be forced upon young Catholics by the National System as shaped by Whately and operating through interdenominational schools. He told William Monsell, the influential convert who as MP for Limerick represented Irish Catholic interests in parliament, that there could be no flagging in the struggle against the National System:

It is clear that if things have to go on as they have done for the past, in the course of a few years the education of the country would be altogether in the hands of a Protestant government. It was time to come to a full stop. The mixed system has been exploded, I think, in every country in Europe. Even Prussia has abandoned it. I think we ought not to submit to it in any way.

(NLI: 7 Dec. 1859)

Although Murray had got along very well with Whately, Cullen kept aloof from the eccentric intellectual Protestant prelate except when Whately directly attacked Catholicism, as he did in a scathing criticism of convents in 1853. This led Cullen to write to Kirby and to threaten retaliation:

Dr Whately has come out this week in great force against nunneries. This will ruin his character with all the Catholics in Ireland. Perhaps it is providential for it may impede him from doing greater mischief. . . . I think I will be out with a pastoral against Dr Whately, though I do not like to make voice yet it is hard to let him pass.

(NK: 11 May 1853)

Cullen's pastoral did little to improve his relationship with Whately, but it offered to help the faithful by forming 'a just estimate of the character of a man who for many years had been insidiously at work to have the management of education in this country in his hands':

We cannot conceal our astonishment and regret when a high Protestant dignitary who resided in our city for nearly thirty years, enjoying ample revenues left to this see by our Catholic forefathers and well acquainted with the advantages conferred upon the poor by the religious communities of Ireland, became an assailant of these Sisters. (*Letters*, I, 241)

Cullen's pastoral attack was more than the beginning of a polemical exercise. It led to the condemnation of Whately's *Evidences of Christianity* and *Scripture Lessons* by the bishops of the Dublin province meeting in provincial synod the following month. When the Board of National Education gave in to this prelatical pressure and removed the offending volumes from their list of books for the schools, Whately retired from the board he had served for so long.

Even when Whately died in 1863 Cullen had little good to say about him. His comment to Kirby on the size of Whately's estate of £300,000 was that it would have funded a grand Catholic seminary. As for Whately's faith, Cullen simply doubted its existence: 'The poor man seemed to have no faith at all — he did not admit the Trinity or the Divinity of Christ.' The man rumoured as Whately's successor, Dr Stanley, a former tutor of the Prince of Wales, was dismissed caustically as having 'every qualification for a bishop except that he is not a Christian'. He ended this rather vindictive letter by gloating over the consternation among the Dublin Protestants when they discovered that he had just bought a Unitarian church. (K: 20 Oct. 1863)

The cause of Cullen's attitude towards Whately was his conviction that the Protestant archbishop at least tolerated a major proselytising campaign in Dublin which was led by the Irish Church Missions. Just before he came to the capital he told his friend William Walshe of Halifax that 'The number of proselytising schools in Dublin is prodigious. . . . seventy or eighty in Dr Murray's own parish, and in St Michan's.' (DAA: 8 Nov. 1851) He knew that the proselytising activities in the capital were linked to the successful campaign the Irish Church Missions was waging in many areas of Connaught and Munster, and his first priority, once he had unity among the Catholic bishops, was to lead them in a Counter-Reformation offensive. In the meantime he was personally going to hit back and hit hard at these enemies of the faith. His early pastorals are filled with references to bold and persistent Protestant missionaries and their insidious work: 'placards posted on our walls, handbills thrust into our houses and scattered through our streets' and Protestant pulpits which resounded 'day by day with invectives against our holy religion'. (*Letters,* I, 238)

Nothing caused Cullen more distress than the persistence of the Protestant missionaries of the Irish Church Missions, who even sent three of their agents to call on him to protest about one of his Lenten pastorals. They were shown the door by a servant, but the attack never ceased. Cullen was furious when a Redemptorist in Kingstown was charged by them in court for publicly burning a bible, but, as he told Kirby, he could sympathise with such foolish overreaction to the 'fury of the Protestants....The devil seems to have got into them corporally.' (NK: 2 Dec. 1855) His advice to the Catholic people, passed on to them through their priests, was simply to practise a kind of religious apartheid — to have nothing to do with Protestants.

Cullen himself resolutely counter-attacked when he thought other than silence would help the Catholic cause. In 1857 he published *A Letter to Lord St Leonards on the Management of the Patriotic Fund and the Application of Public Moneys to Proselytising Purposes*. This was a denunciation of the misappropriation of funds contributed by the general public for the families of those who suffered in the Crimean War; instead of being devoted to this purpose, Cullen alleged, the money was being used for conversion of Catholic children in military schools. He claimed that the scheme was engineered by 'dignitaries of the Established Church and the great confederacy of Orangemen'. In great detail he told of individual cases where the funds were misused, singling out for special treatment the Hibernian School near Dublin. In 1859 he launched another attack on the policies of the Adelaide Hospital in Dublin, which, he claimed, kept priests from bringing the sacraments to dying Catholics.

Cullen in his counter-attack supported strongly St Brigid's Orphanage, founded by Margaret Aylward with the help of her confessor, Father John Gowan, CM. This remarkable lady persuaded destitute Catholic mothers to entrust their children to her association to keep them out of Protestant orphanages or schools. When Aylward went to jail for six months in 1860 for refusing to surrender a child whose mother had converted and wished her offspring to be raised as a Protestant, Cullen visited her despite the loud objections of the Protestant newspapers that such prison levées should be permitted. This move helped to bring Cullen some much-desired public esteem, and this increased further when through Cullen's intercession Piux IX made Aylward a Confessor of the Faith.

The result of this kind of skirmishing was that Cullen gained some popular support and considerable publicity as a strong Ultramontanist champion. On the other hand, it ended once and for all some of the goodwill established between Catholics and Protestants during Murray's time as Archbishop of Dublin. Whenever Cullen could be criticised by the Protestant press he was shown no mercy, as when the *Dublin Evening Mail* of 15 February 1869 excoriated him for forbidding the Parish Priest of Lucan to give any support to a local institution which had been founded with the help of the viceroy and his wife for the maintenance and training of idiots. Cullen's excuse was to say that the asylum had been founded for proselytising purposes. Later the *Express* of 2 September 1869 attacked his 'Ultramontane tyranny' because one of his pastorals implied that the sacraments would be denied to children who attended the Model School in Marlborough Street.

Cullen's militant demands for concessions for Irish Catholics went beyond the winning of simple justice. By the time he appeared before the Powis Commission in 1869 to persuade the government to phase out the Model Schools he so hated, and to replace them with training schools under control of religious bodies and committees, he was showing clearly that what he wanted was Catholic ascendancy in the educational sphere — and wherever else it might be obtained. At that time he admitted that from his own view of the development of the National System in Dublin, and from what he knew of other parts of the country, the evil in the schools was not as great as once had been feared:

In the greater part of the country the schools are in the hands of Catholics, under Catholic managers, under

Catholic teachers and conducted in such a way that they
cannot do much positive evil. The evil they produce is
only negative inasmuch as they deprive Catholic children
of a great deal of that religious education to which they
are entitled. (PM, II, 272)

Nevertheless, nothing was going to satisfy Cullen until complete Catholic ascendancy in Ireland was established, and
even the *Dublin Evening Mail* expressed near admiration for
his indefatigable demands on 15 June 1864 when it commented on the weak administration that so easily gave in to
the incessant demands of the archbishop who had shown
'what he can accomplish by crying ever, more, more'.

Cullen was far from what he wanted even at the end of
his life. Destruction of the Protestant culture which he so
hated was as distant as ever it had seemed to him. In the
Dublin Archdiocesan Archives in Clonliffe College is a large
and impressive collection of Protestant proselytising pamphlets which Cullen collected in the last two years of his life.
They record the opening of new Protestant institutions in
Dublin, the increase in converts in some of them, and the
strong financial position of most of them. Yet Cullen felt
sure that the ultimate victory of his cause was inevitable;
this was the spirit he expressed in a letter to Kirby on 31
March 1873, a day appointed by Protestants throughout the
United Kingdom for prayers for the conversion of Ireland
from popery: 'Their prayers won't do much harm to any
but themselves.' (K)

2. *Triumphalism*
An intriguing question, given Cullen's passionate anti-Protestant
sentiments, and his Ultramontanist ideology which in normal
circumstances welcomed 'legitimacy' in rule, was his relationship with the authorities of the state in Dublin Castle. It was
a question he had to work out for himself almost from the
moment he set foot in Ireland in 1850. On 12 July of that
year he indicated part of his strategy by refusing office on
the Charitable Bequests Board while at the same time encouraging the Castle to maintain friendly communication
with him. On the same day he indicated to Kirby how he
had worded his refusal:

I stated that I refused reluctantly, but as the Bequest Act contained provisions at variance with the spirit of the Catholic Church and hostile to its interests I could not conscientiously act under it nor do anything that would appear to sanction it. (NK)

From this time his policy was to avoid any formal gathering, such as dinners of civic corporations, where his presence might be interpreted as a sanction of contemporary policies. This did not mean that he would never bend to expediency when it came to taking a public part in state functions, but he would only do so when he could appear as the representative of the sovereign power of the papacy, 'flying the Roman Catholic flag', as, for example, on one occasion during the Crimean War:

On Wednesday I visited two French ships of war at present in Kingstown. I was received with all honours by the captain. The men all presented arms. They were then ordered by the captain to kneel down when I . . . gave them my benediction. The vessel then fired a salute of thirteen guns, as many as for the Lord Lieutenant. The Protestants are all furious about this but they dare not say a word against their allies. I have invited the two captains, the chaplain and some officers to dinner today. (NK: 5 May 1856)

To someone nurtured in the triumphalism of Gregory XVI's Rome, pomp and pageantry were easily accepted, and there seems little doubt that Cullen enjoyed formal occasions of state, with persons from the highest ranks of society present, and where he was recognised as representative of the Supreme Pontiff. He particularly enjoyed contact with royalty, and was ready to authorise the sending of an address from the bishops of the Dublin province to the Prince of Wales until Archbishop Leahy of Cashel warned him how an unnatural display of loyalty could be misinterpreted. (CA, 1863/12) On 2 November 1866 he proudly passed on to Rome the news that he had entertained Gladstone's son to dinner: 'a good well-disposed young man . . . about twenty-three years of age and already a MP'. (K) When John Bright, 'the great English agitator', came to Dublin to campaign for the disestablishment of the Church of Ireland, Cullen, who had just been made a cardinal, told Kirby how well he charmed his new political ally. (K: 11 Nov. 1866) So much for Cullen's earlier pride in a policy of never dining with Protestants.

What changed Cullen's policy was his nomination as a cardinal and the public response of Ireland's Catholics to this honour. When the news of his elevation reached Ireland in May 1866 the *Freeman's Journal*, much caught up in Fenian affairs, was at first rather subdued in its reporting of the honour. It noted the 'unprecedented' reception held by Cullen in the papal Quirinal Palace and the elevation ceremonies in the Sistine Chapel, but it left the field to the *Dublin Evening Post*, the organ of the 'Castle Catholics', to extol on 28 May the significance to Ireland, the land of 'unexampled spoliation and unexampled martyrdom', of the 'reward for Irish faithfulness' now bestowed. Now that Ireland had been given its first cardinal, the Irish people were at last brought into the mainstream of European development through Paul Cullen, a *Post* editorial of 26 June proclaimed, for he would assume 'the Roman purple and the cousinship with emperors and kings which it infers'.

The *Freeman's Journal* became more enthusiastic when it recognised the pride felt by Irish Catholics. Finally, after an Orange protest meeting in Dublin had ensured that the procession and illumination planned for the cardinal on his return from Rome in August had to be called off to avoid trouble, the *Freeman* was won over to wholehearted support for Cullen's elevation. On 17 August it gave full details of the reception to be held for Cullen in Holy Cross College at Clonliffe, where all the clergy were to wear Roman uniforms. On the following day its editorial commented on the significance of the honour:

> For the first time an Irish prelate has been raised to the rank of Prince of the Church and a Privy Councillor of the Sovereign Pontiff. . . . Henceforth Ireland takes her place with France, Austria, and other states in directing the ecclesiastical affairs of Christendom.

The paper also extolled Cullen's 'meek and modest nature', 'his suavity and apostolic simplicity of manner', 'his kindly yet firm rule, his prudent toleration'.

In a further comment on the reception at Clonliffe the *Freeman's Journal* editorial of 21 August noted that the Protestant officers of state who paid their respects were the very men who 'by law should convict him and other prelates for assuming ecclesiastical titles'. The writer also said that it was quite within the power of the men assembled at Clonliffe to end the last remnant of 'Catholic disabilities'; this sentiment was pointedly linked with a critical reference to the Established Church, maintained for the 'unholy pride' of a small minority of people.

The *Dublin Evening Mail* took up the theme of nationalism which the *Freeman* had avoided, and opined on 16 June that this exercise in ecclesiastical imperialism revealed that 'the national voice in the selection of Irish bishops has been peremptorily silenced':

> The papal church in Ireland is no longer Irish but in the strictest sense Roman. . . . The Irish Catholic Church of forty years ago has vanished and the people have got an inexorable and mysterious tyranny in its stead. We have never heard that they like the change, and there are symptoms tending to show that they hate it. . . . In the process of stripping it of its ancient national character Dr Cullen has been the great instrument of the Court of Rome. And for this memorable and odious exploit he now receives the scarlet hat.

Castigating Cullen as 'the emissary who has utterly denationalised their church' and 'the unflinching agent of a cruel ambition', the writer of the editorial expressed his compassion for the poor deluded Catholics of Ireland:

> We can only look on and wonder that a people who are perpetually shrieking against the laws of England as incompatible with their ideas of liberty can howl a Jubilate over the infliction of such a real tyranny as the pope and Dr Cullen have forged between them.

Cullen was astute enough to recognise that from the time he became a cardinal the Catholic people wanted him to appear among the mighty, a representative prince of the oldest aristocracy in Europe, yet an Irishman in origins and sympathies. Cullen thoroughly enjoyed satisfying what was probably a true assessment of the longings of the people, for there was remarkably little criticism of his appearance at state functions from this time onward. As for the Protestant ascendancy, they were soon seeking the presence at their various functions of this urbane, sophisticated and charming Irish-Italian prelate. Early in 1867 Cullen described in detail to Kirby the reception at a Lord Lieutenant's banquet where he was given second place at table after the viceroy. The Protestant archbishop chose to absent himself, and Cullen was the focus of all attention as he gave an address on charity which was cheered for almost a quarter of an hour:

> I pleased the people very much. . . . The Lord Lieutenant was most polite. I sat between the Lady Lieutenant and her sister Lady Butler — they are sisters of Lord John Russell and they made themselves most agreeable. . . . Since the dinner I got a message from the Lord Lieutenant expressing his great desire to do anything in his power to please our bishops. (K: 22 Feb. 1867)

In this world of ecclesiastical/political diplomacy Cullen displayed a natural shrewd caution which stood him in good stead. He knew that if he put his foot wrong by visiting the Castle, 'such gentlemen as the writers of the Fenian papers . . . would hold me up as a Castle hack of the worst character'. (K: 18 Mar. 1867) Cullen had an additional reason for being circumspect in his dealings with the Lord Lieutenant, who became the Duke of Abercorn in 1868: the viceroy was a prominent Freemason, who was to succeed the Duke of Leinster as Irish Grand Master in 1874. Cullen told Kirby that he in no way trusted his overtures of friendship.

Just as he abandoned his principle of earlier days never to dine with a Protestant, so Cullen abandoned his pledge never to go to the Castle when it was diplomatically worth while to do so. At the time the Prince of Wales visited Dublin in April 1868 Cullen made a gesture of detachment by not attending St Patrick's Cathedral for the Prince's installation as a Knight of St Patrick, but when the Lord Lieutenant pressed him to dine at the Castle to meet the Prince, Cullen told Kirby that he immediately accepted. He enthusiastically described the occasion in a long letter to Kirby:

The Prince of Wales sat opposite the Lord Lieutenant. The Prince of Saxe-Weimar sat next to the Prince and then I came next. The Princess of Wales sat next the Lord Lieutenant, the Duke of Cambridge next here, and Prince Teck who was opposite me. I suppose I got my proper place as a Cardinal. At all events everyone appeared anxious to treat me with the greatest respect. How things have changed. . . . Ten years ago, Lord Eglinton, the Lord Lieutenant, would not dine with the Lord Mayor because Cardinal Wiseman was to be present. (K: 17 Apr. 1868)

Cullen secretly rejoiced at the various 'bigots', like the Duke of Manchester who sat next to him at dinner, who were obliged to acknowledge his presence and be friendly towards him. He ended his letter by urging Kirby to tell Cardinal Antonelli, the papal Secretary of State, of his social success, which was also in effect a diplomatic triumph.

Ten days later Cullen again recounted the events of the dinner, having forgotten to tell Kirby how the four or five parsons and their wives were completely ignored in the drawing-room after dinner because all attention was focused on himself. Then he proceeded to tell Kirby of another grand social occasion at the Royal Dublin Society gathering to greet the Prince:

About twenty-five years ago the Royal Dublin Society black-beaned Dr Murray when it was proposed to admit him to the society as a member. On this occasion the society invited me to a *conversazione* to meet the Prince and Princess of Wales. I went to it. About 3000 people were present. . . . There were two or three hundred dignitaries of the Protestant Church who looked at my red cloak with horror and amazement. They must have been terribly mortified when they saw me called up to the dais on which the Prince and Princess were placed whilst all the Protestant clergymen were left in the crowd. On this occasion I met the Duke of Cambridge, uncle to the Queen, who apologised for not having been at the Catholic University on the ground that he was engaged with the troops. He came to my home the next day to pay a visit. (K: 27 Apr. 1868)

This was indeed a remarkable triumph for Cullen, and

Cardinal Antonelli was full of praise for his handling of the affair. The nationalist papers attacked him for attending the Castle, but Cullen's only reaction was to express his relief to Kirby that the attempt to murder Prince Alfred in Australia was not known in Ireland, otherwise some similar outrage might have been attempted. As for the *Times*'s criticism of his refusal to attend the ceremonies in St Patrick's, he commented: 'The Protestant Archbishops of Armagh and Dublin were there in official situations – it would not answer me to be a spectator of their doings.' (K: 1 May 1868)

What Cullen was trying to do was to establish in the public mind which church was the real ascendancy church in Ireland. In January 1868 he had been bold enough to invite the Lord Mayor, the aldermen and a great number of prominent Protestants to attend a meeting in the Pro-Cathedral at which he had spoken in support of the pope and his difficulties in Italy. Now he had demonstrated to the Catholic population of Ireland the deference with which the crown was treating the representative of the Holy Father. Patrick Francis Moran, Cullen's nephew who had returned from Rome two years earlier to become his secretary, told Kirby that what had taken place during the Prince's visit represented the coming into public acceptance of the idea of Catholic ascendancy:

> All the respectable Catholics were delighted with it as it completely broke down as if with one blow all the Protestant Ascendancy of the last three hundred years. Everyone treated him with honours. He was placed even before the Lord Chancellor, who takes precedence of all the Dukes and Earls of the kingdom. The other guests were vying with each other who would honour him most. . . . When the Princess of Wales sent the Marchioness of Abercorn to request that he would come and converse with her he did so and remained chatting with her about Rome . . . and everything good. (K: 8 May 1868)

While in Dublin the royal party visited both the Mater Hospital and the Catholic University, and Cullen knew that with this precedent it would be customary for all visiting dignitaries to follow the royal example. His own visit to the Castle had also set a precedent, and from this time he often talked to the Lord Lieutenant, though he was careful to tell Kirby, as he did in a letter of 12 February 1869, that he used the time with the viceroy to advance the Catholic cause: 'Yesterday I spent an hour with his Excellency. I gave him a history of all the proselytising institutions of Dublin and showed how wicked they are.' (NK)

Following the royal visit in the summer of 1868 Cullen was very ill, and when he was recuperating in a rented villa belonging to a parson in Monkstown he told Kirby of the great satisfaction he received from the courtesy calls of several prominent Protestants and their solicitous inquiries after his health. In the following year, when the disestablishment of the Church of Ireland was about to be carried out, Prince Arthur and the Lord Lieutenant were 'hissed and groaned' during a visit to Trinity College; Cullen expressed his strong disapproval of such an affront to the government. His nationalist critics accused him of being a 'Castle Catholic', of course, but Cullen's willingness to be on friendly terms with the government was indicative only of his desire to advance his Ultramontane mission. During Prince Arthur's visit Cullen's admonitions persuaded many Catholics not to attend a Freemasons' ball, even though the Prince and the Lord Lieutenant were to attend. When their absence was noted Cullen told Kirby that it was a 'glorious proof of the faith of our good people'. (NK: 11 Apr. 1869)

Cullen's fascination with high society soon passed, and Moran, writing to Kirby in 1871, described a visit to the Castle in condescending terms: 'The Cardinal and your humble servant dined with the Lord Lieutenant on last Monday. It was very brilliant but seemed to me a poor affair compared with our Roman palaces.' (K: 17 Feb. 1871) It is probable that the Castle's fascination with the cardinal also passed quickly, for he was ever ready to promote the Catholic cause with anyone who would listen to him. Cullen told Kirby of one such meeting with Lord Spencer, who wanted his views on university education in Ireland. Cullen enlightened him about the Queen's Colleges:

> One of the first professors appointed was Vericour, a French infidel, and one of the last made by Lord Spencer himself was an immoral poet by name Armstrong, who

finished a poem against the confessional with the words, 'Now may the good Christ rid us of all priests'. I had the book of poetry in my pocket and I shewed the poem to his excellency. I had a very long interview with him and I am sure I gave him such a dose of truth as he never got before since he came to Ireland. He will look on me as an audacious fanatic for speaking so free. (K: 2 Mar. 1873)

Another way in which Cullen heralded a new era of Catholic ascendancy in Dublin was in his promotion of the large number of churches, schools, hospitals and asylums which were built during his episcopate and staffed by an ever-increasing number of clergy. In 1857 he told Kirby of the splendid reopening of the refurbished Pro-Cathedral in Marlborough Street, which Cullen boasted was 'equal to many of the Roman churches' with its dome modelled on St Peter's: 'You see we are determined to be very grand.' (NK: 6 Dec. 1857) When the Catholic University was opened in 1864 Cullen described how more than a hundred 'respectable people' sat down to dinner in the Mansion House at the invitation of the Lord Mayor:

> The great hall where the glorious and immortal memory used to be drunk re-echoed that night for the first time after centuries with the pope's name. The lord mayor gave the pope's health in the first place, and the queen in the second place. . . . You can imagine what annoyance such a proceeding has given to Protestants. (K: 6 Nov. 1864)

The most notable symbol of Ultramontane triumphalism was the diocesan seminary of Holy Cross at Clonliffe, which was first opened on 1 September 1859 and slowly enlarged year by year. Cullen's brief translating him to Dublin had borne the date of the feast of the Holy Cross, and this day was always specially remembered in the Dublin archdiocese. At Clonliffe on 14 November 1865 in a great display of Ultramontanism ninety guests at dinner drank the pope's health after attending in the Pro-Cathedral the consecration of Cullen's former secretary, James Murray, as Bishop of Maitland in Australia, and of a fellow-alumnus of the Irish College in Rome, Matthew Quinn, as Bishop of Bathurst in the same country. At the consecrations the choir and attending priests were all fully robed in the Roman style, and by this time it was expected that Dublin priests would wear soutanes and even Roman hats. It was also assumed that regular manifestations of such ecclesiastical pageantry would occur at Clonliffe, which became in Cullen's lifetime a recognised centre of Ultramontane display.

The peak of Ultramontane ceremony for Dublin came in 1876 when elaborate plans were laid for the dedication of Clonliffe church in June of that year. The church was built on what was reputed to be the site of the battle of Clontarf. The ornate embellishments, including marble pillars from the Alps, a magnificent high altar, and paintings hung in the fashion of those in St Agatha's in Rome, took so long to install that the opening did not take place until 14 September. The church was dedicated to the Sacred Heart before a huge assembly including Cardinal Franchi and the entire Irish hierarchy. Moran described the scene to Kirby:

> After mass Cardinal Franchi gave the solemn papal benediction from the front of the church with his grand voice, and the number of bishops and clergy kneeling around and the vast assemblage with their banners, etc. it was a scene never to be forgotten. Many who had seen the solemn benediction at St Peter's said that we have transferred that imposing ceremony to Ireland. (K: 19 Sept. 1876)

Two years later, when Paul Cullen died, at his express wish he was buried behind the high altar of Clonliffe church.

3. *The University Question*
Paul Cullen knew that for the Roman Catholic Church to be the presence he wanted it to be in Dublin, and in the whole of Ireland, it had to have a Catholic intellectual life and a university which would rival that of Trinity College. Like no other institution, including the Castle, Trinity symbolised the Protestant ascendancy and fascinated the Catholic middle classes and gentry who sent their sons there. When Cullen wrote to Bernard Smith and others in Rome about the fervent faith of the Dubliners he usually qualified his comment, as he did on 4 October 1852: '. . . with the exception of a few of the aristocrats and lawyers who were ruined in Trinity College'.

(BS) In 1872 he told Gladstone of the evils of Trinity, 'founded as a bulwark of Protestantism, a rallying point for all who might wish to assail the Catholic Church'. Orange lodges met regularly within its gates, its government of provost, fellows and council was exclusively Protestant, and this bastion of the minority was provided for out of the public purse. Worst of all, its members included Catholics who had emerged from the college to become either dignitaries of the Church of Ireland or militant enemies of the Christian religion. (BM, 44433: 25 Mar. 1872)

There was no doubting the native intelligence of Cullen, although, like other Ultramontanists, he was a thorough-going conservative who had no difficulty in giving enthusiastic support to the Syllabus of Errors of Pius IX when it was published in 1864. In the same year he encouraged the founding of the *Irish Ecclesiastical Record* with his nephew, Patrick Francis Moran, as a joint editor as well as one of its major contributors. The purpose of the new publication was frankly stated to be the fostering of closer relations between the Holy See and the Church in Ireland, as well as the raising of the intellectual life of the Irish priests through the reading of approved scholarly writings. Two years later Cullen brought his nephew from Rome to be his personal secretary, hoping at the same time to encourage him in writing Catholic apologetic in the field of church history.

What Cullen took to be an intellectual challenge was presented to him at this time by a report that James Henthorne Todd, one of the most brilliant of Trinity scholars, had purchased seventy-four volumes of the *Acts of the Congregation of the Holy Office* from a continental dealer and deposited them in Trinity's library. Cullen feared that Galileo's trial was in the collection and that Todd intended to make controversial use of this source material. Todd, however, was busy writing a *Life of St Patrick*, which, when it appeared, Cullen described as 'anti-Catholic enough, but so expensive and scholarly not many will read it ... a work of no merit either literary or antiquarian'. (K: 11 Dec. 1863)

At the same time Cullen encouraged his protégé Moran to publish a volume of essays which refuted to Cullen's satisfaction what he believed to be Todd's absurd argument that St Patrick had been a Protestant. When Moran's book appeared Cullen told Kirby that it had shocked the whole intellectual world of Trinity College:

> Dr Todd is very angry, it is said, with Dr Moran. He expected to be let off quite free, and he now thinks it a hardship to have his theories overthrown in so effectual a manner. . . . The people are beginning now to talk about Dr Moran's work. The case here, however, is that no one reads anything except newspapers and novels. Even the priests rarely read anything serious. (K: 19 July 1864)

In a further letter Cullen reported that it was rumoured in Catholic circles that Todd had praised Moran's work as 'worthy of a gentleman and a scholar', and that he himself now wished that he had never published his own work at all. (K: 21 Aug. 1864)

Cullen by now had developed an enthusiastic interest in church history, and he told Kirby that talk of St Patrick being a Protestant, and the claim of Anglicans that they were in the apostolic succession, were not to go unchallenged. Kirby was assured that so long as Cullen was on the scene no one was going 'to give a Protestant colouring to our old Fathers'. (K: 16 Jan. 1867) Again his champion in intellectual combat was his nephew, but he was already looking for possible reinforcement in the form of Protestant scholars who might convert to the one true faith:

> I think Dr Moran has silenced all the Deans and Archdeacons of the Protestant Church on the episcopal succession. They appear all to have retired from the field. The Rev. Dr Brady, nephew of the ex-Chancellor, is writing powerfully against the Protestant Church . . . putting it down. I hope he will become a Catholic. (K: 1 Mar. 1867)

The person Cullen referred to here was William Maziere Brady, Vicar of Clonfert in Co. Cork, who in 1864 had published a massive piece of historical scholarship, *Clerical and Parochial Records of Cork, Cloyne and Ross*. During the Disestablishment controversy his researches convinced him that there was no true succession between the medieval Catholic Church in Ireland and the Protestant establishment set up by Elizabeth in the sixteenth century. This greatly upset his fellow-Protestants, but also brought him to the attention of Moran, who encouraged him and his wife to go to live in Rome after Disestablishment. Kirby received the two of them into the Roman Catholic Church in 1873, and Brady spent the rest of his life in the Eternal City writing voluminously. Leo XIII made him a papal chamberlain for his labours, which included a study of episcopal succession in England, Scotland and Ireland based on hitherto hidden material in Roman archives.

Cullen rejoiced over the conversion of a man like Brady because he had no high opinion of the intellectual calibre of Irish priests. The older generation of continental-trained clergy with wide intellectual interests had been succeeded by Maynooth-trained zealots whom not even their strongest supporters could claim to be men of culture or erudition. Their fervent nationalism reinforced their natural provincialism, and Cullen often wished that more of them could have experienced the enlightenment that would have come to them if only they had studied in the Irish College in Rome, or even in Paris. Cullen would have understood well what Bishop David Moriarty of Kerry was referring to when he asked Kirby on 19 March 1869, on the eve of Vatican Council I:

> Why is it that no Irish theologian has been invited to the Congregation's preparation for the General Council? It seems so strange that England should be asked her opinions through her theologians, and the country in which the laws of the Church are certainly obeyed has no voice in the proposed improvements of law and discipline. (K)

The obvious way to build up Catholic intellectual life was through the new Catholic University for Ireland which Rome had encouraged the hierarchy to establish since 1847. A Catholic University Committee had been set up by the Synod of Thurles, though Murray and his followers, and then the MacHaleites, showed no enthusiasm for the new venture. Cullen, however, was determined to make Irish Catholicism intellectually respectable through the brilliance of young graduates who would emerge from a model Ultramontane university to 'demonstrate to Europe that the country which in former days contributed most to its civilisation is ready once more to vindicate for herself the high position she once held in the literary world'. (PM, II, 74) MacHale, on the other hand, wanted a Catholic university dedicated to the memory of Daniel O'Connell and the cause of Irish nationalism and supported by donations from the Irish overseas. (CA, 1847/92)

John Henry Newman, the famous Oxford convert, had met Cullen in Rome in 1847 when completing his studies for the priesthood in Propaganda College. Rapport was immediately established between them, and Cullen offered Newman the use of his Roman connections if and when difficulties arose for the Oratorian order which Newman was hoping to establish in Birmingham. After Cullen returned to Ireland he asked Newman to advise him about the appointment of academic staff for the Catholic University, but Newman was at first shy about involving himself in Irish affairs. Then he found himself in an unfortunate lawsuit with an apostate Dominican named Achilli whom he had attacked in a public lecture after the latter had given talks on the horrors of the Roman inquisition. Cullen at this juncture tried to use his Roman influence to obtain documents to support Newman's case, and Newman gratefully spoke of 'turning my eyes in devotion and affection to the Primate of that ancient and glorious and much enduring . . . Church of Ireland [*sic*] '. (PM, II, 96)

In the autumn of 1851 Newman obliged Cullen by giving a series of lectures in Dublin, and shortly afterwards Cullen asked him to become first Rector of the Catholic University. Rome confirmed the appointment in February 1852, shortly before the death of Daniel Murray.

Cullen expected a storm over the appointment of a non-Irishman. As he had already told Bernard Smith, this was inevitable, but they were fortunate to get the scholarly Newman:

> Some of the bishops do not like this — but we have no fit person in Ireland. He will be a host in himself. His last lectures are very fine and gave a fatal knock to Protestantism. . . . We are badly off in point of men. We have no educated Catholics ready to do anything. Those who come forward are often times hirelings or adventurers

whom you cannot trust. However, God will raise some one to defend His Church. (BS: 7 Oct. 1851)

The expected opposition did arise, but it was less than Cullen had feared, and he was able to tell William Walshe of Halifax that it was limited to 'a few Young Irelanders who have been steadfast friends of the Queen's Colleges, and enemies of the Catholic University from the beginning'. (DAA: 28 Dec. 1851) Yet many of the bishops felt 'our nationality has been hurt', and he confessed to Bernard Smith that 'half of them are hostile'. (BS: 20 Feb. 1852)

Newman's failing in this Irish venture was that he never appreciated the strong nationalist feelings — and indeed insularity — of so many of the Irish bishops. He was naive enough to consider Henry Manning as a possible vice-rector, and Cardinal Wiseman as the first chancellor, convinced as he was that the Catholic University should be other than merely an Irish institution. Newman's acting vice-rector in the first few months was a professor of mathematics and a layman, Edward Butler, and Cullen was appalled at Newman's suggestion that he be confirmed in this position. Cullen foresaw that if this happened the clergy would cease totally to support a university in which Newman wanted 'to make everything secular'. (NK: 8 July 1857) Cullen must certainly have agreed with the Bishop of Southwark, Thomas Grant, whose parents came from Ulster, when this old friend from Roman times told him on 9 September 1855: 'You have borne and suffered much for taking such interest in an Englishman.' (Molony, *Aust. Ch.,* 25)

Newman gave great cause for complaint to his Irish critics by spending much of his time in England on Oratorian business. Patrick Leahy, the vice-rector, was also absent a great deal, and Cullen became more and more anxious as the new university seemed to have no one with any vision directing it. On 7 February 1857 he confided his concerns to Kirby:

Dr Newman has been absent for the past fortnight — we cannot count on him. Besides he has persuaded himself that young lads ought to be left altogether at their own disposal. One of his French pupils went to hunt and was nearly killed by a fall from his horse. . . . Two other

Belgian nobles who are with him were dancing the other night at the Castle ball. . . . Dr Newman is also allowing his boarders to go to the theatre . . . I do not like to write to the Cardinal on these matters as it would seem I was inclined to persecute. . . . The *Rambler* has come out with a denunciation of Irish pretensions: . . . the Irish are like . . . parents brought up in ignorance who are thus incapable of educating their own offspring. Hence no one but an Englishman is fit to manage a university. (NK)

As it became clear to Cullen that MacHale was going to make use of Newman's failings as rector of the university Cullen was forced to appeal to Cardinal Barnabo, Prefect of Propaganda, in a lengthy letter of 31 August 1858. He said that the rector had not been in Ireland at all that year, that he had spent money recklessly, hiring professors who had nothing to do because students were so few. As for the students, their discipline was deplorable. Cullen had reproached Newman for allowing them to attend dances and to keep horses for hunting, only to be told that these were common practices at Oxford and he could see nothing wrong with them. Matters were so bad that he expected MacHale to launch an attack on the university at a forthcoming meeting of the bishops 'and to attack the archbishop of Dublin who took a principal part in inviting Father Newman to govern this institution'. (PM, II, 264) Cullen was in Rome in the spring of 1859, and from there he indicated to Leahy that he was no defender of Newman. He was drawing up a list of prominent converts and their views on educational matters. From now on Rome would be wary of converts. (CA, 1859/3)

MacHale's onslaught did not come until a meeting of the bishops was held in October 1859, when three entire days were devoted to the university question. Newman had by this time resigned from a university that wished to be narrowly Irish in its concerns, and the bishops had accepted his resignation. Now that they had the task of reorganisation after Newman's disastrous administration, MacHale was determined to be as obstructive as possible, and Cullen was quite shaken by his encounter with 'the Lion' at full wrath.

Cullen had taken the precaution to reinforce his legatine authority with special instructions from Propaganda, personally approved by the pope, and he overruled MacHale, who argued that the meeting had no authority and that no one need be bound by any measures agreed to by the bishops. What 'the Lion' wanted, said Cullen, was to break 'with the other bishops and then to come before the public and justify such a rupture', blaming Cullen for allowing an Englishman to pack an Irish university with his fellow-countrymen, 'excluding Irishmen who were perhaps more deserving'. In another long letter to Barnabo on 11 November 1859 Cullen summed up this traumatic experience by telling the Cardinal Prefect what MacHale had attempted to do:

> In short, he would have condemned the whole system of the same Father Newman who wished to model everything on the pattern of Oxford and to introduce into a Catholic and far from wealthy country customs which were more suitable for a Protestant kingdom like England and for a people of great wealth. (PM, II, 303)

Cullen, however, had patiently heard MacHale out, and finally 'the Lion' had been persuaded to sign the formal address in favour of the university which came out of the meeting. This would, Cullen believed, keep him from taking the issue before the public, but he did not expect any aid for the university to come from Tuam in the future.

Summing up the situation two years after Newman's departure, Cullen began to see that the Englishman's failure had been due to his inability to understand the clerical mind of Ireland and the needs of the people. He told Kirby:

> I think the university will go on. Irish affairs must be managed by Irishmen. Dr Newman put things in such a way that they could not go on, and so the clergy did not like him. When he was asked a question he would give no answer, or say he had a *view* on that point. The real view would be to look to the condition of the people and the country. During the whole time he was here he kept no communication with any of the priests.
>
> (NK: 14 Sept. 1861)

Cullen was convinced that Newman, coming as he did from a lay-dominated Erastian church, had a firm belief in the need for the laity to have a strong voice in university affairs. From what Cullen knew of the pro-government Catholic gentry and aristocracy, the last thing he wanted was their meddling in the affairs of the Catholic University. When Newman's successor, Bartholomew Woodlock, sought to have laymen represented on the board, Cullen revealed to Kirby what he thought of the suggestion:

> I think it is not of any great importance to have the laymen in question. They do without laymen in Belgium — we have scarcely any great laymen who would help to keep up the university and it is on the body of the people we must rely. (K: 11 Aug. 1863)

Newman certainly left Cullen with an uncomfortable legacy. The unwanted English academics hired by Newman were difficult to get rid of, threatening court action for wrongful dismissal. MacHale, now that his opposition to the university was in the open, continued to be as obstructionist as possible, and Cullen's correspondence with Kirby reveals the embarrassment which such tactics were causing him:

> Dr MacHale has not done anything for the Catholic University for the last fifteen years. He condemns everything but gives nothing and will take no part. He verifies the old proverb, the best hurler is always on the ditch. If something is not done at present, the Queen's Colleges will go ahead.... The division among the bishops and Dr MacHale's opposition give ground to the people to withhold their subscriptions — four dioceses gave nothing this year and eight or ten gave little. Some of the priests say that Dr MacHale is right in opposing the university, and then they tell the people not to contribute. This is only for yourself. (K: 14 Aug. 1865)

The division among the bishops meant that Cullen could not press the government for a charter which would give its degrees legal status and allow the Catholic University to compete on an equal footing with Trinity College. Disraeli stood firm against the demand, but after Disestablishment Cullen hoped that Gladstone might be persuaded to grant a charter. He tried to organise a major demonstration in the

Pro-Cathedral in early January 1872 to call for government
support of Catholic education at all levels, but even the
Freeman's Journal had to concede that this 'monster meeting'
was not a great success. There were many empty seats, the
Catholic elite of the city and the country were not there,
and there was no excitement on the streets. The *Times* of
19 January rejoiced that Cullen was failing in his attempt
to further divide Irish society along sectarian lines:

> What the Cardinal says of common schools he extends also
> to intermediate schools and to universities. From stage to
> stage there is the same cry for seclusion and exclusion,
> and we may be sure that the Cardinal, faithful to the
> teaching of the *Syllabus*, thinks, with a sigh, of the ages
> when the presence of a heretic in civil society was regarded
> as we now regard the importation of a beast attacked
> with rinderpest — as something to be stamped out, that
> thereby the safety of the rest of the herd may be secured.

A 'memorial from the Catholic people of Dublin in public
meeting assembled' was duly passed on to the government,
including a request for a university system 'of which Catholics
can conscientiously avail themselves', but its tone was rather
subdued. (BM, 44433)

To Cullen's dismay Gladstone did introduce a university
bill in the following year; it called for support for the Queen's
Colleges and for Trinity, but it gave nothing to the Catholic
foundation except the right to allow its students to go to a
national university for examinations and degrees. It was
Cullen's opinion that 'Altogether the bill would appear to
be worthy of another Bismarck.' (K: 19 Feb. 1873) Then he
arranged a meeting with Lord Spencer, the Lord Lieutenant,
who lent him a sympathetic ear and promised to send his
concerns on to Gladstone. He told Spencer that, if passed,
the new university bill would encourage poor Catholics to
desert 'their denominational tutors' for the endowed colleges
that taught subjects like modern history and moral philosophy.
Cullen made much of a book written by a Cork professor
which seemed to put Christ and Luther on the same level,
and he expressed his horror over a rumour that T. H. Huxley
was to be offered a chair in one of the Queen's Colleges. In

his report to Gladstone the viceroy noted that the cardinal was strong in his criticisms of the new bill, but 'in a good humour and full of gratitude to the government and Mr Gladstone'. (BM, 44307, 161-9)

Although he had put on a good face for the Lord Lieutenant, Cullen told Kirby that if the bill was passed by parliament 'infidelity would soon be spread through the land and the foundations of all faith shaken'. Even Trinity College would be affected, with its academics set free to teach infidelity as well as Protestantism. (K: 5 Mar. 1873) Fortunately for Cullen's peace of mind, the bill was defeated, and special prayers of thanksgiving were ordered to be said in Dublin churches. But when he wrote to report the outcome to Kirby he showed how agitated he had been by the whole affair. No mercy was to be shown for those who had been willing to accept Gladstone's exercise in Bismarckian politics:

> Only two Catholics voted for Gladstone ... Sir Dominic Corrigan, MP for Dublin, for whom I voted at the last election, and Sir Rowland Blennerhasset, MP for Galway and disciple of Dr Dollinger. I hope that at the next election we shall be able to pay off Sir Dominic. I am sure Dr MacEvilly will settle accounts with Sir R. Blennerhasset. ... Mr Gladstone's bill pretended to be favourable to Catholics but was all hostile. We asked for fish and they gave us a serpent. ... (K: 12 Mar. 1873)

Cullen also noted that the Bishop of Kerry, David Moriarty, had been in favour of the bill.

In 1876, two years before Cullen's death, Isaac Butt introduced a university education bill which seemed to Cullen to resurrect much that he had disliked about Gladstone's measure, and this may help to explain in part his lack of interest in Butt's Home Rule movement. Cullen was not to be taken in by any government ploy which would take from the Catholic bishops their influence in university affairs. Nor was he going to tolerate any arrangement which would enable Catholic students to be influenced by the infidel and Protestant spirits to be found in the Queen's Colleges and in Trinity College.

4. *Cullen and the People*

When Cullen came to Dublin he was glad to be rid of Armagh and its religious destitution which demanded that he spend what he considered to be an inordinate amount of time in purely pastoral concerns. He had no pastoral experience as a priest, had been nurtured as a diplomat-administrator in Rome, and found it difficult to apply himself to the direct concern for the religious and social well-being of the people which most diocesan bishops accepted as one of their primary functions. When he did speak of social problems it was usually in the context of some criticism of the secular administration. Because of this aloofness from the immediate needs of the people, he was seldom appreciated as a pastor and never lost the image of being an austere man whose first loyalty was to a cause greater even than that of ministering to the ordinary spiritual needs of the Catholics of Ireland, let alone those of Dublin.

It is almost paradoxical that although Cullen delighted on one level in Ultramontanist triumphal display, as in the building of Clonliffe College, yet his friend William Walshe could write to him from Paris in 1855 to tell him how unpopular he was becoming in Dublin because of his neglect of the Marlborough Street Metropolitan Chapel. People no longer attended it because the staff was considered to be too young and incapable, 'the edifice itself is dirty and very much neglected in the interior', and generally its clergy presented 'a mortifying contrast with those who served it in Dr Murray's day'. (K: 3 May 1855)

Cullen soon remedied these deficiencies in the Pro-Cathedral, but he was generally considered by his contemporaries to be neither a particularly effective pastoral bishop nor a popular one. As time went on he tended to leave diocesan concerns to vicars-general, such as Laurence Forde, Edward McCabe and William Meagher. At the same time, as Forde pointed out in his correspondence more than once, Cullen did not find it easy to delegate authority. Constantly he was overseeing affairs in the archdiocese, not from the standpoint of pastoral efficiency or care for the people, but to ensure that everything was being directed in terms of the Ultramontane mission of the Universal Church.

He was constantly irritated by the regulars, for example, not because of a lack of pastoral zeal, but because they tended to drag their heels over his interpretation of how they should serve the Ultramontane cause. He could sneer on occasion at the Jesuits' acting 'jesuitically', or tell Kirby, as he did several times, that the friars were not much use to him.

His criticism of the legion of clergy under his direction reflected in part his problem of how to keep them all occupied in activities which he could approve. At the time of the Fenian troubles he told Kirby that one reason why the Capuchins in particular gave so much trouble was that they were too numerous and had too little to do, with the inevitable result that they neglected their spiritual mission and got involved in secular politics. He also indicated how expensive it was to maintain the huge number of clergy and religious in Dublin:

In Dublin we have 420 priests or friars, all supported by charity — they cost at least £100 per annum on an average. . . . I think each friar (at least of the old houses) gets more than each secular priest. It is a very dangerous experiment to increase the expense on the people. There are now 1150 nuns. Besides these are three Catholic hospitals and God knows how many orphanages — all supported by charity. The least little upset would reduce priests, friars and nuns to starvation. (K: 19 Jan. 1868)

Directing this vast army in his Ultramontane 'plan of campaign' was Cullen's first priority, and where he failed as a diocesan was in his obsession with the larger affairs of the Church which he considered ought to occupy him, first as Apostolic Delegate and then as cardinal. No one could ever have accused him of being indolent; no one in the archdiocese worked harder or had longer hours than he did. The problem was the focus of his concern. He devoted considerable attention to the affairs of Clonliffe College, securing the appointment of his nephew, Michael Verdon, as its president, then seeking further training for its graduates in Rome, and even appearing frequently in person at the college to conduct examinations. Yet this meant that this showpiece and bastion of Ultramontanism was consuming valuable time that might have been given to domestic diocesan business.

Even when he did focus on local concerns it was apt to be an exercise in ecclesiastical warfare. When he looked at the operation of the Poor Law in his archdiocese, for example, his primary consideration was not the suffering of inmates in the workhouses, but the administration of the law by a Protestant administration. Rates to support the workhouses were, in his view, taxes for preserving Protestantism in Ireland, not for relieving the poor. When he got excited by the need to oppose this part of the Protestant *imperium* he concentrated on it wonderfully, as is apparent from a letter to Kirby in 1861 in which he gave detailed statistics on the working of Rathdrum Union:

> There are 339 inmates of whom thirty only are Protestant, 309 Catholics. Now the master is a Protestant, £60 salary, the matron a Protestant, £20, the clerk a Protestant, £120, Chaplain, Protestant, £30 for attending 30 Protestants, 3 Relieving Officers, Protestant, £30 each, two doctors, £100 each, Protestant, 5 other doctors at £80 each, Protestants, Apothecary, £75, Protestant. . . . So you have £985 paid out of the poor rate to 15 Protestants. The Catholics get £60 for a chaplain, schoolmasters £30, the porter £10, two nurses, one £15, one £12, that is £127. . . . The officials get more than £1000 for starving some 300 poor people. (NK: 21 Mar. 1861)

After he analysed such statistics Cullen did more than to pass them on to Rome in the amazingly voluminous correspondence he kept up with Kirby, with Bernard Smith and with Propaganda. Whenever he could catch the ear of some responsible government official, from the Lord Lieutenant down, Cullen cogently and rationally argued the injustice of denying the majority people a greater say in the administration of the country.

But even while he engaged in this agitation for social justice Cullen was in constant communication with Rome, and his pastoral concern merged with his sense of Ultramontane mission. Probably what first prompted him to devote so much time to the failings of the Poor Law was that it was administered by a heretical anti-Catholic government. The age was one of social reform, the government's conscience was becoming increasingly tender, and perhaps concessions might yet be won for the Catholic Church if only pressure was kept up. It is probable that if the government had been Catholic, Cullen would have had less to say about the Poor Law and its sundry defects and injustices.

Whatever his motives, in this case Cullen served the Catholic poor of Dublin well, for he made a powerful case for reform, as he indicated in a letter to Kirby in 1861:

> In Dublin alone the expenses of the poorhouses have amounted some years to £60,000, and all the good done amounts to this, that some hundreds of women with illegitimate children and prostitutes and bastards are supported and that some four hundreds of poor old women and men are helped to die before their day.
>
> (NK: 12 July 1861)

His strong voice had been added to those of the other reformers of his age, and it was their protests against such social folly and injustice which brought about the changes that were made in Poor Law administration. Cullen's pastoral letters abound with such criticism on behalf of the poor.

Sometimes Cullen's tendency to approach social evils in terms of Ultramontane ideology led him into convolutions of thought that were startling. When he considered the greatest of social evils in the Dublin of his day, the scandalous consumption of alcohol and the horrors that accompanied it, his response was not to consider this curse as an inevitable evil to be opposed only by moral exhortation. Rather he came to the conclusion that Dublin's widespread intemperance was largely a symptom of 'liberalism' in society, especially of the 'freedom of the press'! The only way to solve the drink problem was to restructure society totally, and this would include control of what was printed by newspapers. In 1872 Cullen told Kirby how he was directing three temperance missions, and how the good they sought to do was opposed by 'liberalism' and a wicked press:

The bad newspapers and the whiskey shops destroy all

the good that is done. There are about 2000 whiskey
shops in Dublin. The whiskey consumed and licences
bring in about a million or at least an enormous sum on
duty. Hence to make money the atrocious whiskey trade
is protected and encouraged though it is the origin of every
crime. The newspapers are teaching all arts of villainy,
yet to keep up the liberty of the press and the principles
of the revolution they are let go on and ruin the poor
people. This is liberty of a very bad sort.

(NK: 3 May 1872)

This type of social comment suggests that Cullen harboured
within himself something of the spirit of Savonarola. If his
view had prevailed, Dublin would have had imposed upon it a
very different kind of social order than that which the Protestant administration tolerated for the sake of licence and duty
revenue. At the very least the wicked newspapers would not
have been allowed to advertise dances like the polka, which
Cullen decreed 'repugnant to the purity of Christian morals'.
(NLI, Halliday, 581)

A social issue which also engaged Cullen was the problem
associated with the large number of troops in the Dublin
area, many of whom were Catholics. As far as Cullen was
concerned, these men were under his spiritual authority when
they were in the city, and he spent a great deal of time
attempting to impress this fact upon the government. He
especially objected to Catholic soldiers attending mass said
in 'mixed churches', and by 1865 his constant pressure
resulted in separate Catholic chapels appearing at the Curragh
and later in the Hibernian Military School. By 1872 Cullen
proudly told Kirby that this particular battle was won and
mixed chapels had disappeared in Ireland. Also he pressured
the government for better treatment of the dependants of
Catholic soldiers, working with Patrick Leahy to gather information about Catholic troops in camps such as the Curragh
and Newbridge. (CA, 1858/59) He enjoyed such 'agitation',
and as early as 1857 he told Kirby with some amusement
that the Protestant press was even blaming him for stirring up
mutiny in the army in India: 'When one of the British regiments refused to obey orders, an old Orangeman here in

Dublin said very seriously it was Cullen's letter that did all that.' (NK: 6 Dec. 1857)

Of particular interest to him in terms of authority were the Catholic chaplains in the army. He protested about the small number of Catholic chaplains who accompanied the army to the Crimea. Because of his pressure more were appointed, and then he objected to their being posted in and out of barracks in the Dublin area without his being consulted. He also questioned the high rate of pay they received from the army, which, he claimed, was part of a general plot to prepare the clergy generally for 'pensioning' by the state:

> This system of giving large salaries to the professors in Maynooth and to army chaplains and allowances to students will damage us very much. The country is becoming very poor, but the training given by government will so dispose the clergy that they will not be satisfied to live in poverty and some day or other they will be caught with a golden bait. (K: 21 Apr. 1865)

Cullen's pressure on the government was so relentless that finally it was agreed that, in spite of statute law and army regulations, Cullen was to have the *de facto* right to appoint and to remove military chaplains in his archdiocese. He told Kirby: 'The public authorities by act of parliament have a right to appoint and remove all those chaplains. Of course we do not allow that right. I nominate and remove all the chaplains without asking anyone's permission.' (K: 12 Sept. 1872)

Where Cullen wanted to serve the people most directly was, of course, on the religious level. One way of doing this, he was convinced, was by bringing into the archdiocese he governed every possible visible sign of religious and ecclesiastical triumphalism that would stir the people to engage in greater spiritual exercise. Although he had tended to neglect this aspect of pastoral superintendence when he first came to Dublin, as in the case of the Pro-Cathedral, he soon began to encourage the importation of Italianate Counter-Reformation artifacts for the churches and to assist any priest who wished to beautify his church. When he was in Rome he had befriended an Irish ecclesiastical sculptor of some genius, John Hogan, who worked for some twenty-five years in the Eternal City.

Hogan returned to Ireland in the same year as Cullen, and until he died in 1858 Cullen helped him in every way possible to adorn Dublin churches with art in the Italianate style.

Even before Cullen began to show this interest in refurbishing Dublin churches in a way that would display to the faithful the new militant spirit that was coming from Rome, he had determined to promote the new devotions of the Ultramontane revival, such as the *quarantore*, or 'forty hours'. As early as 1852 he wrote to Cardinal Fransoni to indicate his desire to raise the religious enthusiasm of the people through the new religious exercises that had done so much to promote piety among the masses elsewhere in the Church:

> The devotion of the forty hours will be held in all the churches of this city during the Jubilee and I hope for the greatest results from it. Already the forty hours have been held in the cathedral church and the crowds who attended were without number, and the devotion which they displayed was most edifying. Father Faber of the Oratory preached in the aforesaid church at the opening of the Jubilee. He is endowed with extraordinary eloquence and has done much to arouse the devotion of the people to the Most Holy Sacrament as also to due veneration towards the successors of St Peter. (PM, III, 139: 4 Oct. 1852)

Cullen as a pastor never won the hearts of the Catholic people of Dublin in the way that Daniel Murray had, nor did he ever win the respect and even admiration extended by Protestants to his saintly predecessor. Yet he was passionately concerned in an abstract way for their spiritual welfare; and according to his rather narrow and Roman view of what they needed, he gave himself totally to his mission to lead them in the way of salvation. In fact, considering the demands made upon him as Apostolic Delegate and then as cardinal, it is remarkable how much he achieved for the Catholics of Dublin as their diocesan. He served them less well — though according to his precepts he could do no other — in persuading them to separate themselves so radically from their Protestant neighbours. Coming to Dublin as he did at the height of the Irish Church Missions advance, perhaps he had no alternative. Yet many liberal Catholics had no wish for religious apartheid and sectarian bitterness in Ireland and deplored what Cullen accomplished. They were not interested in seeing a Catholic ascendancy or triumphalism succeed the Protestant rule that came to an end with Disestablishment. Perhaps this very success of Cullen's Ultramontane war against everything Protestant in Dublin denied him popularity with the people. They were used to, and were willing to live with, a pluralist society which this Ultramontane zealot in their midst could never tolerate. Instinctively they distanced themselves from this austere cleric who at times seemed to have forgotten the biblical reminder that the sabbath is made for man, not man for the sabbath.

VI

The Legatine Commission

1. *Cullen's Counter-Reformation War*

Paul Cullen had come to Ireland as Apostolic Delegate, his appointment to Armagh being a convenience, as was his translation to Dublin. His task was to restore the authority of the papacy in a church that threatened, from the Roman standpoint, to become ungovernable. Cullen's brief was to persuade the Irish Roman Catholics to join in the Ultramontane mission of the Universal Church against Protestantism, liberalism in its many forms, and the other evils which the pope was to list for the faithful in his Syllabus of Errors. He was to carry out his task doggedly, patiently and ruthlessly, slowly replacing the men who exercised authority in the Church by those who shared his sense of mission. He was to be so successful in his task that his critics were to refer to his achievement as the 'Cullenisation' of Ireland. Indirectly his influence also extended to the Catholic Church in Australia, which was largely staffed by émigré Irish priests. 'In one way or another all the prelates appointed to these sees until 1878 were Cullen's men . . . who left a lasting stamp on the Catholic Church.' (Molony, *Aust. Ch.,* 5)

It was because of this national mission that Cullen at times did not focus as he might have as a diocesan on affairs in Armagh or in Dublin. He said, for example, little about the problem of mixed marriages in the metropolitan city, though this error was of as much concern to him as mixed education, or the use of mixed chapels by the military. Cullen saw this as a national problem, and he knew that if he said too much about it his episcopal opponents would dismiss it as a problem peculiar only to his own territory. For tactical reasons he was in Dublin less assertive about this vexed question than he might otherwise have been, and in terms of advancing his mission nationally he was willing to assist, or even at times to encourage, intermarriage with Protestants, as we shall see shortly.

Much of the success of Cullen's legatine mission in Ireland reflected the support he was given in Rome by his friend Pio Nono, by Propaganda, and above all by Tobias Kirby, who had succeeded Cullen as Rector of the Irish College and Roman agent for the Irish bishops. Without the loyal unflagging support of Kirby, Cullen would not easily have known what British agents in Rome were doing to counteract his mission, or what the MacHaleites and other enemies were up to in their efforts to oppose him in the Roman tribunals. He also counted on Kirby to reinforce his mission by sending him the eager young zealots who came out of the Irish College in Rome and returned home as convinced Ultramontanists.

Kirby had been in Rome since 1827, where he was known as a fervent Ultramontanist and a disciple of the French historian and defender of the papacy, René Rohrbacher. This meant that his understanding of Irish affairs was very limited, which did not help his work as agent for the Irish bishops after Cullen went to Armagh. In 1851 he asked the astonished Archbishop of Cashel, Michael Slattery, to send him a report on the progress of 'socialism' in Munster. Slattery replied:

> In your letter you requested me to publish a pastoral against Socialism but I can assure you most solemnly that not only is such a thing altogether without existence amongst my people but even the very meaning of the word is unknown, so that to address them upon it would be perfectly useless and a complete waste of both words and time. (K: 18 Feb. 1851)

To remedy at least in part this ignorance of Irish affairs Cullen arranged in the autumn of 1851 for Bernard Smith to run the Irish College while Kirby came home to recuperate from an illness and to gain some insight into the true state of the Irish Church. Kirby learned much from this visit, especially about affairs in Connaught, where John MacHale was trying to cope with the major incursion into his territories made by Protestant proselytising societies.

Cullen did not make as much use of Kirby in the early years of his mission as he did later, this being perhaps a reflection of Kirby's early ignorance of Irish affairs. Slowly, however, his correspondence shows a growth of confidence in Kirby, and in the last decade of his life almost a reliance on the help that Kirby could give him. What bound the two men together personally was not so much friendship as a strong concern for the affairs of the Irish College, which always meant much to Cullen. Long letters, for example, were exchanged with both Kirby and Moran in 1866, at the height of the Fenian troubles, over the disastrous effects accompanying the use of too small pipes in the water-closets of the college. Cullen also worried about matters like the disposal of the college's vineyards, or its external appearance. When the Italian government threatened annexation in 1873 Cullen did not hesitate to urge Kirby to plead British identity and seek help from the government:

> Get a good legal document drawn up by a lawyer and send it to the Italian government and to the English ambassador — Put nothing but mere facts and legal documents — Don't let anything doubtful be put in, or anything exaggerated or declamatory — we shall be able to get a documentation of that kind brought before parliament. (K: 4 Dec. 1873)

Above all, Cullen counted on Kirby to carry on the Ultramontane spirit of the Irish College and to send him dedicated recruits for his Irish mission, such as his nephew Patrick Francis Moran, the future Archbishop of Sydney, or the three Quinn brothers: James, subsequently Bishop of Brisbane, Matthew, Bishop of Bathurst, and Andrew, who became one of Cullen's vicars-general. Intelligent yet narrow and zealous, these men confronted the hated liberalism of their age with a frame of mind not very different from that of their Counter-Reformation predecessors. One of these alumni, the gifted William Hutch, who in 1866 returned to Ireland to serve in St Colman's College, Fermoy, wrote to Kirby during his homeward journey. He expressed his disgust over 'the worldliness of Florence'. (K: 16 Apr. 1866) When he got to Ireland he scorned the rebellious spirit of the 'terrible Fenians', as well as the spiritual sloth and anti-intellectualism of those

Irish priests who had been 'denied the blessings of a Roman education'. (K: 26 June 1866)

These narrow, bigoted and able Irish College graduates were exactly the men that Cullen needed in his mission, for on his arrival he found the Irish Catholic Church under fierce attack. Archbishops like MacHale and Slattery and bishops like Egan in Kerry had dioceses filled with proselytising Protestant missionaries who were making thousands of converts among the demoralised people, many of whom in the wake of the famine felt that their church had abandoned them. Cullen wanted to help the besieged prelates to withstand the English-directed proselytisers; they, however, were reluctant to call upon the services of Cullen, whom they looked upon as a kind of inquisitor. They were very aware of the pastoral and other scandals, the lack of educational provisions, and the many deficiencies which made their territories so vulnerable for penetration by the proselytisers. The last thing they wanted was for Cullen or Rome to know the full extent of the crisis which was upon them, or to accept help from the graduates of the Irish College in Rome or the other Counter-Reformation missionaries whom Cullen wanted to send them.

Rome knew how desperate the situation was, for Cullen himself in 1847 had visited Ireland and prepared a detailed report outlining what was happening in the west and south. He sent this document to Kirby on 29 October, asking him to pass it on to Cardinal Fransoni of Propaganda:

> It would be well that Cardinal Fransoni should write to Dr Slattery and Dr MacHale to take care . . . from the proselytising of the parsons — thousands have lost their faith in Kerry and Cork. The PP of Berehaven writes to Dr Renihan that in one day lately 150 heads of families went *in toto* to church for the purpose of getting relief, in Kerry matters are worse, and in the city of Cork Michael O'Sullivan told me that much mischief had been done. Dr Egan would not speak for the world about the mischief — he is endeavouring to conceal it from the eyes of all. A letter from the Cardinal will put an end to all the impious doings. (NK)

Little was done before Cullen's arrival to stem the Protestant advance, however, and while Cullen was dealing with the Synod of Thurles and archdiocesan affairs in Armagh, English Evangelical societies were pouring money and men into the field. The situation began to look critical, particularly in Connaught, which seemed as if it might become another Protestant-dominated Ulster. James Maher tried to assure Kirby that, as he had told his nephew, there was a simple reason for the mass defection: the proselytisers were bribing the people, engaging in 'souperism': 'Holding out relief for the body, they hope to infect the soul with their impious heresies.' (K: 3 Aug. 1850) Cullen, however, was too intelligent to look for a single explanation for what was happening, and he paid particular attention to the views of the Catholic *Dublin Evening Post*, which argued on 11 November 1851 that Connaught had been chosen as the main area of proselytising advance because there the people, long denied the blessings of the National System of Education, were peculiarly ignorant and peculiarly vulnerable to activities of the missionary societies.

On 16 June 1851 Cullen sent Propaganda a long and detailed report on the seriousness of the situation, especially in MacHale's territories, where the establishment of well-financed proselytising schools showed that Protestantism was there to stay among the people. The political bishops in the province were hopeless and gave little or no spiritual guidance to their flocks. Higgins of Ardagh, for example, completely neglected his diocese, and French, the Bishop of Kilmacduagh, had not visited his diocese for several years. A place like Oughterard was 'no longer a parish of Catholics, it has literally become a parish of Jumpers and Bible Readers'. The parish priest, William Kirwan, had never resigned his ecclesiastical appointment, but had literally abandoned his people by becoming President of the Queen's College in Galway. Since his death in 1849 no parish priest had been appointed, and the two curates were at each other's throats; and furthermore, the vicar-general and two of the most important local priests had fled the distressed area and were in London. It was so bad that recently the Protestant Bishop of Tuam had arrived with a Bianconi car full of parsons to confirm hundreds of 'perverts'. (PFS, XXX, 662-5)

A result of Cullen's visit to Ireland in 1847 was Rome's request to Michael Slattery to send in reports on the successes of the proselytisers in the western part of his archdiocese and in Cork and Kerry. (CA, 1847/95) Lengthy accounts given by the parish priests and curates in parishes such as Doon, Cappamore and Pallasgreen indicate how serious the situation had become by 1853. Protestant successes were attributed to the threat of eviction by the landlords, to the use of bribery by missionaries who were supported by Robert Daly, the Protestant Bishop of Cashel, and to the funds of Exeter Hall, the Evangelical headquarters in London. (CA, 1853/18/35)

The only bright spot Cullen saw in the west was in Clonfert with its new bishop, John Derry. In 1854 he persuaded Derry to write to Propaganda directly to seek help in his parish of Ballinasloe, where he was waging a strong resistance to the proselytising supported by the Earl of Clancarty, brother of the much-hated Protestant Archdeacon of Ardagh, the Ven. Charles le Poer Trench:

> Here Sunday Schools for both boys and girls (and splendidly equipped) are to be found in abundance both in Ballinasloe and round about. There is a campaign on to get the Catholic children to go to them, and the aforesaid Lord of Clancarty will not take on workmen if they don't send their children to these schools. . . . While the enemy presses on with all this activity, past and present, we must admit to our lasting shame and disgrace that on the Catholic side there has been enormous supinity, much of which is still with us. (PFS. XXXII, 284-7: 17 July 1854)

In another letter to Propaganda Derry said that the only hope in a place like Ballinasloe was for the bishop himself to supervise local affairs by daily visits. Cullen knew, of course, that it was inconceivable that MacHale would personally encourage a Counter-Reformation mission in a place like Oughterard, or even admit that such a problem existed in his province. He might appeal to the public, as he did in a letter to the *Freeman's Journal* which was reproduced as a pamphlet entitled *An Apostolic Letter from His Grace the Most Rev. Dr MacHale, Lord Archbishop of Tuam, to the*

Rt Hon. Earl of Derby on the Fact of the Jumper Tribe now Prowling through Ireland (1852). Such bombast was not going to help the situation, however, and in fact it played into the hands of the Protestants who wanted confrontation and controversy. Nothing helped more to raise funds in Exeter Hall than stories of missionaries harassed by a popish bishop in far-away Connaught.

During the time that Cullen was adjusting to the new demands made upon him as Archbishop of Dublin the news from Connaught became ever more alarming. The Protestant *Dublin Evening Mail* of 18 February 1852 rejoiced that because of MacHale's misrule in Connemara over 10,000 people had renounced popery. Kirby and Cullen exchanged letters over 'statistics of perverts around Dingle' sent by Mother Mary T. Collins of the Presentation Convent in that community. (K: 7 Nov. 1852) Cullen told Kirby, as he had already told Bernard Smith, that around Clifden the falling away of the people in some parishes was 'awful', but that MacHale was still refusing to recognise that there was a problem:

> His Grace seems to think it would be a slur on himself to let in strangers. He had invited missionaries to Clifden — but he wrote afterwards that things were so well that he did not want them. . . . I am told that a mission is very much wanted. Perhaps *a poco a poco* his Grace will come over. (NK: 13 June 1852)

Propaganda was made aware of Cullen's anxiety, but was unsure how to deal with the obdurate and unpredictable Archbishop of Tuam. Finally, however, Pius IX followed up a general admonition in the autumn of 1852 with an expression in February 1853 of his grave concern over affairs in Tuam. This was brought to MacHale by the Archbishop of Calcutta, Patrick Carew, who was visiting Ireland. Carew also passed on the pope's suggestion that MacHale go to Rome to explain what was happening in his territories. The pope did not press the invitation, however, when MacHale pleaded his reluctance to leave his hard-pressed flock when the wolf was literally upon them. (PFS, XXXI, 384-6)

In thus answering the pope MacHale had admitted there

was trouble among his people, and he did allow two Ros-
minian missionaries to visit the Clifden area. To Cullen's
intense chagrin they found nothing to complain about:

> They spent but two weeks there in the midst of frost and
> snow so I strongly suspect they did not understand how
> things really were. They are to return again to Clifden after
> Easter. Dr MacHale has a complete triumph over all those
> who said there were perversions in his province since the
> two . . . missionaries published their declamation.
>
> (NK: 24 Mar. 1853)

MacHale did allow the Rosminians to return, but they accomplished little, and MacHale continued to exclude any outside
attempt to reform affairs within his domain. He also blocked
any reforming measures initiated by the clergy under his
control, as Cullen reported after a personal visit to Connaught:

> Dr MacHale has a controversy with Dean Burke. The Dean
> wishes to be allowed to take a grant for the nuns' school
> on the grounds of their poverty. The nuns are extremely
> poor and the children cannot get books. The Board would
> give them £100 per annum without any interference, but
> Dr MacHale would not consent. There will be trouble about
> the matter. (NK: 23 Sept. 1853)

The dean referred to was Bernard Burke, who had been
MacHale's chief rival in the election to the see of Tuam in
1834 in succession to Oliver Kelly. Burke had actually been
preferred by the clergy over MacHale, and the latter never
forgave him for this. Burke had wanted National Schools in
Tuam, but he told Kirby in a series of letters in the autumn
of 1853 that he had never had the courage to withstand the
roaring of 'the Lion' whenever he brought the subject up. If
he had taken a firm stand, he admitted, 'perversion of our
youth would not have gone to the extent it unfortunately
has'. The real tragedy was that because there were so few
Protestants in the province the schools would have been
almost totally in Catholic hands. Seven years later Burke,
having announced to Kirby that he was going to resign, said
that MacHale had persecuted him for thirty years: 'nor has
his Grace ever lost an opportunity of torturing me almost to
death when he could do so'. (K: 11 June 1860)

Neither Propaganda nor Cullen wished to force reform measures upon MacHale except through 'gentle persuasion', for they did not want him appealing to the prejudices of the people over their heads. They knew what use the recalcitrant archbishop could make of the charge of Roman legatine interference in Irish affairs. Cullen was well aware that this would only play into the hands of the Protestant administration, particularly those who were resisting his pressure for concessions in so many areas. Above all, Propaganda and Cullen had to retain a united episcopate if any kind of Ultramontane advance was to be sustained.

As we shall see, Cullen's tactic was to ensure that each of MacHale's suffragans was persuaded to accept a reforming coadjutor with right of succession as soon as their physical or mental powers were called into question. Slowly MacHale was isolated through this manoeuvring, and wherever a see was taken over by a Cullenite bishop the full authority of Ultramontane ideology was used to withstand the Protestant proselytisers.

Even this device gave Cullen no more than a partial victory, however. In 1858 John MacEvilly, who had become Bishop of Galway in the previous year with the help of Cullen, said that Oughterard was still filled with active proselytisers: 'I fail not to call there myself on Sundays to rouse the feelings of the people against the emissaries of Satan.' (K: 13 July 1858) The situation was no better in the rest of MacHale's dominions, and as late as 1869 MacEvilly was telling Kirby of stubborn Protestant resistance to the Catholic counter-offensive, with orphanages, schools and churches still filled and sustained by English Evangelical funds. (NK: 26 Apr. 1869) As for Dublin, as we have seen, the Protestant resistance was just as strong as in Connaught. The only positive thing MacEvilly could say to Kirby was that most of the numerous perversions in the city were the result of mixed marriages. (K: 2 Jan. 1863)

When the census of figures of 1861, with their disclosures of religious affiliation, were released Cullen pored over them to see what they revealed about the religious war, especially in the west. About all he could say was that there was no remarkable increase in the number of Protestants in Connaught in spite of all the wealth poured into the proselytising missions. The census did give evidence of the injustice of public money being used to sustain a minority ecclesiastical institution such as the Established Church, an alien body in a land that was clearly Catholic. He told Propaganda: 'An abuse like this in Naples or Modena would have the whole of the English rise in protest.' (PFS, XXXIV, 156: 10 Aug. 1861) From this time Cullen was intent upon his great project to have the Church of Ireland disestablished and disendowed. At the same time he kept up his pressure for denominational Catholic schools supported by the state, and never eased his attacks on the 'godless colleges', Trinity College and every bastion of Protestant privilege. Cullen was convinced that the best means of defence was attack, and he never ceased his pressure against the Protestant presence wherever it had taken root in the land.

Sometimes his anti-Protestant campaign led him to make use of men whose orthodoxy in Ultramontane terms he questioned. One of these was the immensely able David Moriarty, who had served in the Irish College in Paris and then became the second president of All Hallows College in Dublin in 1847. Cullen never liked his tolerant treatment of the National System and other signs of independence in his thinking. On the other hand, he was able and energetic, and from the time he became coadjutor to Cornelius Egan of Ardfert in 1854 Moriarty directed a singularly effective counter-attack against the proselytisers in the Dingle peninsula, asking for a special plenary indulgence for all children who attended schools run by the Presentation Sisters or Christian Brothers. He asked Rome to 'delight the people' by making their anti-proselytising parish priest a Doctor of Divinity, and Moriarty was soon telling Kirby of a Protestant rout as he and the missionaries he had brought in 'peppered them with red-hot Roman shot'. (K: 9 Nov. 1854) This was a grand boast, but the 'perverts' in Dingle continued to hold out for years to come.

Cullen's anti-Protestant zeal also led him to some compromise when it came to the vexed problem of mixed marriages. He considered that the Protestant view of marriage was hardly Christian, and when he heard that Richard Whately had

approved of Bishop Colenso's ideas on polygamy he said he
was not surprised. He also boasted that he had never once in
his life given a dispensation for a mixed marriage. Yet he was
not completely inflexible on the matter; the truth was that
his attitude to such a union was conditional upon certain
social factors. If a mixed marriage brought wealth to the
Catholic partner, and hopefully to the Church, Cullen was
prone to be less intransigent than he might otherwise have
been. He was always accommodating when there was even a
faint hope of financial gain for the Church. In 1868 he wrote
to Kirby about a young man, John Power, son of a baronet
and heir to an estate, who wished to join the pope's army.
Assuring Kirby that the young man was 'not clever, but very
good', he urged that everything be done to keep him from
Protestant influences. (K: 5 Feb. 1868) In 1869 he commended
to Kirby an 'old lady' named O'Ferrall, worth about £60,000,
who wished to visit Rome before marrying a Protestant eager
'to lay his hands on so large a sum'. Cullen urged that Kirby
pay particular attention to her: 'Don't let the old lady know
that I have written, or that I have called her an old lady.'
(K: 26 Apr. 1869) Another wealthy 'old lady' brought to
Kirby's notice was the daughter of the bigoted Judge Keating
who had converted to Catholicism at the cost of ostracisation
by her Protestant friends. She was now eager for social
acceptance, and Cullen had promised he would help her to
gain entry to Catholic circles in England or France:

> In either country she imagines that she would be well
> received if she had the title of baroness or countess, or any
> other title. She is very zealous and I believe has plenty of
> money. Would it be possible to get a title for her from the
> Pope? If you think it possible, make a petition for her in
> my name. (K: 21 Jan. 1874)

Probably Cullen felt a little uneasy about such worldly
calculation, but such was his dedication to the struggle against
the Protestant 'enemy' that any expedient to advance his
mission would be considered, if it could possibly be justified
morally. Using the 'wisdom of the serpent' in his battle with
the powers of darkness was not beyond Paul Cullen.

2. *The Problem of Protestant Ulster*

When it came to his struggle with Protestantism, Cullen knew that he had a particular problem to deal with in Ulster, where in many parts of the ecclesiastical province Protestants were not only the ascendancy but also the majority people. Traditionally they had intimidated their Catholic neighbours, and in this part of the Irish Church Cullen wanted strong men to stand up to such bullying. For this reason he had some reservations about Joseph Dixon, who succeeded him as Archbishop of Armagh and Primate. Dixon was a pious and a good man, but he had a conciliatory nature and during his Maynooth days had been a friend of such Gallican figures as William Crolly and Daniel Murray.

Cullen determined to strengthen Dixon, however, and he arranged for him to go to Rome in 1854 for the Immaculate Conception ceremonies of that year. Dixon was astonished and delighted both at the invitation and the reception he experienced when he met with great ecclesiastics like Cardinal Fransoni, the Prefect of Propaganda, and Cardinal Antonelli, the Secretary of State. The result of this total immersion in Rome's triumphalist atmosphere was that he returned to Ireland a convinced and, as far as his gentle nature would allow him, a militant Ultramontanist.

At the same time he had no intention of allowing any open conflict to arise between the faithful and the Orangemen of Armagh who were turbulent after the fracas at Dolly's Brae in 1849. He had been taught in Rome and never forgot that sooner or later revolutionary nationalists turned on the Church: 'To Satan's seed belong those Carbonari, or Freemasons, who laboured so strenuously to revolutionise Italy, to overturn the Church, and destroy religion.' (Dixon, *Bl. Cornelius*, 39)

Dixon's tactic was to focus on south Armagh, where the Catholics were strongest, and to press for the reversal of objectionable local customs, such as the burial of Catholics in Protestant graveyards. To press his reforms he held a provincial council at Drogheda in May 1854, the first since the reign of Queen Mary. After the synod Dixon told Cullen proudly how the hundred clergy present had toasted Pius IX at dinner and had then issued a spirited public address pro-

testing at the attacks on the pope made by Palmerston and
Gladstone. By the time Dixon died in 1866 a new Catholic
spirit was beginning to appear in Armagh.

Cullen was determined that Dixon's tentative exercises in
self-assertion by Catholics should not lapse. When the consecration of Dixon's successor, Michael Kieran, took place in
1867 Cullen took part as cardinal, attended by several bishops,
nearly two hundred priests, and members of the Catholic
nobility and gentry, some of them displaying papal decorations
such as those of the Knights of Malta. This prompted the
Protestant writer James Godkin to sneer that 'If Protestant
gentlemen were so silly as to appear at the consecration of a
bishop of the Established Church dressed in the uniform of
deputy-lieutenants, they would be laughed at.' (Godkin,
Churches, 457) There was, however, a note of unease in what
was said by Godkin and other critics. They were aware of
Dixon's impressive programme of church-building, and they
recognised that Kieran was going to continue to build up the
Catholic presence in Armagh. It was almost inevitable that
Cullen would report to Kirby that after the grand opening of
Armagh Cathedral visiting bishops experienced something of
the realities of Ulster life on their way home: 'The Orangemen
pelted the trains with stones and broke the windows of the
railway carriages — what scoundrels.' (K: 26 Aug. 1873)

The most southerly part of the Armagh province was
Meath, where John Cantwell, MacHale's ally and lieutenant,
had long held religious and political sway. Cullen reported
in detail the degree of agitation that was tolerated in the
Meath diocese, and in 1855 Cantwell was asking Kirby to
assure the Prefect of Propaganda that the tales about him
reaching Rome were exaggerated:

> The clergy of Meath are not second to the clergy of any
> diocese in Ireland in scrupulous attention to all the duties
> of their sacred office, in zeal for the interests of religion,
> and in devoted attachment to the centre of Catholic unity.
> (K: 3 Dec. 1855)

Cantwell's Ultramontane assertions were not taken seriously
by the papal delegate, however, and he pressed for a reforming coadjutor to be appointed in Meath. Unfortunately the

man appointed, Thomas Nulty, a Maynooth graduate who had acquired a reputation for tolerating agitation when he was Parish Priest of Trim, was elevated against the advice of Cullen. In his first pastoral in 1865 he urged the Meath priests to publicise evictions to coerce the landlords, and Cullen noted: 'It is the good landlord they generally denounce.' (K: 10 Mar. 1865) A year later Cullen told Kirby that Nulty was openly opposing him by objecting to the attempt being made to raise money for the pope in his difficulties:

> He calls on his flock not to give any assistance to any good work outside his diocese, and he cautions them expressly against giving anything to the charitable institutions of Dublin. You will scarcely credit this, but he actually mentions Dublin. I fear it was a misfortune that he was raised to the mitre. (K: 16 Feb. 1866)

After Cantwell died in 1866 Nulty was obliged to turn to Cullen for help against priests in open revolt against him, and Cullen later told Kirby: 'I suppose in the last years of Dr Cantwell's episcopacy some of the priests did as they liked.' (NK: 29 Apr. 1869)

The other southernmost diocese of the Armagh province, Ardagh, like Meath, did not have the preponderance of Protestants found in the true 'Black North', but its non-Catholic population had been large enough for sectarian tension to be significant. The area was filled with Protestant proselytisers, and government of the diocese had been almost totally abandoned by MacHale's old lieutenant William Higgins, who had shut himself up in his residence, received no one and was drinking heavily. (PFS, XXX, 712-13) Cullen ensured that here a real reformer was appointed to succeed Higgins when he died in 1853. This was John Kilduff, an alumnus of the Irish College in Rome, who had worked with the Vincentians in Paris and Castleknock. Although his name was not on the *terna*, Propaganda nominated him for the appointment. Immediately he began to get the political priests of the diocese back into their pulpits, condemned the secret societies which abounded in the area, brought in religious, and organised missions against the proselytisers. After his death from typhus in 1867 Propaganda secured the appoint-

ment of Neale MacCabe, a Vincentian who had received his
training in the Irish College in Paris. For more than two years
he also carried on the war with the Protestants, to be succeeded
in 1871 by the Roman-trained George Conroy, who had been
Cullen's secretary. An able man who had served the Holy See
in Canada, Conroy governed Ardagh to Cullen's satisfaction,
making sure that the reforming decrees of the Maynooth
synod of 1875 were implemented in his diocese.

Cullen had no trouble in the diocese of Kilmore, where
the bishop, James Browne, a former dean and Professor of
Scripture in Maynooth, was a quiet man who kept his clergy
in tight control. Browne had been bishop since 1827 and
belonged to Daniel Murray's school. He was on relatively
good terms with Cullen, although he always remained a strong
supporter of the National System. His successor, a Maynooth
graduate, Nicholas Conaty, carried on quietly the reform
measures suggested by Cullen from the time he became bishop
in 1865. None of the other northern dioceses were as amenable
to Cullen's wishes as Kilmore, however, especially those in
the true 'Black North', where there were greater numbers of
Protestants and where sectarian antagonism was increasing.

In the diocese of Clogher relations between Catholics and
Protestants had been very good early in the century. When
James Murphy, who was bishop from 1801 to 1824, reported
to Rome on the state of his diocese in 1804 he praised the
help given by Protestants to the Catholics of Clogher who
were without proper chapels. He could cheerfully report
that because of this 'substantial assistance', 'We have lately
got many good chapels erected, and covered with the best of
slate.' (PFS, XVIII, 262-3: 23 Nov. 1804) However, during
the episcopate of his successor, Edward Kernan, who was not
a strong diocesan, the clergy got out of hand in the Catholic
Emancipation era, and great sectarian tension arose in the
area. Then, to add to the troubles in the diocese, the prefect of
the Dunboyne establishment at Maynooth, Charles MacNally,
was appointed coadjutor, succeeding to the see when Kernan
died in 1844.

MacNally was in almost all ways a disaster as a bishop,
allying himself with MacHale and displaying what Cullen
regarded as the very worst characteristics of the new nationalist

form of Gallicanism that was being fostered in Maynooth. He regularly attacked Roman intervention in Irish affairs, while at the same time he avoided duties like a visitation of his diocese, which was not carried out for ten years after his consecration. When he did send Rome a report on the state of Clogher and its clergy in 1853 it was hardly reassuring to Propaganda. The diocese was almost under siege by proselytisers preaching in the Irish language. Towns like Clogher and Enniskillen were dominated by wealthy Protestants, renowned for their bigotry. Although MacNally hoped to establish nuns soon in Enniskillen, there were as yet no religious of any sort in the diocese. As for the clergy, more of them were now resident than formerly, and MacNally thought he was helping them over their great moral weakness, 'habitual intoxication'. Rather than admonishing them for this fault, he now indicated that he understood the reason for it: 'the peculiar circumstances in the country'. These included intimidation by the Protestants, which was so severe that 'we dare not as yet venture to keep the adorable Eucharist in any chapel or church permanently, with the exception of my own oratory, and the chapel of the seminary'. (PFS, XXXI, 649-55: 18 Oct. 1853)

What was especially shocking to Cullen was that as the years went by MacNally seldom held confirmations, associated with his clergy less and less, and spent more and more time in the company of Protestants. His nationalist ideas seemed to have totally disappeared, and at one time he suspended some of his rough-and-ready priests because of their social behaviour at a dinner attended by local gentry. The suspension of priests for trivial misdemeanours soon became habitual; MacNally further annoyed Cullen by keeping diocesan funds in his own name; and on 12 August 1864 Archbishop Dixon reported to Kirby his opinion about MacNally after visiting him:

To speak plainly, Dr MacNally is fitter to be the inmate of some quiet asylum than to occupy his present position. His mind is becoming weaker every day, and his extravagant eccentricities which make Protestants laugh are well calculated to draw tears from reflecting Catholics. (K)

Fortunately for Cullen, MacNally died late in 1864, and his successor, James Donnelly, who had been a professor in the Irish College in Paris, was willing to promote the Ultramontane reform programme. Cullen had earlier sent Donnelly to America to raise funds for the Catholic University, and he was not surprised when under his government some degree of Roman law and order was brought to Clogher.

Another area of Ulster where there was a tradition of Catholic/Protestant accord which Cullen could not appreciate was the diocese of Derry. On 7 December 1788, for example, there had been a great celebration to mark the Protestant rebellion a hundred years earlier, and at a civic dinner over a thousand people, both Catholic and Protestant, had attended. During the day, in a custom that was to last almost to the eve of Catholic Emancipation, the Catholic clergy had marched in procession with their Protestant neighbours:

> Religious dissensions, in particular, seem to be buried in oblivion, and Roman Catholics vied with Protestants in expressing by every possible mark their sense of the blessings secured to them by our happy constitution, and the cordial part they took in the celebration of this joyful day. (*Derriana*, 65)

This accord was to continue to a remarkable degree until the coming of the railways brought this distant part of Ulster more into the mainstream of Irish development.

When John MacLaughlin, who was bishop during the Repeal agitation years, became insane the diocese was administered from 1845 to 1849 by the fiery nationalist Edward Maginn, but circumstances did not allow him to build up a lasting influence. When the unfortunate Bishop MacLaughlin finally died in 1864 his successor was a Maynooth graduate, Francis Kelly, whom Cullen considered to be a traditional Gallican because he had sung the anniversary mass for the obsequies of Archbishop William Crolly. Cullen could never get a satisfactory reply from him about the affairs of Magee College, and generally Cullen had little success in promoting Ultramontanism in the Derry diocese.

West of the Derry diocese was the wild area of Raphoe whose bishop, Patrick McGettigan, belonged to Murray's party, strongly supported the National System, and, as Cullen told Propaganda in 1851, was a garrulous old man who drank too much and mortally offended him by acting as a Charitable Bequests commissioner. (PFS, XXX, 712-13: 28 Sept. 1851) In 1856 Cullen rejoiced that Daniel McGettigan, the vicar-general of the diocese, was elected coadjutor to his namesake. He succeeded to the see in 1861, and although Cullen had disliked him personally from his days at the Irish College in Rome, where he had displayed an unusually independent spirit, he felt he was bound to be an improvement on his predecessor.

Cullen's suspicion that Daniel McGettigan was at heart a traditional Gallican was reinforced when he was assured that not only was there no serious trouble with the Protestants in Raphoe, but there was 'no crime, no processions, no secret societies'. (K: 31 Dec. 1867) Added to this, McGettigan proved to be a friend of Newman, who asked him to preach on occasion. Worst of all from Cullen's viewpoint, the Bishop of Raphoe opposed the infallibilist party at Vatican Council I. When this prelate, who never became a Cullenite, was translated to Armagh in 1870, denying the primacy to Cullen's secretary, George Conroy, Kirby was warned that this would mean 'hard times there and many troubles'. (PM, V, 29) Cullen had had no contact with McGettigan's successor in Raphoe, James MacDevitt, a professor in All Hallows College, and to the end of his life he felt that little in terms of Ultramontane reform had been advanced in the diocese.

Apart from Armagh and Ardagh, Cullen never felt happy about the advance of his mission in Ulster, but the only dioceses where he experienced real despair were those which served the minority Catholic population east of the River Bann, in the counties of Down and Antrim.

The diocese of Dromore, which included the western part of Co. Down, had as its bishop Michael Blake, who had been instrumental in opening the Irish College in Rome after the Napoleonic Wars. Blake belonged to the generation of clergy trained in continental Gallican seminaries late in the eighteenth century, and he strongly supported both the National System and the Queen's Colleges. Cullen was unusually tolerant towards him, however, because of his early work for the Irish

College, and he helped Blake in Propaganda when he had diocesan problems and asked him to preach the opening sermon at the Synod of Thurles.

Although Blake was very old — indeed, close to senility, according to Cullen's informants — he had no intention of accepting the coadjutor that the papal delegate wanted to impose upon him. He had always been a strong Gallican, and in his youth had won considerable notoriety for a debate he had with O'Connell about papal interference in Irish ecclesiastical affairs. Blake was sure that Cullen would force into his diocese an Ultramontanist, and until ill-health forced him to accept as coadjutor with right of succession John Pius Leahy, a Dominican from Cork, he thwarted Cullen's plans for Dromore. Even when Cullen managed the appointment of Leahy, Blake refused to surrender administration of the diocese until the time of his final illness in 1860, when he was eighty-six years of age. Leahy had been President of the Dominican Irish College in Lisbon, had been provincial of his order in Ireland, was renowned as a preacher, and soon showed his willingness to advance Cullen's reform programme in Dromore. In 1872 he reported in quietly triumphalist terms how very Catholic Newry was becoming, and that a new spirit was spreading among the minority people so long considered in Ulster as 'an inferior race'. (K: 24 Oct. 1872)

Cullen's greatest cross to bear in Ulster was the sprawling diocese of Down and Connor in Counties Antrim and Down. When Patrick MacMullan, the bishop, made a report to Propaganda on the state of his diocese in 1814 he noted that there were few 'middling Catholics' in the diocese. Most parishes contained 400 to 500 poor families, and the whole diocese was served by about thirty-five parish priests and a few curates, according to MacMullan's rather vague accounting. The people had absorbed unfortunate ideas from their Protestant neighbours and insisted, among other things, on nominating their parish priests. MacMullan had tried to oppose this 'dangerous precedent', but he confessed to Propaganda that he did not want to displease his unruly flock. (PFS, XIX, 177-8: 12 Oct. 1814)

One popular appointment that MacMullan agreed to was that of William Crolly, a professor at Maynooth who came to

be Parish Priest of Belfast in 1812. Crolly was highly successful in building churches in the predominantly Protestant
town with its growing Catholic population. This programme
was carried out only at the cost of Crolly living frugally with
his curates in one house and enduring continual outrages such
as the breaking of the windows of the presbytery by Orangemen. Crolly himself was absent from his parish for no more
than one month in ten years, and was by any account a conscientious and effective parish priest.

Crolly was also so popular with the Belfast middle classes
that when he was appointed as bishop in succession to
MacMullan in 1825 public dinners were held to celebrate the
occasion, and these were well attended by Protestants. Crolly
then appointed as Parish Priest of Belfast Cornelius Denvir,
who had succeeded the Abbé Darré as a Professor of Theology
in Maynooth. The bishop and the new parish priest shared
the same Gallican theology, worked well together, and did
much to improve the Catholic presence in the community,
particularly in terms of ecclesiastical buildings.

In Rome, however, little appreciation was shown for
Crolly's erecting a new church in almost every parish in the
diocese, the building of a seminary, and the classical college,
St Malachy's, to serve the children of the growing number of
Catholic middle classes that were appearing. When Crolly was
translated to Armagh and received the pallium his letter
to Cullen acknowledging the gift was cold and formal:

> You will have the goodness to ensure His Holiness of my
> unalterable fidelity, prompt obedience at all times, and
> on all occasions, to the venerable successor of St Peter,
> the visible and unerring Head of the Holy Catholic Church.
> (C: 31 Aug. 1836)

Cullen's replies to Crolly were just as distant, particularly
when the new Primate approved the National System, the
Charitable Bequests Act and the Queen's Colleges, as we have
seen.

Neither did Cullen have any friendly feelings towards
Crolly's friend Cornelius Denvir, who succeeded him as
Bishop of Down and Connor by popular local demand. Denvir
had been a moderate during the agitation of the Emancipation

years, but Cullen labelled his attitude 'timidity'. In 1826
Denvir had taken part in a mammoth eight-day debate with
Protestant controversialists, and Cullen never forgot that
during this exercise he had expressed his personal belief that
Protestants could be saved. (*Authentic Report*, 281) Reports
reached Cullen of Protestants attending his consecration
dinner, and Cullen suspected not only Denvir's relationship
with heretics, but even his orthodoxy, for Bishop John
Cantwell had assured Rome that Denvir had cast doubts on
the doctrine of the divinity of Christ as one of 'the weakest
inventions of the human mind'. (C: 24 Feb. 1846)

In reality Denvir was not a timid man. He dealt firmly
with his Protestant counterpart, Richard Mant, during the
famine years, and when serving as a Charitable Bequests
commissioner even called him to account for the suspicious
handling of a Catholic legacy. He was never appreciated by
the Cullenites, however, who considered his good relations
with the government and local Protestants as ideological
weakness. When he succeeded Daniel Murray as a member of
the Board of National Education calumny against him rose
to the point where, in 1857, Denvir was obliged to resign this
commission. Cullen never forgave Denvir for his urging 'united
education as tending to extinguish party animosities and
generating kindly feelings' in evidence he gave to parliamentary
commissioners investigating the state of Belfast Academical
Institute:

> I think it must be an effectual means of suppressing the
> spirit of party, particularly if proper precautions were
> taken to prevent any undue influence or predominant
> power on one side or the other. (Crolly, *Life*, lvii)

Poor Denvir knew that neither Propaganda nor Cullen
really understood the kind of bullying the minority Catholics
had to endure in this part of Ulster as they increased in numbers
and appeared to threaten Protestant supremacy. He tried to
explain his position and his horror of sectarian warfare in a
detailed report he sent to Propaganda in 1845, 'Diocesan
Statistics on Down and Connor'. In it he said the diocesan
seminary was in his own house because of Protestant threats,
and that the chief means of education had to be the National

Schools because there had been no monasteries or convents in the diocese since the time of the Reformation. (BV: 20 Dec. 1845) Cullen, however, ignored such apologetic and listened to the multitude of Denvir's critics, whose letters were so numerous that Cullen told Bernard Smith that he was 'tormented with letters from people there'. (BS: 13 Mar. 1852) Typical of these was one passed on to Smith from a wealthy Belfast merchant, James Canning, who contributed handsomely to the Catholic University:

> It would seem, my Lord, that the Sacrament of Confirmation was to be done away with altogether in this diocese. It is about seven years since the bishop went around and at that time the one fourth of those who were present were not confirmed. The children were examined in such a bullying, threatening, outrageous manner that even those who were well prepared could hardly answer a word. The great majority of them were ordered to stand aside, and they have stood aside from that day to this. Mr O'Loughlin, one of the priests, said in St Malachy's parish chapel today: 'There are 50,000 Catholics in Belfast,' and, said he, 'It is well known that there are only three priests of us to attend to such a number.' (BS: 21 Sept. 1851)

Through Archbishop Dixon Cullen tried to persuade Denvir to give up all his connections with the state and to press on with reform, dividing the huge parish of Belfast to begin with, and doubling the number of priests. Denvir hoped he might have a sympathetic ear in Kirby, and he wrote to him to say that only an Ulster Catholic could understand what 'Orange terror' could mean. He recounted in detail events like O'Connell being driven out of the North, or what happened when religious orders tried to hold missions in Lisburn while two companies of soldiers protected them from a howling mob of Orangemen. (K: 12 June 1854)

Kirby actually was not unsympathetic to the old bishop, who twice refused an invitation to visit Rome because, he said, he had to remain to try to control local sectarian violence which had arisen from a bad beating given to Scripture Readers by irate Catholic countrywomen. Also sympathetic was a long confidential report sent to Rome by Dixon on 10 June

1857; this was based on information given to him by an older priest, who was not an enemy of Denvir. Much of Denvir's trouble came from the 'Presbyterian spirit' among the clergy, who wished to bully the old bishop. Dixon suggested that Rome be cautious in listening to lay reports about him:

> Dr Denvir's natural turn of mind would not, I think, relish what he considered dictation from the laity, and thus their disappointment at times may give rise to some unreasonable murmurings. (PFS, XXXIII, 358-9)

Cullen kept up his pressure, however, indicating that it was no longer possible for Denvir to manage even Belfast affairs with the four curates who lived in his own house. A new spirit had appeared in the Catholic Church even in Ulster, and Thomas McGivern of Ballynahinch, an old Roman friend of Kirby, wrote to say how bewildering this was to old Gallican bishops like Michael Blake and Cornelius Denvir:

> Some of the old bishops of the North who heretofore were wont to visit the royal castle in Dublin say they would continue to do so still but they are afraid of Dr Cullen; indeed, they say, they cannot understand what he means: though in the due course of nature these may be said to be on the eve of being gathered to their fathers.
>
> (K: 1 Dec. 1858)

The usual tactic was then tried to have a reforming co-adjutor appointed, but to Cullen's horror the choice of the clergy was Charles William Russell, the President of Maynooth. He came from near Downpatrick, a breeding-ground for Ulster bishops, knew the North well, and was a remarkably intelligent individual. He was also, in Cullen's eyes, too friendly with the government, had many Protestant friends in high society, showed no enthusiasm for the Catholic University, and was a strong Gallican. Fortunately for the Ultramontanists, Russell pleaded to be excused the appointment. His request was readily heard, and the appointment in June 1860 went to the second choice on the *terna*, Patrick Dorrian, another native of Downpatrick.

Dorrian in earlier years had been enough of a Maynooth patriot for Cullen to harbour suspicions about him, but he was then only forty-six, very energetic, a strong sectarian Catholic, and he promised to give the diocese the firm leadership it needed. Although he came from the Lecale barony, he was not from the same social class as the old well-to-do Catholic farming families, like the Crollys or the Denvirs, and was less likely to fit in with the Protestant ascendancy.

Unfortunately for Cullen, Denvir followed the example of Michael Blake and refused to pass complete administration of the diocese over to Dorrian. He publicly embarrassed nuns brought into the diocese without his consent, refused to allow missions which might provoke the Orangemen, and avoided celebrating high mass or engaging in any ceremony which might provoke the Protestants. On 31 October 1863 Dixon wrote to Kirby begging him to approach Cardinal Barnabo to get a pension for the aged bishop which would enable him to retire, even though he admitted that the shock of losing control of his diocese would hasten Denvir's death:

> Dr Denvir is a man of very good intentions, but the *spiritus timoris* as regards the Orangemen among whom he lives so predominates in him that he is utterly unfit to be left in the administration of the Church in Belfast. Indeed it may be said to a great extent that Dr Denvir's administration has ruined Belfast. . . . Oh for the pen of a Bernard or a Malachy to describe its prostrate condition, its people left as a sheep without a shepherd. (K)

Finally Propaganda acted, and Cullen and Dixon informed the aged bishop in 1865 that he had to surrender administration to Dorrian. A new order now began to appear in Down and Connor — one that was very satisfying to Cullen. A year earlier Dorrian had reported in a letter to Kirby: 'We have some Orange rioting in this town, but if necessary we will be able to keep the fellows quiet.' (K: 10 Aug. 1864) Dorrian proved to be an effective administrator, and Cullen watched with gratification while the new regime he had long wanted was established in Catholic Belfast. Cornelius Denvir died in 1866.

On 31 May 1865 Dorrian told Kirby that he was holding a jubilee in the city, with twenty-four confessors working ten hours a day and many Protestants converting to the true faith: 'a good omen with God's help for our future in Belfast — the stronghold of heresy'. (K) A year later Cullen himself came to Belfast for a triumphal opening of St Peter's Church, and Moran reported to Kirby that a crowd of 10,000 assembled to cheer their newly created cardinal 'in that capital of Orangeism'. (K: 19 Oct. 1866) This event passed without Orange intimidation, and Dorrian pressed on with his reform programme, which included firm measures against the 'Presbyterian' tendency of the laity to dictate to the clergy.

Dorrian was certainly a strong Catholic, and he could make appropriate Ultramontane noises, as he did in the almost ecstatic welcome which he gave to Pius IX's encyclical *Quanta cura* with its Syllabus of Errors:

> I look upon the encyclical and accompanying Syllabus of Errors as the most glorious event of modern times. . . . The Whigs and their supporters must now see the ground taken from under their feet by the condemnation of their views on the questions of Education and the Temporal Power. All who wish to be right will now have no excuse, and I hope bishops and priests will be faithful. They want to be *more consistent*. (K: 6 Feb. 1865)

Dorrian also pleased Cullen by pouring his scorn on ecclesiastical Whiggery and the accommodation politics of the 'Castle Catholics': 'the evil genius of Ireland — a few offices for traitors and starvation and oppression for the rest of the Catholic people', as he told Kirby. (K: 10 Aug. 1864) He kept Rome well supplied with accounts of prelates who dined with officials like the Chief Secretary or helped to elect men who contributed to the Garibaldi fund. Yet Dorrian did have Protestant friends, for example Lord Dufferin, the Lord Lieutenant of Down, a powerful yet benevolent landlord. On occasion Dorrian tried to use this friendship to obtain secular appointments for Catholics who supported him, although he tried to avoid public meetings with Dufferin or, as he said, 'to go where some over-fastidious persons might think I had no business'. (PRONI, D 107/H/B/F: 3 Nov. 1871) This policy of direct negotiation on behalf of Ulster Catholics was not much different from Cullen's own visits to the Castle as cardinal, but Cullen was not very happy about such local initiative.

Neither was he pleased about Dorrian's views on the vexed question of the 'priest in politics'. In 1865 Dorrian expressed his opinion on this matter to Kirby: 'It was unfortunate that the priests were for a time withdrawn from politics for people were thus driven to despair, to combine illegally.' (K: 6 Feb. 1865) Dorrian did not support the Fenians, with their desire for a secular political settlement, but he had no hesitation in encouraging his priests to engage in the kind of political militancy which added to the sectarian divisions in Belfast. He founded a paper, the *Ulster Examiner*, to promote 'the legitimate aspirations' of the Catholic people. This was just the kind of outspoken sectarian publication which gave Protestant extremists the excuse to reply in kind. Dorrian spent thousands of pounds on the paper, which on occasion viciously attacked even Catholics who did not agree with its policies. Eventually local protest against it became so strong that finally Dorrian dissociated himself from it.

In Patrick Dorrian Cullen had what he had long wanted in Ulster — a strong Catholic bishop who would stand up to the Protestants and carry the war into their camp. Cullen rejoiced as he heard of the battling for Catholic cemetery privileges, the building of churches in Down and Connor, and the increasing number of religious brought into Belfast to man its new schools. At Vatican Council I Dorrian sided with the infallibilists, and Cullen should have been well pleased with this able prelate. Dorrian came from the Lecale barony, however, where the Catholics of the well-to-do farming class lived very much like their Protestant neighbours. To a Roman like Cullen their independence of spirit and thought looked as 'Presbyterian' as that displayed on occasion by Belfast's Catholic laity. It seemed to Cullen that, at times, Dorrian presumed like his predecessor that a southern Catholic like Cullen who had spent most of his life in Rome could tell Ulster Catholics very little about their problem of trying to live with their fierce Protestant neighbours. To the end of his days Cullen never felt comfortable over what was happening in Down and Connor, nor did he ever assume that Patrick Dorrian was ever in the true sense an Ultramontanist.

3. *The Disestablishment of the Church of Ireland*

When the religious census of 1861 revealed no great increase in the number of Protestants in Ireland, in spite of the intensive proselytising campaign of the missionaries supported by massive English funds, the conviction grew among many that the religious establishment in the country could no longer be supported. In an age of political reform the propping up of an institution serving only a minority of the population appeared unjust and embarrassing. The problem was what to do with the wealth of the Church of Ireland, for it was clear that disendowment would accompany any act for disestablishment.

In 1865 Lord John Russell sent an envoy to Rome to discuss what Rome would suggest should be done with the wealth of the Church of Ireland if it was disestablished. (DAA: 29 Nov. 1865) In England the movement for disestablishment became significant among the dissenters, who formed the Nonconformist Liberation Society. Manning persuaded the English Catholics to lend support to what these unlikely allies were seeking, but Cullen told Kirby that he thought the establishment would find some way of surviving:

> The great question now occupying public attention is the disendowment of the Protestant Church. I fear little will be obtained. The Protestants will set their opponents to fight about the application of church revenues.
>
> (K: 2 Jan. 1867)

He could not resist joining in the assault, however, and as he began skilfully to direct the Irish Catholics in the disestablishment campaign, uniting them in support of the English Nonconformists, the *Times* of 16 November 1868 commented on the strange 'union of Cullen with Knox'.

Direction of the Irish campaign to serve the Ultramontane mission was not easy for Cullen. Many plans were suggested about how to dispose of the wealth of the Church of Ireland, one of the more interesting being that of Aubrey de Vere, the famous convert friend of Manning, Newman, Monsell and Lord Dunraven. He had to be taken seriously, but Cullen was very uneasy over what de Vere suggested — that at least some of the Protestant revenues should be given to the Catholic Church in Ireland. Cullen was further upset when de Vere's suggestion was supported by David Moriarty, the Bishop of Kerry.

Cullen saw instantly that such a move would bring about that which he had fought against for so long, at least a partial 'pensioning' of the Irish clergy. This would divide the Irish Catholics, and if the Protestants took advantage of the division, as they surely would, disestablishment might be postponed indefinitely. In the spring of 1867 he developed his thought for Kirby, urging that his opposition to accepting any Protestant revenues be passed on to Propaganda:

> If we ask for anything, all parties will agree to leave things as they are rather than consent to endow us. The best thing for us is to look on and do nothing — we cannot approve of the application of the ancient church property to secular purposes — but much less can we be satisfied that it should remain in the hands of those who use it for the injury of religion. If the parliament take it from its present holders, and apply it to good services, they render us a service, though we cannot approve of such a thing. At all events no one asked our opinion, so we need incur no responsibility. (K: 22 Mar. 1867)

The problem for Cullen, however, was the insistence of Manning and other English Catholics, who wanted to make sure some of the wealth at least was used to help Irish Catholicism. Cullen was furious over the meddling of the English Catholics, sharing the opinion of Moran, who told Kirby: 'I hope the good English gentlemen will mind their own business and not be allowed to interfere at all in our Irish questions.' (K: 12 Apr. 1867)

Fortunately for Cullen, Rome accepted the wisdom of what he was suggesting, and when the bishops met on 1 October 1867 to discuss the disendowment options Cullen revealed that his own brief was endorsed by Cardinal Antonelli, the papal Secretary of State. Cullen had worried how MacHale might react to the suggestion that the Protestant wealth should be applied only to public services, but 'the Lion', having registered his disapproval, left quietly after the first of the three days of the meeting. He did not object to joining with the others to give tacit agreement to Cullen's plan, however; Moriarty also agreed, and Moran wrote to Kirby that evening to say: 'It was a glorious thing to see all unanimously adopting the principle of sacrifice in order to preserve unsullied the liberty and independence of their sacred ministry.' (K)

MacHale's reluctant endorsement of Cullen's plan turned to active support early in 1868, once the Anglicans in England and Ireland began to rally in support of their religious establishment. With considerable satisfaction Cullen told Kirby that the 'John Bull' party, by supporting their 'politico-ecclesiastical institution', were provoking 'a great roar from the Lion'. He knew now that if there was no wavering over the question of endowment, steady pressure on Gladstone and his party would finally bring down the much-hated Established Church in Ireland. (K: 13 Feb. 1868)

To Cullen the coming victory was but one triumph in the advance of the universal Counter-Reformation directed by the Supreme Pontiff. He sent Kirby a letter to be passed on to Cardinal Antonelli thanking him for directing the strategy in Ireland, for it was only in the light of Rome's wisdom and protection that Cullen could proceed. Success now seemed certain, he declared, and once more Catholics would be ascendant in their own land: 'If the [Established] Church be put down, all Ireland will soon become Catholic.' (K: 27 Apr. 1868) With this great victory apparently about to become a reality, the Catholic press began to laud Cullen as a religious tribune of the people. The *Dublin Evening Post* of 31 July 1868 also reminded its readers that Cullen 'held the highest spiritual dignity short of the supreme pontificate'. When he fell ill the same paper indicated the international importance of Cullen, for whose return to health public prayers were offered in Italy, France, Belgium, Spain, Portugal and Germany, as well as in Ireland.

When Disraeli in debate said that the Catholics were trying to hand the very government of England over to the pope, Cullen told Kirby that at last this enemy of the faith was showing 'the cloven hoof'. (K: 8 Oct. 1868) In fact, he was delighted when in both England and Ireland disestablishment was viewed as a papal victory, and he welcomed the inevitable

Protestant 'No Popery' rallies when they began. What they did was to confirm for Cullen how few friends the Church of Ireland really had. The *Dublin Evening Post* of 6 February 1868 had reported a poorly attended meeting of the Protestant Defence Association at which 'less than a fourth of the Protestant peerage, and less than a fifth of the Protestant magistracy was represented'. As for the rank and file of Protestants, their absence showed clearly that they were no longer willing to stand up and fight to defend exploitation of Ireland by the Coles and Knoxes of Ulster or the Beresfords and Bernards of Munster. Yet Cullen knew that the victory was more than an Irish one. Disestablishment meant the end of Protestant ascendancy, and the increase of papal influence in the land as Catholic ascendancy came into being. He would have agreed with the prognosis of Bishop William Delany of Cork, who told Kirby:

> Now men of wealth will not send their sons into the Protestant Church. The labourers in their fold will become proportionate to the numbers of their congregations and must in many districts of this part of the country dwindle for a long time and finally die out. (K: 2 June 1868)

Cullen well knew what was heralded by the disestablishment of the Church of Ireland.

Many of the Irish Protestants also knew what this Cullenite victory signified. In an editorial comment on 30 January 1869 the *Dublin Evening Mail* warned the jubilant Catholics that in the long run they would gain 'little from the church which the pontiff rules'. Its agents, like Cullen, served the cause of Rome, not Ireland. When Cullen won so many concessions through his tactic of controlled agitation, 'give what we ask, or else', he served not the Catholics of Ireland, but the papacy. His policy 'cuts itself off from the nation' and operates against 'the nation from a point outside it, and always will do so'.

On 13 March 1869, shortly before the first reading of the bill to disestablish and disendow the Church of Ireland, Cullen was triumphalist enough to suggest to Gladstone that one of the two Dublin cathedrals should be given to the Roman Catholics: 'We would fill it and preserve it at our expense.' (BM, 44419) He told Kirby about this suggestion eleven days later, but also warned the Irish agent that this should be kept quiet. Kirby agreed, adding that he hoped that other cathedrals, such as St Canice's in Kilkenny, would also be surrendered to the Catholics. One of Kirby's Kilkenny correspondents wondered how the edifice could be reconsecrated: 'If it comes into Catholic hands, they will have no small difficulty in knowing what to do with the foul Protestant carcasses buried in the floor.' (K: 8 May 1869) The hopes of Cullen and Kirby were not to be realised, but from this time Cullen hoped that more concessions might be won from Gladstone. He told Monsell on 21 May 1869 that it might be expected that he would be made Secretary of State for Ireland, as 'Mr Gladstone is so anxious to do justice for Ireland'. (NLI, 8317) Cullen soon found, however, that Gladstone was not to be influenced in any way that was not of benefit to his party. Cullen was never to begin to approach what the *Dublin Evening Mail* of 19 November 1869 said he really wanted, complete ascendancy 'not alone over the Protestants of Ireland, but over the legitimate authority of the state itself. . . . Mr Gladstone must kiss the dust at the feet of the pope's representative or he does nothing.'

Cullen's promise to control Irish Catholics in return for further concessions helped for a time to maintain his association with Gladstone and the Liberals. But the brief alliance ended when it became clear to the government that Ulster Protestants threatened to be more of a problem than Cullen and his followers. Until Disestablishment the Orange Order had had limited appeal to Presbyterians, but after 1870 more and more of them joined, bringing new financial support to the organisation. For a few years, from 1869 to 1873, some Orangemen in places like Monaghan, thoroughly disenchanted with the Liberals who had sacrificed the Church of Ireland, even became anti-British Home Rulers. (*Times*, 9 Sept. 1869) This extreme reaction soon passed with the Conservative victory of 1874, but by that time the Liberals had realised that their future support for Cullen had to be limited indeed. Long before this, however, Cullen had decided that nothing more could be gained from Gladstone, who had in addition mortally offended the cardinal by his criticisms of Vatican Council I.

After the Disestablishment victory Cullen showed little compassion for the humbled Church of Ireland, whose members were in a state of psychological shock after this significant change in the articles of the Act of Union which had so long protected them. Cullen told Kirby that although many had advised against it, he could not resist the temptation to hold a 'Te Deum for the downfall of the old church of Elizabeth'. (NK: 13 Aug. 1869) When the reorganisation of the Church of Ireland began he wrote to Kirby to gloat over the Protestants 'fighting gloriously' over the form of their new free church, which, Cullen prophesied, 'would become a Babylon':

> I am trying to prepare another letter in which I will recommend that Protestants not be wearying themselves endeavouring to make up a new church. I will advise them to try to find out the church which Christ intended, which can be known by the notes, one, holy, Catholic and apostolic. (NK: 9 Sept. 1869)

A week later Kirby was informed that while the Protestants were holding their first synod, 'which was a scene of discord', Cullen with the Lord Mayor and other dignitaries were attending a 'grand dinner' at Clonliffe, where the cardinal 'gave the health first of the Pope, then the Queen . . . Mr Gladstone and all who contributed to pass the church bill'. The food for this feast, 'half a buck', was provided by the Lord Lieutenant, to Cullen's immense pleasure. (NK: 16 Sept. 1869)

4. *The Defence of the Papacy*
Some Irish Catholics compared Cullen's Disestablishment victory to O'Connell's Catholic Emancipation triumph, but whatever euphoria Cullen allowed himself was qualified by his knowledge of the desperate situation of the papacy at that time. This resulted from what Cullen saw as the long and bitter war against the temporal power of the papacy which had been waged by Italian nationalists supported by Protestant funds. At the very time that Cullen had won his local victory in Ireland the Eternal City itself was threatened by the enemies of the Supreme Pontiff.

From 1850 to 1859, when Cullen was establishing his

authority in Ireland, affairs in the papal states were relatively peaceful because of Austrian aid and a French garrison in Rome. But Pio Nono had been hissed in the streets of Bologna in 1857, and the pope's temporal power was denounced by the liberal press throughout Europe. In England papers like the *Times* encouraged prominent Evangelicals like Lord Shaftesbury or political rulers like Palmerston in their criticisms of the despotic misrule of Pio Nono in his territories. At the same time European and British liberals praised Count Cavour's build-up of power in Piedmont and warmly endorsed his intention of putting Victor Emmanuel on the throne of a united Italy.

In 1859 a crisis came when Napoleon III announced that he could no longer protect the papal states and Cavour announced their annexation. This development thrilled British Protestants, and Kirby's cousin set him an account of what was happening in Ireland:

> I am roused from my usual lethargy by the virulence of the articles with which the Protestant press of this country now teems in consequence of the sudden change which affairs in Italy have taken. During the past month every Protestant, no matter what his station in life . . . predicted the fall of the Pope, or, as they call him, the man of sin.
>
> (K: 31 July 1859)

Cullen's immediate response to the 'rabid bigots' and their unholy joy was a long pastoral in the autumn of 1859 defending the temporal power of the papacy. It was widely distributed not only in Ireland and England but also on the continent. Its major argument was hat there would be no discontent in the papal states but for 'foreign influences' such as Bible societies, and secret political organisations, both of which were financed by English Protestant money. Now, as in the days of Arnoldo da Brescia, Hus, Wyclif, Luther and Voltaire, the teachers of falsehood were those who wanted the destruction of the pope's temporal power:

> Were Rome delivered up to the domination of infidels, were the aspirations of Lord Shaftesbury and the evangelicals realised and Gavazzi and Mazzini enthroned in the

Vatican, who can contemplate the consequences without being sorely afflicted? (*Dublin Letter*, 31)

In Ireland Cullenite bishops like Laurence Gillooly of Elphin, John Kilduff of Ardagh and John MacEvilly of Galway held large popular meetings to protest against British interference in papal affairs. Even the mild Joseph Dixon in isolated Armagh stood up to local Orangemen and made a public statement in support of the pope, telling Kirby of his action in a subsequent letter:

> It is the first time, indeed, that I have taken on my own account, in a public document of this kind the title of Primate of All Ireland. I did so because I thought it would give more affect [*sic*] to my protest against the treatment of the Holy Father. Indeed, I intended this principally for the newspapers as a demonstration, such as it is, against the conduct of our English neighbours. (K: 25 Oct. 1859)

Special prayers and intentions of the rosary were offered at a legion of altars throughout the land, and the excitement among the people rapidly mounted.

Cullen usually avoided controversy with the proselytisers, but when it came to defence of the papacy his tactic was to obtain as much publicity as possible for the cause of the pontiff in the hope of winning the support of Ireland's Catholic population. When Sir Culling Eardley, a prominent Evangelical, wrote to ask him what evidence he had that Shaftesbury and other Protestants were collecting money to arm outlaws and banditti in the papal states, Cullen published several long letters in reply that were obviously written for public consumption. Essentially what Cullen said was that it was common knowledge that Shaftesbury was president of a committee dedicated to such a purpose, and that 'it was great hypocrisy for men to call themselves evangelicals whilst they were fomenting treason and sedition and trampling on the Gospel which recommends obedience and submission to higher powers'. (PM, II, 320) When a report reached Cullen later of a ship stopping in Cork harbour loaded with 28,000 muskets for Garibaldi's followers, he told Kirby that the whole cargo was probably paid for by Sir Culling Eardley and his friends.

After these exchanges in December 1859 Cullen was fully at war, deluging the Irish College in Rome with speeches he had made in defence of the pope, and similar apologies made by men like Lord Normanby, a former Lord Lieutenant of Ireland, which attacked Palmerston, Russell and the Italian revolutionaries. At the same time he organised a Confraternity of St Peter's to raise money for the papal forces, and he began to harry those bishops like John Cantwell of Meath who dragged their heels over the papal cause. As for MacHale, Cullen watched him carefully, telling Kirby: 'Dr MacHale is croaking, but we do not see what he is doing.' (K: 10 Feb. 1860) When Sir John Pope Hennessy, MP for King's County, was hesitant in his support of Cullen's crusade, scorn was heaped on him as a graduate of the Queen's Colleges, an apologist for the Orangemen rather than a representative of the Catholics of Ireland. Protestants generally looked on in stunned amazement at the sheer fury of Cullen's attack. After one Dublin meeting whipped up by the Ultramontanists the *Belfast Newsletter* of 3 January 1860 recorded one correspondent: 'Rome was saved from the Gauls in ancient days by its geese. Some Irish Romanists of the present day do not see why they should not have their turn.'

The support for the papal cause was not all that Cullen wanted, however. George Butler, then Dean of St Mary's, Limerick, told Kirby that whereas most of the priests and 'the rabble' were on the side of the pope, much less enthusiasm for Italian affairs was being shown by the Catholic aristocracy, gentry, merchants and professional men. (K: 7 Mar. 1860) These were the Catholics who had substantial means, and Cullen knew that what support of a financial nature the papacy received from Ireland would of necessity come from the common people. The *Belfast Newsletter* of 7 February 1860 had noted that the attempt to charm the money out of the pockets of poor Catholics was initiated by Cullen acting not as Archbishop of Dublin but 'in his real character as Legate of the pope'. Nevertheless, the amounts garnered were significant. Poverty-stricken Kilmacduagh and Kilfenora sent £565 and Achonry raised £672, according to Kirby. (K: 5 July 1860) The wealthier diocese of Kildare and Leighlin sent £2000 of the £5000 to be raised during the year. While the collecting went on Cullen carried on his polemical war with the Protestant press, which pointed out that the large sums leaving Ireland were being used to prop up a despotic regime dedicated to the denial of liberty and a constitution for the people of Italy.

Meanwhile a volunteer papal army had been raised by Major Myles O'Reilly, and the thousand or so men who formed the Irish Brigade arrived in Italy safely, heard mass in St Agatha's, the Irish College chapel, and prepared themselves to meet the Piedmontese forces who were crossing the papal frontier. The actual fighting lasted only a few weeks, with the Irish taking part in the siege of Perugia, a battle at Spoleto, a major engagement at Castelfidardo, and the final surrender of the papal forces at Ancona in September 1860. They had substantial casualties, and those taken prisoner suffered greatly.

Before the actual fighting Cullen was in high hopes of a papal victory, and on 10 July 1860 he regaled Kirby with stories of the fighting spirit of those about to go to Italy as 'emigrants' to enlist as soldiers in the papal army:

> One of the emigrants before going was travelling in a railway carriage with an attorney from Drogheda by name Rowland – a great Orangeman, who cursed the Pope most heartily. The emigrant after a long dispute closed proceedings by saying: 'Well as you are such a friend of the Pope, I must leave you his blessing before we part', and with that he gave Rowland such a blow between the eyes that he left him senseless on the railway. (NK)

Cullen had little to say about the Irish soldiers who fell in the fighting, however, or those captured after the sieges of Spoleto and Perugia, and it is interesting that the prelate who at times could be so precise remained vague about Irish casualties, even when he was trying to raise funds to help their return to Ireland in the autumn of 1860.

This venture into militarism shocked Cullen because it cost the pope so much and gained him so little. On 22 November 1860 he wrote to Kirby to discuss the state of the papal treasury and to express his fear that after their ordeal the returning soldiers would have little use for the papacy:

> I suppose the whole expedition must have cost the pope

£70-80,000. I was afraid at the beginning that great mischief would be done by the men returning to Ireland. They
appear to be all satisfied — so we shall not have to complain
that religion has been impaired. All however speak with
the greatest contempt of the Italians. The people will
always return that feeling towards their southern brethren.

(NK)

It cost another £10,000 to get the surviving troops back to
Ireland, and Cullen wondered where the money would come
from when the country was so impoverished and the expected
payments of Peter's Pence were still uncollected. On 27
December, when the final cost of the Irish Brigade had become
clear, Cullen vowed to Kirby that never again would he
support military adventures. (NK)

Cullen nevertheless resolved to raise as much money as
possible for the pope in his difficulties, in spite of a major
depression in the country between 1859 and 1864. Bad
weather added to the falling off of trade because of the
American Civil War, and the people suffered greatly. Kirby
received letter after letter from bishops apologising for their
inability to get money out of the distressed people to help
the papacy. Typical of these letters was one from the Cullenite
Laurence Gillooly of Elphin, who reported in 1861 that he
could send only £84 to the pope:

> The distress now is so great . . . throughout this diocese
> that I must to my great regret suspend for some time the
> monthly collections for His Holiness — or rather I should
> wish to have the permission of His Holiness to continue
> the collections and to give the amount as from him to the
> parochial relief committee which I have established.

(K: 17 Dec. 1861)

Another Ultramontanist, William Keane, who had been Vice-
Rector of the Irish College in Paris, told Kirby in 1862 that
although he had published a special pastoral urging the people
to give all they could for the papacy, such was their distress
that 'this state of things must greatly affect the Peter's Pence
collection'. (K: 12 Mar. 1862) The situation was then so bad
that prayers were being said in Paris for the starving people of
Ireland.

When the papal delegate could send only 12,500 francs to Rome in the summer of 1862 he blamed the small amount on the failure of three harvests in a row because of incesssant rain. In his report to Propaganda he also noted that without the cost of keeping up the Established Church the people would have had more to give, and he observed that the English were doing little to help the distressed Catholics of Ireland. (PFS, XXXIV, 510-11: 11 Aug. 1862)

In 1863 Cullen thought up a new scheme to raise funds for the Holy See — a papal lottery. It seems to have had considerable success, and William Keane was able to tell Kirby proudly how some of the poor people 'pawned their clothes in order to raise money for the purchase of bazaar tickets'. (K: 9 Feb. 1863) Charles MacNally of Clogher suggested that an engraving of the pope should also be given to everyone who bought a papal lottery ticket. In spite of this tactic, and unrelenting pressure on bishops and priests alike, the poverty of the country defeated Cullen's best efforts to raise funds for the papacy at a time when the economic situation was causing people to leave Ireland in their thousands. Cullen's protégé in Connaught, John MacEvilly, writing to Kirby in 1866 to apologise for the 'widow's mite' that Galway was able to send to the papacy that year, described the desperate plight of the people in his city at that time:

> The peculiar poverty of Galway is owing to the fact that one half at least of its population is made up of the evicted from their lands in Connemara. These poor people are thrown into boats, are conveyed to Galway and flung on our quays to provide for themselves as best they can. These poor people — good Catholics, greatly resigned to God's holy will — endeavour to find shelter in our lanes and alleys and live upon the chance providence may cast in their way. In this diocese we have prayer without intermission for the Holy Father. (K: 6 Oct. 1866)

This plea for the needs of the poor did not deter Cullen's resolve to help the pope in any way that he could. He told Archbishop Spalding of Baltimore in 1864 that although there was 'a great deal of distress' in the Dublin archdiocese, £2200 had been collected there and sent to the pope during

the year. (DAA: 12 Nov. 1864) During 1867 his letters to
Kirby show his great concern over the activities of the Fenians
and the presence of cholera in the land. Of more immediate
importance to him at this time, however, was the raising of
£2000 in Peter's Pence from Kildare, and another £1000
from Ferns. The war against the Italian nationalists was going
badly, and the regiments of Papal Zouaves raised throughout
the Catholic world seemed no match for the insurgents. Young
Irishmen were serving in Franco-Belgian regiments rather
than serve under Englishmen, and Cullen told Kirby that he
was concerned that they would return to Ireland as embittered
as those who had served the papacy earlier in the Irish Brigade:

> They all went out enthusiastically for the Pope, what way
> will they come home? Probably filled with hatred of
> everything Roman. They will produce a bad impression,
> and this imperfection will be widely felt as the men are
> from every part of the country. (K: 20 Feb. 1868)

Cullen's worst fears were realised when some of the Irish
Papal Zouaves proved to be as ill-disciplined and hard to control as had the Irish in Italy in 1860. He tried to get Kirby to
send the malcontents home as quickly as possible before news
of how they were being treated in the papal army became
widely known. The news could not be contained, however,
and by the time the papal army was making its last stand
before Rome Cullen realised how unpopular the war had
become in Ireland:

> Our Peter's Pence has run dry since the account of the
> Zouaves arrived. We got from June to January about
> £6000 — since the beginning of the year scarcely anything.
> (K: 22 Mar. 1868)

5. *The Vatican Council*
By 1869 almost all the bishops in the Church had been
appointed by Pius IX during his long reign, and, as in Ireland,
the great majority of them now shared something of his
spirit of militant Ultramontanism. It was thus with considerable assurance that the pontiff called for the meeting of
the bishops in Vatican Council I to further the centralising of

authority and to intensify the battle against liberalism in the
Church and in society. Cullen knew of the plans for the
council from early 1869, and he took a prominent part in
organising the agenda for the 700 bishops who assembled in
Rome in December of that year. As he informed Kirby, he
was also one of those who were strongly in favour of a
declaration of papal infallibility being made at the council.
(K: 2 Nov. 1869)

Only twenty-one bishops from Ireland attended the council,
though the bishops from overseas dioceses raised the number
of Irish present to almost a tenth of those assembled. Most of
the Irish bishops were infallibilists, but Cullen suspected that
Gallican ideas were still harboured by MacHale, Derry, Furlong, McGettigan, Leahy of Dromore, and Moriarty, all of
whom 'kept aloof' from infallibilist cabals. They seemed to
be aligned with those liberal bishops who, Cullen believed,
hoped that a revolution in France or a war in Europe would
put an end to the council before any legislation could be
passed. Cullen was particularly uneasy when informants told
him of meetings between Moriarty and the liberal Bishop
Dupanloup of Orléans.

Cullen was completely in his element during the council.
(Mac Suibhne, *Ireland*) His letters home to his secretary George
Conroy show him marvelling at the cost of an exhibition of
Christian art organised by the pope: 'I am afraid that the
Roman finances are not equal to so gigantic an undertaking.
A pity the pope has not funds at his disposal; if he had he
would surpass Sixtus V.' (PM, V, 64) He also loved the political
in-fighting, telling Conroy in detail of the shifting alliances
which developed as the debates went on: 'Our kind bishops
have become quite hot on the infallibility, and Dr Moriarty
and Dr Leahy are in Coventry. Dr MacHale scarcely mixes
with the Irish bishops at all.' (PM, V, 66)

Cullen spoke for the first time on infallibility on 19 May
1870, lashing out at his opponents, as he told Conroy, 'like
an Irishman at Donnybrook Fair and I knocked them to
pieces'. (PM, V, 103) Included in his argument was the 'proof'
that from the Synod of Thurles back to the days of Queen
Elizabeth the bishops of Ireland had been supporters of infallibility. On the following day the Gallicans had their

opportunity to put their case, one of them being MacHale, whose speech was disdainfully described by Cullen as 'lame and undecided', a defence of Gallicanism, 'a compendium of Delahogue'. Later Cullen reported that MacHale's exposition of old Gallicanism was considered by almost all the bishops as 'a terrible failure': 'Some of the French bishops said they always heard he was a giant, but that they now find he is a mere pigmy.' (PM, V, 109) When MacHale made a second speech in June, arguing from the evidence in parliamentary papers that Murray, Doyle and other important Irish prelates had never been Ultramontanists, Cullen dismissed the speech as confusing and 'childish', and so bad generally that the Irish bishops were furious with him for making such a fool of himself.

Although Cullen also tried to dismiss Moriarty's speech in June as a long and 'very tiresome web of sophistry' which 'did a great deal to lower the character of Ireland', he was worried by the fact that Moriarty and MacHale were now supported by Irish-born overseas bishops such as Peter Kenrick of St Louis and Thomas Connolly of Halifax. He confessed to Conroy that at this stage of the council he felt that 'after all our orthodoxy . . . Ireland takes a worse place in the Council than any other country'. (PM, V, 131) To counteract this negative impression Cullen made a second speech which included a new and simpler definition of infallibility. This was the definition eventually adopted by the council. The pope personally told Cullen how indebted they all were to him for this contribution. As for the Irish dissidents, they all absented themselves from the council when final approval was given to the doctrine of papal infallibility.

After the bishops returned to Ireland Cullen told Kirby that all the prelates, including MacHale and Moriarty, finally agreed to sign a letter to the people referring to the pope as infallible teacher in the Church, and this Cullen believed was enough to show that they 'publicly proclaimed their faith'. (NK: 4 Aug. 1870) He was still worried lest MacHale might make a public statement against infallibility, however, and he indicated to Kirby how closely he was having 'the Lion' watched when he made a triumphant return to Tuam to meet his clergy and laity:

The priests presented a flaming address but they say nothing about the Council. His Grace in his reply to the address and his afternoon speech refers to the Council. In one place he speaks of an infallible executive in the Church always admitted by all — but he appears to pass over the infallibility of the Pope. His speeches will mislead the people. . . . I think it would be well if Dr MacHale could be induced to come out more distinctly. (NK: 22 Aug. 1870)

His anxiety over what MacHale might do about infallibility never lessened, and after a Dublin placard appeared asking 'Who is right on the infallibility, Dr MacHale or Dr Cullen?' Kirby was told that 'Whatever Dr MacHale may say in defence of his silence, he ought not to let his name be used as a cloak for heresy.' (NK: 9 Sept. 1870)

Cullen made sure that the faithful knew now with what great respect the Supreme Pontiff was regarded by all the Church. When meetings were held by Protestants to support Bismarck in his attack on the Catholic Church, Cullen ordered papal encyclicals to be read in all churches so that 'everyone will know what Peter says'. (K: 9 Dec. 1873) On hearing that the new Italian government had taken over church property in Rome, he encouraged the organisation of parish meetings to protest against this 'spoliation' of the property of the Holy See. He also began to press for further collections of money for the pope, though the economic plight of the people had hardly improved since the disastrous years of the 1860s.

One indirect outcome of the Vatican Council was Cullen's final disenchantment with Gladstone after the latter's publication of *The Vatican Decrees* in 1874. Cullen was shocked by the work, telling Kirby that it was 'most wicked and malicious' and 'animated with the spirit of Bismarck' in the unmeasured language it used to attack the pope:

Lord Palmerston said at one time of Gladstone that the man will terminate his career either in a madhouse or in the Catholic Church. It is very probable that he is going mad, but humanly speaking there is no hope for his conversion. But God may take him as he did St Paul and make him a good Catholic whether he likes it or not — Gladstone's pamphlets all seem to indicate that he is sinning knowingly and willfully. (K: 25 Jan. 1875)

Gladstone's work also had the side-effect of arousing deeper suspicion of Newman's orthodoxy, occasioned by the appearance of his *Letter to the Duke of Norfolk on Occasion of Mr Gladstone's Recent Expostulation* (1875). Cullen was not at all happy about this pamplet and told Kirby that in it Newman clearly 'lays down principles or makes assertions which are calculated to weaken the authority of the Vatican Council'. In no way could Cullen see Newman's work as a real criticism of Gladstone's ideas:

> Among other things you will see that he seems to put the authority of a Council more on the acceptance of the world than on the confirmation of the Pope. He also assumes that Honorius was condemned as a heretic by the General Council. The *Times* of yesterday reviews it in seven columns and concludes that it is a splendid defence of Gladstone's pamphlet. (K: 17 Jan. 1875)

The worst was yet to come, however. Gladstone seized upon the rejoinders of Newman and others as an excuse to publish *Vaticanism: An Answer to Replies and Reproofs* in 1875. He included a summary of how Catholic thought in Ireland had developed from the time of James Doyle and his Gallicanism, and he directly attacked Ultramontanism as a threat to liberalism in the world because it sought to control the minds of men:

> It is, in my opinion, an entire mistake to suppose that theories like those of which Rome is the centre are not operative on the thoughts and actions of men. An array of teachers, the largest and most compact in the world, is ever sedulously at work to bring them into practice. Within our own time they have most powerfully, as well as most injuriously, altered the spirit and feeling of the Roman Church at large; and it will be strange indeed if having done so much in the last half century, they shall effect nothing in the next. (*Vaticanism*, 16)

However furious Cullen was over this attack on Ultramontanism by the English statesman who had served his cause so well in the past, he was too good a general to waste his time in attacking Gladstone. His concern was the Roman reformation of the Irish Church, and matters like the Liberal alliance simply ceased to be of great concern to him once he was sure it was no longer of benefit to his advance. In late August and early September 1875 Cullen held a plenary council at Maynooth to consolidate the initiatives began at Thurles twenty-five years earlier. Describing the meeting to Kirby, Cullen allowed himself one of his rare moments of satisfaction over what had happened:

> I have just returned from Maynooth where we finished the work of the synod yesterday. All the bishops of Ireland were present except for Dr Walshe of Kildare who was unwell, and Dr Flannery who lives in France . . . everything harmonious . . . no dissensions. Dr MacHale . . . quite complacent and made no resistance . . . he was near dying on one of the days . . . dropped down and remained senseless . . . but recovered. . . . We made many new decrees . . . kept the Synod of Thurles as our guide . . . adding new ones. . . . Dr Croke was of the greatest service . . . a fortunate circumstance that he was appointed.
>
> (K: 21 Sept. 1875)

Cullen would have been less enthusiastic about Croke if he could have foreseen his future resurrection of Gallican nationalism to the vexation of Rome, but in 1875 it appeared that the 'Cullenisation' of the Irish Catholic Church was a *fait accompli*. Cullen's report to Rome on 1 December 1875 reveals his personal satisfaction that his twenty-five years' use of legatine authority was finally beginning to bring results. (PFS, XXXVI, 449-58)

In spite of his quiet feeling of triumph over the new Roman spirit he had nurtured in the Irish Church, Cullen indicated in the year before his death that he had no intention of relaxing his vigilant watch over the enemies of the faith, including Mr Gladstone. He warned the Lord Mayor of Dublin how dangerous an enemy the English statesman was:

> I beg to state that Mr Gladstone for several years has made it his business to assail and misrepresent in a most offensive manner our present venerable pontiff. . . . I think I may safely say that no other statesman, however hostile, ever ventured to treat Pius IX as he has thought fit to do.

Besides, Mr Gladstone has been incessant in his attacks on the Vatican Council. Though Mr Gladstone rendered or attempted to render great services to Ireland, for which she is most undoubtedly grateful, yet it cannot be forgotten that for the last five years he has displayed a wonderful activity in injuring our religious interests.

(PM, V, 246: 5 Nov. 1877)

The 'religious interests' that were of primary concern to Cullen were those connected not with Ireland but with the authority of the papacy. However signal the service Gladstone may have rendered to Irish Catholicism through the disestablishment and disendowment of the Church of Ireland, once he displayed his anti-papal animus he was Cullen's foe. By the end of the Vatican Council the Irish cardinal who had been so instrumental in presenting the compromise formula of papal infallibility was generally recognised as 'excessively reactionary' even among the conservatives who supported Pio Nono. Many believed that Cullen would have been viewed as a 'potential candidate' for the papal throne if Pius IX had died in the early 1870s. (Walsh, *Vat. Council*, 58) Fortunately, from the standpoint of liberal Catholicism, Cullen was too ill to be considered in the conclave following the death of Pius IX in February 1878; but if he had become pope, it is likely that his policies would have been very similar to those of his predecessor. In the universal mission of the Church the extension of Roman authority would have been given the same kind of priority that Paul Cullen gave it in Ireland.

VII

The Inquisition

1. *Munster and the Limits of Legatine Authority*

Cullen had considerable satisfaction over the surface accord
that he had brought about by the time of the Maynooth
synod of 1875, but he knew that Gallicanism in its traditional
form, or its mutation into revolutionary Irish Catholic
nationalism, was still to be reckoned with in all parts of the
country. He knew, for example, that his authority in Ulster
was inhibited by the traditional Gallican tendency to try to
come to terms with the majority Protestant people, except
perhaps in Down and Connor, where he had hope that Patrick
Dorrian was initiating a new era. Elsewhere Cullen knew he
had to battle with the essence of Gallicanism, for most Irish
churchmen the assertion of local authority over and against
that of the papacy. When the Primate, Patrick Curtis, and
Oliver Kelly, the Archbishop of Tuam, and James Doyle of
Kildare and Leighlin gave evidence before the parliamentary
commissioners investigating the state of Ireland in 1825, they
all appeared shockingly Gallican to Cullen because they
insisted upon the inviolability of local custom. Archbishop
Kelly had said bluntly that if papal bulls or rescripts were not
compatible with local traditions, then Irish bishops felt it
their duty to 'remonstrate respectfully and not to receive
their regulations'. (PP, 1825, VIII, 240)

To someone as zealous as Cullen local custom was not to
be tolerated, but the problem was how to deal with it without alienating bishops and clergy from the mission he was
trying to promote through his legatine authority. None of
them was going to welcome a Roman 'inquisition' into
diocesan affairs, even if the object was the proclaimed one
of delivering them from that superstition or any other 'state

of bondage' which Cullen found so prevalent in the Irish Church, as he told Propaganda on 31 January 1852. (PFS, XXXI, 78-81) The problem was that many of them did not recognise their 'state of bondage', as Cullen found out when he tried to press for reforms in the province of Munster.

His original tactic on arriving in Ireland was similar to that which he had used successfully as Roman agent. To win the allegiance of bishops to his cause rather than to that of Murray or MacHale, Cullen used every possible Roman influence to put them into a position of indebtedness to him. One of those whom Cullen deliberately courted was Timothy Murphy, who had become Bishop of Cloyne the year before Cullen came to Ireland. Murphy was important to Cullen because he might be persuaded to oppose local Catholic support of the Queen's College in Cork, which was strongly defended by William Delany, the Bishop of Cork. The opportunity to help Murphy came when Kirby let Cullen know of a request Murphy had made to him:

> I have at one period suffered much from colds in the head, and whether it be in consequence I know not, but it has so happened that my hair has fallen off and therefore I have humbly and respectfully to solicit from the Holy See permission to avail myself of the very desired covering and protection of a wig. (K: 6 Sept. 1850)

Cullen, of course, was only too willing to help the ailing Murphy and spoke highly of him as a man of zeal and apostolic spirit. When Murphy wanted to separate the diocese of Ross from his administration, and to have as its bishop his vicar-general, William Keane, Cullen agreed and also helped him when he went to Rome in 1854 for the definition of the Immaculate Conception. The most that Cullen could get out of Murphy over the issue of the Queen's College in Cork, however, were the letters expressing concern which were passed on to Kirby on 16 November 1853. Murphy admitted that the new institutions were causing 'invidious comparisons', 'morbid jealousies' and 'ungenerous suspicions' among the bishops, and he deplored that such feelings inevitably led to 'heartburnings and scandals'. (K) But Murphy showed no inclination to oppose this popular local college, in spite of

Cullen's expressions of goodwill, though he did support Cullen on other issues, such as suppressing 'stations'.

William Keane, who became Bishop of Ross in 1850, was to end his days as a fervent Ultramontanist, dying in January 1874 after receiving the apostolic benediction sent through Kirby. He had been for fourteen years Vice-Rector of the Irish College in Paris, and Cullen believed he would be obedient to the Holy See. Yet on 20 October 1853 Keane joined Delany of Cork in a deputation to Rome to complain about Cullen's attempt to end the 'stations' in Munster, and the papal delegate was far from happy over this attempt to defend 'local liberties and customs'. Cullen for a long time felt that Keane was an instinctive Gallican, a bishop who would seek authority from the populace rather than Rome, and who would protect local customs rather than serve the reforms begun at Thurles.

Cullen's opinion of Keane was revealed when Timothy Murphy of the balding pate died in 1856 and an immediate struggle began in the Munster community to find his successor. One of the candidates was William Keane, who addressed an election dinner in Fermoy to promote his translation to Cloyne. Cullen in disgust told Kirby what took place at the gathering:

> He spoke exactly as if he came to canvass for votes. He praised the parish priests etc., and then he proclaimed that he would not be the man to curtail the just rights of the priests, that in Ireland politics and religion were synonymous. In the end he said, of course, that priests should conduct themselves properly and according to the dignity of their state. The political part of the speech was received with thunders of applause. I could not but look on such a way of acting as rather low. (NK: 17 Jan. 1857)

In spite of this opinion of local ecclesiastical electioneering and all that it implied in terms of his ultimate control of Keane, Cullen approved of the choice of the priests, who nominated the Bishop of Ross as *dignissimus* on their *terna*. After his election no bishop was more faithful than Keane in building and staffing religious schools in the Cork diocese. He founded St Colman's, Fermoy, as a diocesan college and con-

tributed much to the Catholic University. He was an infallibilist
at the Vatican Council, and in later years Cullen made increasing use of him, especially in the field of primary education.

In the Munster diocese of Waterford and Lismore Cullen
found how troublesome a bishop could be when he was
popular in the community. This was the case with Nicholas
Foran, who had succeeded the Gallican William Abraham in
1837 and tried to maintain order in the diocese until his
death in 1855. Very much a local man, he had many friends,
but also many enemies, and by the time Cullen came to
Ireland it was clear that the diocese was in a state of near
anarchy. Dominic O'Brien, the President of St John's College,
Waterford, commented on the 'cold and apathetic' attitude
of the bishop and criticised his failure to control the attendance of Catholic children at the Model School in the town.
(K: 26 Feb. 1852) Michael Walsh, Vicar-General of Ossory,
whose parish bordered with Waterford, also reported on the
scandals in the neighbouring diocese where there were no
poorhouse chaplains, the money for the purpose being
pocketed by the parish priests. The priests, said Walsh, were
generally a bad lot, neglecting the countryside which was
filled with proselytisers, and ignoring the reforming statutes
of Thurles:

> The parish priests monopolise all and generally speaking do
> no duty. They merely give a slender support to the curates,
> and £10 a year salary, whereas the salaries of the parish
> priests average £400 per annum, notwithstanding emigration
> etc. (K: 31 May 1853)

As for the bishop, he was ignored by the factions of parish
priests who had long established a kind of ascendancy over him.

Kirby came from Waterford, and Cullen also knew well
what the local situation was. His choice of a successor to
Foran was Dominic O'Brien, who had studied at Propaganda
College in Rome and who promised to be a reliable reformer.
He certainly made a good beginning, harrying the Catholic
families whose children attended the Model School and
encouraging much church-building. In November 1859 he
reported to Cullen and Kirby how well the diocese was
progressing:

We are going on here, thanks be to God, as well as ought to be expected. Our seminary flourishes, our religious houses are prosperous and improved in observance, new churches of a superior style of architecture are rising in several parts of the diocese, and what is better still, devotional practices are carried on with as much fervour as ever.

(K: 23 Nov. 1859)

O'Brien did not mention the faction-fighting among the clergy, however, nor the tradition of defying their bishops which had existed since the days of William Abraham. O'Brien had been born in Waterford, and when it came to an issue like the management of farming charities he found himself caught up in local political passions. His deep roots in the community did not allow him to transcend the clerical warfare, and by 1872 Cullen was telling Kirby that O'Brien was very much in need of a reforming coadjutor:

Poor O'Brien was unable to do anything for some years and it is said that things are in disorder — drinking, playing cards, etc. common among priests. . . . Hear if you can what Propaganda thinks of the matter. (K: 23 Nov. 1872)

Propaganda agreed that a coadjutor was needed in Waterford, and as soon as O'Brien heard of this he tried to persuade Cullen that one of his own supporters should be appointed.

Cullen, of course, knew what a disaster would follow from such a move, and on 23 December 1872 he forwarded to Rome a letter from the Parish Priest of Cahir, who indicated the dangers of such an appointment, apart from the fact that O'Brien's nominee was sixty-four years old and already rather feeble:

He would be dependent too much upon the wisdom and control of *his friends*. He would not urge on the progress of religion and education as the present crisis demands. . . . The future will be a dull, monotonous, lifeless continuance of the past. We need an infusion of a new animation of the spirit of the priesthood. *Can any one* who may have shared in or witnessed our lethargy be the fit one to lead in the dispelling of the same? (K)

The coadjutor eventually agreed to by Propaganda was John Power, a native of Cappoquin, who succeeded as diocesan on the death of O'Brien in 1873. Power had been recommended by Archbishop Patrick Leahy of Cashel, and during his episcopate he conscientiously and patiently advanced the Ultramontane reform programme among the unruly clergy of the Waterford diocese.

Patrick Leahy, who had succeeded Michael Slattery as Archbishop of Cashel in 1857, was one of Cullen's most dependable supporters. A good theologian, an eloquent preacher and an accomplished scholar, he had been Professor of Scripture and then Vice-Rector of the Catholic University until his elevation. Leahy befriended Cullen, urging him to be cautious when he was injudiciously inclined to give too much support to John Miley in the Irish College imbroglio in Paris. This monition brought from Cullen a request that Leahy, with his deep understanding of Irish prejudices, keep him from further false steps: 'I am so weak and so timid that any little thing might put me wrong.' (CA, 1858/34) Leahy served Cullen well in the Disestablishment debate and made an excellent speech at the Vatican Council, and Cullen missed him greatly when he died in 1875. In spite of all his fine qualities, Leahy had little aptitude as a diocesan reformer, and Cullen therefore resolved to secure the appointment of a strong administrator who would carry on the Ultramontane mission after Cullen himself was gone.

One person to be considered for the post was Thomas William Croke, a native of the Cloyne diocese, who had studied at the Irish Colleges in both Paris and Rome. Distinguished as an eloquent preacher and an administrator, he had been appointed Bishop of Auckland, New Zealand. When ill-health made him available for the appointment to Cashel he was immediately considered by Cullen, who had first met him as a brilliant student in Rome and had consecrated him before he left for New Zealand. (CA, 1870/6) While the appointment was pending, John MacEvilly, the Bishop of Galway, wrote to Kirby to assure him that 'His Ultramontane views are I believe very decided.' MacEvilly went on to stress how very pro-Roman Croke was:

In these days it is not sufficient that a subject be learned
or pious, qualities no doubt absolutely necessary, but his
principles should be well known to be in perfect accordance
with the teaching and spirit of the Apostolic See on the
leading question of the day, education and kindred subjects.

(K: 3 Apr. 1875)

Cullen, after consulting Kirby about how Croke might control
the Cashel clergy who paid scant attention to the reforming
decrees of Thurles, concluded it would be a good thing if the
appointment went to Croke. Such was Croke's confidence in
the authority of Cullen that once he knew he had the cardinal's
favour he wrote to Kirby to say that he would wait at Ancona
until he heard he should go to Rome for the pallium. (K:
18 Apr. 1875) Croke was to prove to be an effective diocesan,
and Cullen was not to live to witness his vehement nationalism
which greatly embarrassed Rome in the future.

The most able of all the Munster bishops with whom Cullen
had to deal, with the possible exception of Croke, was David
Moriarty, who became Coadjutor Bishop of Ardfert and
Aghadoe, or Kerry as it was generally known, in 1854. Before
his elevation he had been Vice-Rector of the Irish College in
Paris, and President of All Hallows, the missionary college in
Drumcondra. By the time he became diocesan on the death
of Cornelius Egan in 1856 he had begun a very successful
counter-mission against the proselytisers in the Dingle peninsula, and it would have been expected that Cullen would be
pleased with the energetic labours of this young and energetic
bishop. Such was not the case, however.

Although Moriarty told Kirby that he hoped Rome would
back him fully in his attempts to get the highly politicised
priests of Kerry back into spiritual mission (K: 17 Jan. 1855),
Cullen always suspected him of being at heart a Young
Irelander, largely because of his friendly relations with Protestants. Shortly after Moriarty had taken control of diocesan
administration Cullen wrote to Kirby complaining about the
new bishop making a contribution to an old-established Protestant orphan society. This gesture, said Cullen, was typical
of Moriarty, who had once been a Young Irelander and was
now showing the pro-Protestant sympathies of that group of
liberal Catholics:

> To contribute to a Protestant orphan asylum in Kerry is worse than elsewhere because there are numbers of apostates there who should not receive any sanction whatsoever. . . . His justification is that he wishes to separate the old Protestants from their modern missionaries and he says his contribution tends to do so effectually.
>
> (NK: 21 Aug. 1856)

Moriarty also offended Cullen by his ideas on education. He thought little of Cullen's policy of 'condemning it in theory and adopting it in practice' and told Kirby that in Kerry 'the children were admirably instructed wherever there were National Schools, and where there were not the people are in ignorance of the catechism'. (K: 1 Sept. 1859) He hoped that the Holy See would 'tread lightly' in condemnation of a system that greatly helped the Catholics. Cullen, of course, was informed of Moriarty's sentiments, which he attributed to a Gallican bias, as he did his tendency to be less critical than other bishops about the Poor Law system. (PFS, XXXIV, 131) When Moriarty joined with C. W. Russell of Maynooth and other Gallicans to resist Cullen's attack on the Model Schools the papal delegate was sure that he was somehow in collusion with the government.

After the death of Archbishop Dixon in April 1866 Cullen feared that the government might exert pressure in Rome to have Moriarty translated to the primacy. Both Cullen and Moran wrote to Kirby begging him to use all his influence to ensure that this did not happen:

> If the government had a voice they would translate Dr Moriarty who sides to a great extent with them on the educational question. He has been lately in London for several days treating, I believe, with the government about education and the marriage laws. I have not been able to discover what recommendations he has made.
>
> (K: 15 May 1866)

Cullen's anxiety increased when the *Dublin Evening Mail* on 15 August 1866 in a very conciliatory editorial praised the peaceful campaign of 'zeal, tact, ability and unwearying energy' of Bishop Moriarty which was bringing great benefits to the Catholics of Kerry, including a new cathedral, a new

Franciscan church and even a 'falling off of everything Protestant . . . in this county'.

The primacy did not come to Moriarty, but he attempted to remain as conciliatory with Cullen as he was with the Protestants, describing the newly created cardinal as 'a Borromeo for the Irish Church'. (K: 22 June 1866) Earlier he had told Kirby how much he encouraged support for the papal cause in his diocese, describing how a crowd of 20,000 had gathered in front of the cathedral to listen to orations in both English and Irish in support of the Holy See:

> In one of these Fr Matt O'Connor asked them if they had arms in their hands where they would put them. An Irish shout from the crowd answered him — 'into the guts of the enemies of the Holy Father'. I never enjoyed such a day of real fun. (K: 14 Dec. 1859)

Cullen, however, had no intention of being misled by such blandishments. Moriarty remained in his eyes very much a Gallican, and he knew that the Bishop of Kerry had pleaded the authority of 'local custom', as in a letter to Kirby in which he opposed the law that nuns' confessors should be changed every three years. (K: 20 Mar. 1862) Nothing convinced him more that Moriarty served the government than his famous diatribe against the Fenians after their abortive rising in Kerry in early 1867. Full of indignation at this overreaction, which Cullen considered farcical after what he had experienced in Rome, he wrote to Kirby to condemn Moriarty's folly:

> Dr Moriarty's saying that eternity was not long enough and hell not hot enough for the Fenians has given great offence. I wish he could be called to account for it. He is now publishing a letter to the clergy of Kerry in which he praises the parsons as models of every virtue, whereas we all know that they are the greatest enemies of everything good. I just happened to see a proof sheet where these outrageous praises are given. As it was shown to me in confidence I cannot write to Dr Moriarty about it — but if I get it in any other way I will write to him — I will send you a copy as soon as I get one. Dr Moriarty was first an ardent Young Irelander, now he has gone into the

opposite extreme. In the *Connaught Ranger* of last week
there is a fierce letter against him signed Patrick Lavelle.
The worst of the letter is that it tells a good deal of truth.

(K: 22 Feb. 1867)

The cardinal's own hostility to the Fenians, and to Patrick
Lavelle, was such that he was in no position to press his
charge against Moriarty's intemperate sermon, and it is
probable that what he most resented here was the independent action taken by the Bishop of Kerry — as well as his
friendship with Protestants. He also heartily disliked a plan
Moriarty advanced for disestablishment and disendowment
of the Church of Ireland, and was no less displeased with the
evidence he gave to a parliamentary committee on the Ecclesiastical Titles Bill, in which, Cullen told Kirby, 'he said plenty
of foolish things'. (K: 29 July 1867) Then Cullen heard
rumours that the government was trying to persuade Moriarty
to become one of the royal commissioners looking into
primary education in Ireland. He told Kirby:

I fear Dr Moriarty will be put forward by the high Catholics
as the representative of the Christian body — he would
perhaps defend mixed education and propose that Catholics
should take a portion of the income of the Protestant
Church. (K: 18 Aug. 1867)

When the rest of the hierarchy persuaded Moriarty and C. W.
Russell of Maynooth not to act as commissioners Cullen
expressed his relief to Kirby, noting that with such 'weak and
yielding men' the commission 'would probably have gone
great lengths with the government'. (K: 1 Oct. 1867)

Moriarty was of concern to Cullen not because he had
once been a Young Irelander, as Cullen always claimed, but
because he threatened to affirm once more the kind of
traditional Gallicanism that seemed to have disappeared with
the death of Daniel Murray. Although Moriarty had not
originally been happy about being sent to 'the bogs of Kerry',
he soon developed a deep love for the people he was called
upon to serve; and whatever the issue which challenged him,
his concern was the welfare of the Kerry people, not the
furthering of Cullen's Ultramontane mission. In fact, as he
told Kirby many years later, he could never appreciate Cullen's

fear that the Church would indebt itself to the demonic state: 'to put our neck into the halter'. (NK: 13 May 1870) When the Board of National Education suggested curtailing some of the rights of clerical managers of schools Moriarty, together with Delany of Cork and Butler of Limerick, was willing to consider the suggestion on its merits rather than ideologically. Fortunately for episcopal unity, the government dropped this suggestion, but only after tension had increased between Cullen and Moriarty. The latter's alliance with the anti-infallibilists at the Vatican Council did nothing to bridge the gap between the two men, nor was Moriarty's friendship with Newman, nor his continuing correspondence with Kirby, ever appreciated by Cullen.

Cullen would have argued from his lessons in Munster that the really dangerous Gallican element in the Irish Catholic Church in his day only appeared when a bishop allied himself not with the government as the old Gallicans had done, but with local prejudices and passions. When that occurred it took all his legatine authority and administrative skills to deal with the situation, as occurred in the early 1860s in Limerick, where the bishop, John Ryan, was senile to the point of childishness. When Cullen was made aware of the situation in 1861 he employed his usual tactic of prevailing upon Propaganda to nominate a reforming coadjutor with right of succession. This was George Butler, Dean of Limerick, who had impressed Cullen by raising funds for the Irish Brigade, by supplying figures on the numbers of Protestants and Catholics in high places in Limerick, and by opposing the Model Schools.

Poor senile John Ryan was dominated by some of the local clergy, and they had no intention of allowing Butler to take over administration of the diocese. They persuaded Ryan to oppose Butler's reforms, and Butler soon found that he was resented by most of the local population. One of them was an unsavoury young priest, James Hickie, a relative of the old bishop. Having been forced to leave Maynooth, Hickie had later obtained ordination in France, but when he applied to enter the Dublin archdiocese Cullen had refused him because of his 'bold or impudent appearance'. (K: 27 Mar. 1863) Hickie had then gone to Limerick and persuaded his 'feeble and not of sound mind' relative to appoint him to one of the chief parishes of the diocese, Rathkeale. Butler told Hickie that because of the old bishop's mental incapacity the collation would be considered invalid. Hickie, however, ignored this warning, hurried down to Rathkeale, where the previous incumbent had just been buried, and had himself inducted.

A further development in the scandal arose from the fact that Bishop Ryan was very wealthy. Cullen told Kirby on 27 March 1863 that his estate was based partly on his own savings, 'but very much of trust monies received by him from time to time for charitable and diocesan purposes'. (K) Hickie also knew of the bishop's wealth and persuaded him to change his will in his favour and to make him the will's sole executor. When Butler intervened in the affair local passions were aroused, and soon Butler was reporting to Kirby that the question had become a very serious one: 'Dr Ryan's grand-nephew, a dissolute, drunken creature who lives at the bishop's and a young woman who lives there as a quasi-housekeeper — whether these two or myself shall have the administration of the diocese'. Butler went on to say that when he sent an administrator to take over Rathkeale and to oust Hickie from the parish there was almost a riot. Butler described this incident to Kirby on 10 April, by which time it was clear that he was not in control of the situation:

> A large mob of the worst characters, the scum of the town, paraded the streets in a violent manner crying out that Fr Hickie should not be disturbed. They afterward proceeded to the chapel and nailed the door of the House of God. The curate of the place who was a partisan of Fr Hickie was quietly looking on at this outrage which a word from him would have stopped. (K)

Cullen's advice to Kirby was for Rome to be very careful in its handling of the affair: 'The opponents of Dr Butler are all from Cashel, and in some parts of Ireland the spirit of clanship runs very high.' (K: 15 May 1863) The truth of this was realised when Archbishop Patrick Leahy of Cashel tried to tidy up the affair and Cullen discovered how much Leahy was resented because all three families, Ryans, Hickies and Leahys, came from the same area.

Popular resistance of this kind was the greatest impediment

to Cullen's legatine 'inquisition'. What was to be done, he asked Kirby, when gambling and drunkenness were common among the Limerick clergy and many of them managed by one way or another to amass as much wealth as Dr Ryan?: 'What a shocking thing to hoard up so much money in these times of misery.' (K: 18 May 1863) Or what was to be done when at a second attempt by Butler to install an administrator at Rathkeale the clergy were completely cowed by a mob that again nailed up the door of the church, denying the people mass on the following Sunday? (K: 23 Aug. 1863)

George Butler fell greatly in Cullen's estimation when he displayed a lack of resolution during the Ryan/Hickie imbroglio, and Cullen was not surprised when the new Bishop of Limerick supported David Moriarty in some of the disputes relating to the National System. Cullen, however, was not to be intimidated by the Limerick mob which tried to defend local custom, any more than he was impressed by those who argued for an ecclesiastical rapprochement with the government. Gallicanism in any form was anathema to him, and he used every possible pressure to ensure that Hickie submitted to Butler and that the 'miscreants' who had seized the chapel were compelled to surrender it. Bishop Ryan was then persuaded to draw up a new will. Cullen told Kirby how shocked he was at the great wealth of the Hickie family, with Father Patrick Hickie, the Parish Priest of Doon, where the proselytisers had made such an advance, being almost as rich as John Ryan: 'He must have been a wonderful man to put together such a sum in these bad times.' (K: 6 Aug. 1864)

2. *The Harrying of 'the Lion'*

The political situation in Connaught presented Cullen with a challenge of such peculiar magnitude that we will leave it to the next chapter for detailed study. The problem of the 'priest in politics' was, however, only one aspect of John MacHale's lack of government in his province. There were many other abuses resulting from his Gallican tendency to accommodate ecclesiastical policies to the demands of the local populace which was divided into belligerent factions over such issues as the Protestant proselytisers, the success of the Queen's College in Galway, and the barring of National Schools from the area.

Yet Cullen could do little to control the situation in Connaught directly. He knew well that if he could be found guilty of direct intervention in MacHale's disastrous administration an appeal would be made to local prejudices against the tyranny of Cullen's 'Italian mission'.

Cullen could, however, attempt to reinforce those clergy in MacHale's province who welcomed the assistance of Rome, and he could make use of his tactic of appointing reforming coadjutors whenever the opportunity presented itself. One area where the MacHaleite bishop had many enemies was Killala, where there was still a bitter legacy among the clergy who had been on the losing side in the O'Finan crisis. Bishop Thomas Feeny, who succeeded O'Finan, was always opposed by, among others, the poor mad priest of Kilfian, Edward Murray, who had earlier been removed by Feeny from Crossmolina. When Murray was not writing to Propaganda about mystical experiences or visions, he was reporting on the bishop's activities with a 'concubine', his indiscreet visits with her to Liverpool, his simony and his tyrannical rule of the diocese. (PFS, XXXV, 801: 25 Aug. 1866) In spite of Murray's watch-dog activities, he was never able to obtain sufficient evidence to persuade Propaganda to depose Feeny, but other reports indicated to Cullen that the Bishop of Killala's rule of his diocese was far from ideal. He finally managed to impose a coadjutor upon Feeny in 1871, two years before the old bishop's death, but he was shocked to learn later that the new bishop, Hugh Conway, received only £250 a year for his labours in Killala.

MacHale did little to protect Feeny, perhaps because the latter's way of life bordered on the scandalous, but also because Cullen pressed his attack against 'the Lion' on other fronts besides that of Killala. One of these was the diocese of Elphin, whose bishop, George Browne, had ruled since coming from Galway in 1844. Browne recognised Cullen's power when he came to Ireland, and on 15 January 1853 he had tried to curry Roman favour by sending Propaganda a report on the shocking state in the neighbouring diocese of Ardagh, whose bishop, William Higgins, had just died. (PFS, XXXI, 362) Other reports to Propaganda were made by Archbishop Dixon and Cullen himself, and Browne's offering was gratuitous, though it did indicate to Cullen that the Bishop of Elphin was willing to distance himself from MacHale and support the Ultramontane mission. Browne made this decision very clear to Kirby a few months later when he wrote to him after a visit to Rome, where his conversion to Ultramontanism was completed, and expressed his new resolve to support the Catholic University and the papal delegate:

> Some few bishops are not disposed to be co-operative with him in the university matter as they should and ought. There is great jealousy. I hear much but do not wish to become an accuser of any of my brethren. O what a blessing that I went to Rome where my eyes were opened or I might be caught in the . . . resistance. (K: 15 Nov. 1853)

Cullen and Kirby were not impressed by Browne's courage in defecting from the MacHaleite camp, however, for they knew how much he feared what a legatine inquisition in Elphin was bound to discover. The Elphin priests were renowned for violent political agitation, and the extent of their failings as pastors was made abundantly clear by the countless scandal-mongering letters which were sent to Kirby and Cullen when it became obvious that Browne's loss of health and control would necessitate the appointment of a coadjutor.

When the MacHaleite nationalists tried to promote the cause of the Maynooth patriot John O'Hanlon, Bishop Browne indicated that O'Hanlon's supporters in Elphin were a pack of immoral scoundrels notable only for their 'concubinage'. (K: 2 Nov. 1855) Archbishop Dixon had already supported Browne's opposition to O'Hanlon by reminding Kirby and Cullen of his lack of piety and other failings. (K: 13 June 1855) This correspondence helped Cullen to persuade Propaganda that the appointment should go to a sound Ultramontanist, Laurence Gillooly, an alumnus of the Irish College in Paris and a Vincentian.

Gillooly soon found he was very much in need of Roman support in his attempt to initiate reform in Elphin, for he soon found that the 'immoral scoundrels' among the clergy were not prepared to accept reform without a struggle. Almost as soon as he was appointed a printed broadsheet was distributed in the diocese, and a copy was sent to Rome. Written by an 'Elphin Priest' on 22 July 1856, it claimed that during the time the newly appointed bishop and his brother were students in Paris they had been financially supported by the immoral earnings of a prostitute sister who plied her trade in both Roscommon and Dublin. (PFS, XXXII, 837)

A vicious attack on Bishop Browne was also launched by the extreme nationalist Henry Brennan, Parish Priest of Dysart and Tessara, who sent his accusations not only to Propaganda but also to Cardinal Fransoni and even the pope. In a long recitation of past grievances Brennan described Browne's administration as 'most overbearing, insolent, harsh and tyrannical in the extreme'. As for Browne himself, he was said to be completely dominated by a group of drunken priests led by Martin O'Reilly of Athlone, renowned as a seducer who regularly shipped his pregnant victims off to America. Browne had never opposed O'Reilly, not even when he deliberately encouraged a wealthy alcoholic to drink himself to death after making his property over to him. When the will was published it caused such a scandal that a faction-fight had followed in which one man was killed. Browne had long persecuted Brennan, forcing on him a curate who had denounced him to his parishioners as morally unfit to hear confessions. Furthermore, he had accused Brennan of having an immoral relationship with his housekeeper, whom he referred to publicly as 'Queen Bess', and had even tried to kill Brennan by running him down with his coach. What had finally driven Brennan to appeal to Rome was a denunciation by Bishop Browne from the altar of his own church at Tessara:

> His lordship told my people there from the altar that it would not be expected they would bend the knee to confess to one whom they hated, that his lordship came there to establish liberty of conscience, and that his lordship would by and by take the vote of the people to see if a majority of them were for writing to Rome against continuing me as their parish priest.
>
> (PFS, XXXII, 643-9, 657: 7 Apr., 10 Dec. 1856)

When Gillooly was questioned by Propaganda about the truth of these charges he had to admit that there were some 'intriguing, selfish and crafty priests' who were opposed to any attempt to implement the reforming decrees of the Synod of Thurles:

> The selfish, the slothful, the ignorant, the ambitious, will cheerfully return to the old system made for and by themselves. . . . I am represented by Dr Browne's friends . . . as stern and imprudently zealous, and the coercive measures which I threatened to employ in one case are sedulously held forth as a sample of my system of government. With a clergy so habituated for years to cabals, dissensions and contempt of authority, and with a bishop . . . who has no fixed rule or principle of administration . . . it would be impossible for me at any time or under any circumstances to govern the diocese with and under Dr Browne.
>
> (PFS, XXXIII, 145: 10 Feb. 1857)

On the other hand, the enemies of Browne were highly politicised priests who had no intention of accepting the new coadjutor who wished to promote Cullen's 'inquisition' in the Irish Church. Henry Brennan for one seemed intent upon opposing every reforming measure.

MacHale kept out of Elphin affairs until Browne died in 1858, leaving the agitation against reform to Henry Brennan and his followers. By 1862, however, Gillooly had to admit to open warfare between himself and 'the Lion':

> The archbishop's feelings are anything but friendly towards me. He regards me as his adversary in the province and attributes to my influence the control he has lost over the majority of the other bishops of this province — in a word my opinions and feelings on many public questions do not agree with him — I have been obliged to oppose him even in our synods and did so successfully and these are crimes which he can never forget nor forgive. (K: 26 Oct. 1862)

A few months later Gillooly told Kirby how much he was under attack by MacHale, who was doing everything in his power to oppose the reforms that were needed in Elphin: 'It is not a pleasant thing for me to grapple with the Lion, but seeing there was no other way of protecting my clergy and flock from great spiritual evil I could not hesitate to do so at any risk.' (K: 10 Jan. 1863)

The trouble in Elphin entered a more critical phase in the summer of 1863 when Gillooly reported that anonymous letters attacking him and his family were in general circulation throughout Connaught, and that the most probable author of them was MacHale himself. On 12 September he reported further that MacHale was saying that if Rome was brought into the dispute, 'he would publish an account of the entire proceedings and justify his conduct before the country'. (K) This challenge was too much to bear, and MacHale was reproved by the pope himself for his imprudent support of Henry Brennan and the other Elphin dissidents. Brennan himself was obliged to submit to Gillooly and to express publicly regret for his disobedience. The result was a sadly disaffected diocese, and it was now widely recognised, as in the *Times* on 24 January 1872, that Gillooly was an out-and-out Cullenite. Still Gillooly pressed ahead with his reforms, using even the extreme measure of denouncing from the altar those who opposed him, a practice which was bitterly complained of in a letter sent to Propaganda. (PFS, XXXVI, 143: 29 June 1874)

Cullen's real base for the containment of MacHale was the diocese of Galway, from where he could monitor directly developments in neighbouring Tuam. There he arranged for Propaganda to nominate as bishop in 1856 a Mayo priest, John MacEvilly, who after a brilliant course at Maynooth had become a Professor of Scripture in the Tuam seminary. His predecessor as Bishop of Galway was the ineffectual Laurence O'Donnell, who had practically abandoned Oughterard to the proselytisers and paid no attention to Roman rescripts about the Queen's Colleges. In Cullen's eyes the only good ever performed by O'Donnell was in bringing MacEvilly with him to Thurles, where the latter caught the eye of the papal delegate. Shortly afterwards MacHale, who also thought highly of MacEvilly's abilities, appointed him president of the Tuam seminary.

When O'Donnell died in June 1855 Cullen approached MacHale about an administrator for Galway, mentioning as his choice John Derry, the Bishop of Clonfert. MacHale's reply was to suggest either his own nephew Thomas, of the Irish College in Paris, or Peter Daly, a staunch Gallican and

a supporter of the National System who for political purposes occasionally allied himself with MacHale. When Cullen
took advantage of the confusion among the Connaught
bishops and clergy to ensure the nomination of MacEvilly,
MacHale was furious; and Cullen reported that ever since
MacEvilly's appointment had become certain 'the Lion' had
turned against him. (K: 13 Dec. 1856)

One of the undesired innovations that O'Donnell had
tolerated was a Model School in Galway, which by 1863 was
well established with over 300 pupils. Such schools had no
local managers, and Cullen had opposed them strongly from
the time he came to Ireland, using the argument that they
were Queen's Colleges in miniature. MacEvilly agreed with
Cullen, and from the time he became bishop he sought to
build up a Catholic school system staffed by religious, and to
dissuade Catholic parents from sending their children to the
local Model School. Attendance there was to be considered a
reserved sin for which parents would be called to account.

MacEvilly's attack on the Model School brought into the
lists against him Peter Daly of the parish of St Nicholas
North. He refused to take a census of Catholic children attending the school, refused to read pastorals attacking it, and
boldly attended meetings at the Mechanics' Institute which
MacEvilly had forbidden. The bishop described to Kirby in
detail how contumacious Daly was:

> I sent him the circular to be read on Sunday 4 January.
> He took it up on the public altar, and looking at it said in
> a scornful tone — 'there is a paper here about schools
> which I have nothing to say to', etc. and then flung it
> from him. (K: 6 Mar. 1863)

The result of this action by Daly was a badly divided Catholic
community, with those who attended the Model Schools
being accused of accepting government bribes. Worst of all,
MacHale began to support Daly, promising an investigation of
what was going on in Galway. In the summer of 1864 MacEvilly
told Kirby that he was being attacked in the *Patriot*, 'the
avowed organ of Dr MacHale', which MacEvilly further
characterised as a 'malicious Garibaldean rag . . . sometimes
heretical, sometimes schismatical, and at all times personally
offensive to the head of the Church'. (K: 14 June 1864)

Cullen expressed to Kirby and MacEvilly his amazement that MacHale would support Model Schools, part of the National System against which he had battled for so long, and put the aberration down to 'the Lion's' natural truculence. As for Daly, Cullen had no sympathy for a priest who wrote in the Orange *Galway Express* and was seen attending a ball at a Protestant mansion. Unfortunately for the supporters of Cullen, however, when MacEvilly finally suspended Daly, Propaganda's confirmation of the suspension was vague about the date when it would become effective. According to MacEvilly, this allowed Daly to continue his 'dodgery' and to be 'as obdurate as ever'. (K: 4 Dec. 1864) Daly's campaign included publishing in the *Freeman's Journal* of 24 December 1864 an apology for upsetting his bishop. This was passed on to Propaganda, together with long letters about his sufferings at the hands of his diocesan, who 'without cause harassed my old age by a constant persecution, and never ceased to inflict the most unprovoked insults and injuries on me to the open scandal of the faithful and the ruin of ecclesiastical discipline'. (PFS, XXXIV, 1210-18)

By this time the Model School was almost deserted of Catholics, so MacEvilly lifted his suspension of Daly. This did nothing to change the old priest's behaviour, and, as MacEvilly was soon reporting to Kirby, he continued to 'conduct himself outrageously':

> Think of a parish priest going into a Protestant church with the remains of a young Protestant gentleman, and within the church standing by the coffin next to the parson with his head reverently uncovered while the latter was performing the funeral service. . . . The deceased young gentleman was a Queen's College student. The coffin was carried into the church by the students, Catholic and Protestant. *All* of whom remained during the service. But what blame to them with the example of an old priest before their eyes. (K: 10 Mar. 1865)

Three years later Peter Daly died, but during the months before his death he did all he could to annoy MacEvilly, giving balls and dinners at which 'the chief guests are the low Protestants, the chief agents of proselytism', and at the dances

the execrated polka was often part of the entertainment.
Daly could well afford these extravagances, MacEvilly pointed
out to Kirby, because of his great wealth:

> He is a shocking old man eaten up with pride and avarice.
> He is worth £30,000 and never contributed a farthing to
> any charity. He is becoming worse every day. I endeavour
> to ignore all he does. (K: 6 Oct. 1866)

A direct result of the publicity given to the MacEvilly/Daly
feud was the notoriety given to the Bishop of Galway as the
chief agent of Ultramontanism in Connaught. He encouraged
meetings in the city in support of the pope, who was pictured
as the victim of 'English bigotry'. The *Daily Express* of 2
January 1872 described an election meeting at which local
MPs were reminded of their obligation to support Catholic
interests in education and other matters: 'The sentiments
expressed by the speeches were Ultramontane in conception
and uttered in the well-known style and spirit of the Vatican.'
When the election took place the successful candidate was
unseated by Judge William Keogh, who accused the Galway
priests of intimidation of voters. The *Freeman's Journal* of
28 and 29 May 1872 carried an account of the judge's 'tirade'
against the 'organised attempt to defeat the free franchise' by
the Galway priests, who put up a candidate who would be
but an instrument 'in the hands of ecclesiastical despots'.
MacEvilly had no trouble defending his actions to Cullen,
while Kirby was informed that the priests had merely protected the people from electing anyone who would be a
'false guide' to the populace. It was their Christian duty to
intervene in the election, 'to exercise their influence for
good' rather than retiring 'to their sacristies as nobodies in
society':

> A greater evil could not befall religion and society in Ire-
> land than the latter alternative. Put the priest aside and
> God help the people. No one could contemplate the result
> without a shudder. Fenianism, Carbonarism, Communism,
> every wicked *ism* would soon be in the ascendant with our
> impulsive warm-hearted people. It is this the priests sought
> to prevent, and hence the cry against them. Moreover they
> could not begin to have a son of Lord Clancarty, whose

family is noted for their hatred of Catholicity in every part
of the kingdom, as the representative of the Catholic
Church of Galway. (K: 4 Aug. 1872)

In the face of this attack by the establishment, Cullen's
Ultramontane and MacHale's nationalist forces briefly closed
ranks, but division between them over who would control the
Catholic population of Connaught soon returned. MacHale,
however, was by now a very old man, and in 1875 he requested
Propaganda to let him have a coadjutor. Immediately MacEvilly
began to promote his own cause with Cullen, arguing that a
strong hand was needed in the archdiocese to halt the as yet
unchecked Protestant proselytisers, the outrageous Fenians,
and the insubordinate and drunken Tuam priests. (DAA:
23 Jan. 1877) Only someone who was completely devoted
to the Roman cause could bring the situation in Connaught
under control and redirect Catholic resources in a way that
would advance the faith.

Although MacHale did everything in his power to promote
the cause of his nephew Thomas MacHale of the Irish College
in Paris, writing to both Cullen and Cardinal Franchi on his
behalf, MacEvilly was appointed his coadjutor. MacHale
refused to surrender administration to the new appointee,
however, and his resistance received some support when the
Primate, Daniel McGettigan, after a visit to Tuam reported
to Propaganda that the situation was not as bad as some
reports said it was. (O'Reilly, *MacHale*, II, 621-3) It is possible
that MacEvilly exaggerated conditions to strengthen his
own case, yet in 1878, shortly before Cullen's death, he told
Kirby how little the efforts made by either himself or the
cardinal had altered conditions in MacHale's territories. In
the remote region of Joyce's Country there were five chapels
served by one aged priest and one curate; priests regularly
denounced each other in the public press and from their
altars; bloodshed among them was not uncommon; curates
'with impunity' defied their parish priests; the seminary was a
'nest of Fenianism'; and proselytism was still a problem:
(K: 14 Jan. 1878) The real Ultramontane advance in Connaught
was not to take place until after the deaths of Cullen in 1878
and MacHale in 1881.

3. *Leinster: the Siege of Callan*

Some of the fiercest resistance to Cullen's inquisition took place in the area of the papal delegate's birthplace. The inhabitants of the old Pale were strongly independent in their thinking, and they did not take kindly to Roman interference in their affairs. Cullen complained to Kirby that 'There is not a Roman of any weight to be found among them.' (NK: 18 Aug. 1856) After a visit to Kildare he informed Kirby that the clergy generally were lax in their religious life, and the people resentful of their extortionate marriage fees, while the bishop, James Walshe, a former President of Carlow College, was a local man little inclined to stir up animosities by trying to change local clerical customs. (K: 6 Mar. 1862) Cullen's response to this situation was his usual one of trying to appoint a reforming coadjutor.

The priest chosen was James Lynch, an old friend of the Cullen family and a Vincentian, who had succeeded John Miley as Rector of the Irish College in Paris. It was on Cullen's recommendation that Lynch had in 1866 been appointed coadjutor to the Vicar Apostolic of the Western District of Scotland, an area teeming with Irish immigrants, including those in the city of Glasgow. In his new position Lynch soon fell out with his Scots diocesan bishop, and his activities encouraged religious and cultural division between the Irish and Scots clergy. When appeals were made to Rome, Propaganda commissioned Cardinal Manning to make an apostolic visitation of the very divided Western District. Manning interpreted Lynch's work as an exercise in Irish religious and cultural imperialism, directed by Cullen, and feared that the next move might be a demand for an Irish bishop in Liverpool; according to a recent historian of Scottish Catholicism:

> Manning had to watch helplessly as Paul Cullen appointed his relatives and friends to Brisbane, Maitland, Bathurst, Hobart and Adelaide at the beginning of what was a virtual takeover of the Australasian hierarchy and ... feared that if Cullen's adventure in Scotland was successful some similar ploy might be attempted in England, for in the early summer he had written to Dr Alexander Grant, Rector of the Scots College in Rome, to say 'that he will

do all in his power in the matter to check this Irish nomination which threatens England as well as Scotland'.

(McRoberts, *Catholicism*, 20)

Manning in his report to Propaganda suggested that both the warring prelates resign. This was done, and to oblige Cullen once more Propaganda in 1869 secured the appointment of the difficult James Lynch as coadjutor bishop in Kildare and Leighlin to assist the ailing James Walshe. (McRoberts, *Catholicism*, 22) The latter was furious over the appointment, which was made without any kind of election, although Walshe had twice requested he be granted a coadjutor. 'He thinks I am persecuting him,' commented Cullen. (K: 23 Sept. 1869) Walshe and Cullen were of the same age and came from the same part of the country, and there had been trouble between them in 1866 when Carlow College, of which Walshe had been president, had some communication with the senate of the Queen's Colleges about the conferring of degrees. There was further tension between the two when, shortly after Walshe's arrival, pressure was used to close down the Carlow College magazine because a serial story by William Carleton, a convert to Protestantism, was reproduced in it. (PM, V, 309)

To the chagrin of both Cullen and Lynch the sickly James Walshe surprised everyone by living until 1888, during which time he kept a vigilant eye on the unwanted and unpopular coadjutor that Cullen and Rome had foisted on the diocese. Cullen was aware of this situation, and whenever he wrote to Lynch he did so through an intermediary in case Walshe got hold of the correspondence and caused trouble. Walshe was very vigilant against any inquisition in his diocese, and Cullen tried to ensure that no grounds were given for the charge of 'persecution' to be made. (PM, V, 99) The result of this was that although Lynch outlived Walshe by eight years, he was then well into his eighties, his reforming days were past, and the Ultramontane mission advanced very slowly in Kildare and Leighlin.

Cullen had comparatively little trouble in the diocese of Ferns, where a peace-loving bishop, Myles Murphy, who was one of Murray's supporters at Thurles, offended Cullen only by his failure to stand up to the agitators in his diocese, as Cullen told Kirby on 16 August 1856, three days after Murphy's death. (K) His successor, Thomas Furlong, a former professor at Maynooth who had acted as Murphy's theologian at Thurles, was held in some suspicion by Cullen because his testimony before the recent Maynooth Commission had been considered Gallican. He proved to be a good pastoral bishop, however, serving the cause of temperance and establishing industrial schools within his diocese. His greatest service to Cullen was that he was so conscientious in his diocesan administration that the cardinal could focus his attention on affairs in neighbouring Ossory, where open resistance to his inquisition caused him considerable anguish.

The opposition to Cullen's policies in Ossory came not from a bishop but from a stubborn old Gallican priest, Robert O'Keeffe of Callan, a man as difficult to control as MacEvilly had found Peter Daly in Galway. Born in 1814, O'Keeffe had taught school in Kilkenny for ten years before moving to the parish of Callan, where he became an enthusiastic supporter of the male National School. He not only acted as patron, but taught several subjects, kept in touch with the latest educational developments in London, and helped the school to develop a reputation for excellence. In his zeal for education he also encouraged some French nuns to come to Callan and open a school in 1868.

O'Keeffe had been a close friend of Bishop William Kinsella, who died in 1845, and never got along with his successor, Edward Walsh. When Walsh opposed the opening of the nuns' school a bitter quarrel began which ended with O'Keeffe threatening to sue the bishop. Although this affair was settled out of court, O'Keeffe's two curates shortly afterwards began to attack the male National School as a 'godless institution' and to hint that O'Keeffe was misappropriating the money raised in the parish for education. On Bishop Walsh's refusal to discipline the curates when requested to do so by O'Keeffe, the latter accused the bishop of encouraging them and brought him to court on a charge of slander. He also wrote to Cullen and Cardinal Barnabo demanding that the bishop be tried in a Roman court for forty years of 'infamous traffic' in sacraments and dispensations. The result of all this was that Walsh suspended O'Keeffe. (Scrutator, *Ultramontanism*, 1-3) Walsh then wrote to Cullen:

I am at a loss how to treat him. His head, I fear, is gone astray, and the reports of his immorality are fearful. Your Eminence will be pleased to advise me what to do in my present predicament. (DAA: 20 June 1869)

Cullen was particularly upset by the fact that O'Keeffe was making use of the secular courts; but he already had sufficient experience of how difficult Irish priests could be, as in the cases of James Hickie in Limerick and Peter Daly in Galway, to know that he must proceed with caution. So he made no direct moves, but instead wrote to Propaganda to obtain special authority as papal delegate to inquire into the scandal. Future events were to justify this prudent action.

Twice in July 1871 Cullen summoned O'Keeffe to appear in Dublin, only to receive replies from the old priest indicating that such a meeting would be of no use to anyone. If Cullen really wanted to help the situation, let him send O'Keeffe £700 which he needed for legal expenses, and let him also replace the wicked and drunken curates that Walsh had forced on him; then they could all make a fresh start. Cullen reminded O'Keeffe of the ecclesiastical penalties facing those who brought bishops into lay courts, but O'Keeffe refused to apologise for the action he had taken. When they finally met in Cullen's Eccles Street office, with Laurence Forde present, O'Keeffe insisted that the cardinal recognise him as the injured party. Cullen finally suspended him, only to receive a letter in December 1871 from O'Keeffe warning him of the consequences:

My Lord Cardinal — A document was read in the Friary Chapel here on last Sunday which pretended to be a letter of suspension passed on me by Your Eminence. You have thus for the sixth time passed censure on me behind my back, without any trial or citation to me, and without alleging any crime, as far as I have been able to learn, except that I went to law with Dr Walsh. I think in the circumstances no one can reasonably expect me to make an apology for going to law with Your Eminence.

(O'Keeffe, *Trial*, xxviii)

Cullen was now thoroughly alarmed, for he knew well the use the Protestant establishment would make of Ireland's cardinal and Apostolic Delegate being arraigned before a lay tribunal over an issue of ecclesiastical authority. Bishop Walsh could not handle O'Keeffe, so Cullen decided to use his tactic of appointing a reforming coadjutor in the diocese of Ossory, someone with the intelligence and authority to control the rebellious priest.

The priest Cullen had in mind was the one person who was really close to him, his nephew, friend and secretary, Patrick Francis Moran. After a visit home in 1842 Cullen had brought Moran, then aged twelve, back to the Irish College in Rome. Moran had remained with his uncle for twenty-four years, during which time he had also served as Vice-Rector of the Irish College and as a professor of Propaganda. The bond between Cullen and his nephew was very close, to the extent that they shared the same prejudices. The ascetic Moran often wrote to Kirby from Eccles Street, passing on gossip he had heard about Irish College students back in Rome not walking *in camerata*, or going into cafés on their way back from Propaganda. When Queen Victoria visited Dublin he wrote to Bernard Smith commenting on her ruddy complexion (which he attributed to drink) and delightedly describing how the crowd had hissed her and how the Catholic bishops had refused to go out on a verandah to watch while she passed. (BS: 30 Aug. 1853) Other prejudices which he shared with his uncle reflected Moran's Co. Carlow strong-farmer background. Moran's home at Leighlinbridge was not far from Callan, and the ecclesiastical struggle between the two men soon took on the added dimension of a feud between members of the Cullen/Moran clan and their O'Keeffe neighbours.

When the election for coadjutor was held O'Keeffe was denied a vote because he was suspended. Moran was the victor, but only by one vote; and his victory was at the expense of a cousin of Robert O'Keeffe. Now the struggle in Callan openly took on the character of a feud between two rival ecclesiastical farming families, and Cullen himself feared the appearance of a schism like that which had occurred in Birr in the 1830s.

O'Keeffe greeted Moran's victory by putting up placards with the heading 'Rev. Robert O'Keeffe *vs* Cardinal Cullen, a Real Papal Aggression' and sending others to Protestant clergymen with a statement that he intended to take the cardinal to court. Cullen's riposte was to place O'Keeffe's chapel under interdict. He also pointed out to the state authorities that as O'Keeffe was now an officially suspended priest, he could not act or receive his usual income as patron of the National School and chaplain of the poorhouse. Cullen justified this action to Kirby: 'Fr O'Keeffe appears to be devoured with the love of money — the loss of his salary may help to convert him.' (NK: 20 Mar. 1872) Moran, however, told Kirby that O'Keeffe owned three shops in the community, that half the population supported him, and that money came to him from them and Protestant sources. It looked as if he could carry on his litigation for some time yet.

A *de facto* schism did appear in the community when Cullen in March 1872 appointed Moran administrator of the parish of Callan. O'Keeffe immediately occupied the parish church, and Moran and two curates assisting him were obliged to set up their altars and confessionals in the friary chapel. Then local toughs began to come into the town to brawl on behalf of their ecclesiastical champions. O'Keeffe proclaimed that the chief support for Moran came from local Fenians led by a notorious character, Heffernan Dunne. Soon the press was reporting widely the acrimonious ecclesiastical faction-fighting in Callan, and Cullen's embarrassment grew.

O'Keeffe was a formidable opponent for Cullen, and he soon showed that his position was well worked out, both theologically and ecclesiastically. On 8 May 1872 he announced his platform in a printed public letter which was passed on to Kirby:

> If I have not an Ultramontane cap on my head, I have in my brain an acceptance of more than thirty-five years' standing with the Canon Law and theology of the Cisalpine school of divinity. My knowledge of the law and theology teaches me loyalty to my Queen as well as to the Head of the Church. It teaches me to disavow and abjure the temporal while I respect and reverence the spiritual supremacy of the Head of the Church. This

Canon Law and this theology of the Lingards, the Lanigans, the Carews, the Doyles, the MacHales and the O'Hanlons will ignore the pretensions of a Pius IX, as it would those of a St Pius V, or an Adrian IV, when these pretensions are inconsistent with the civil rights of the sovereign, or the subjects of this realm; and if you pronounce me degraded for giving expression to these sentiments, I tell you that you exalt me in the opinion of every right-minded man in the community. (O'Keeffe, *PP Callan*, 54)

O'Keeffe ended his broadside by announcing he would change his opinions only when he could be convinced that the authorities he had quoted were wrong in theirs. MacHale and O'Hanlon might not have appreciated O'Keeffe's old-fashioned Gallican view of their opposition to Roman 'pretensions', but they would have certainly applauded O'Keeffe's determination to oppose a non-Irish view of the Church being forced on them by an 'Italian monk'.

Moran told Cullen that he had tried to reason with O'Keeffe, offering him 'paternal affection' as he pointed out how the *Belfast Newsletter*, the *Dublin Evening Mail* and the *Express* were praising the rebellion of the Parish Priest of Callan, but O'Keeffe was as obdurate as ever. John O'Hanlon had begun to support him, giving him advice about canon law, and it was clear that fundamental problems of church/state relations would soon be under discussion. On 12 April 1872 Cullen told Kirby that the real enemy behind the whole affair was Freemasonry (K), having made comparisons in an earlier letter with the rebellion of the Old Catholics in Germany. (NK) Cullen also made sure that Cardinal Barnabo knew of every development in the struggle as O'Keeffe went on with his preparation to bring Cullen to trial on a charge of libel before the Court of Queen's Bench.

By the time that the aged Edward Walsh died in the summer of 1872 and Moran succeeded him as diocesan bishop Cullen was almost in a panic. His impulse was to go to Rome; he told Kirby cn 29 August: 'It would give me great confidence to hear *viva voce* what the pope thinks.' (K) On 12 September he reported the alarming news that O'Keeffe claimed to have the support of MacHale, Moriarty and C. W. Russell of Maynooth, and that he was boasting that 'posterity will wonder how an old man . . . was able to vanquish both the Pope of Rome and the Queen of England'. (K) Then, to add to Cullen's dismay, Laurence Forde, 'the most accomplished ecclesiastic in Ireland', who had hitherto guided him in his handling of affairs in Callan, became seriously ill.

Forde's illness was actually a blessing for Cullen, for it gave his lawyers an excuse to postpone Cullen's trial until early 1873. Tactically this was of great advantage to him. Cullen told Kirby on 24 November 1872:

> The jury law at present in force which gives a Protestant High Sheriff the right to select an Orange jury ceases to exist this year and the system of drawing the names of the jury by lot will commence on the next 11th of January. In Dublin the Catholics entitled to be on the jury are about 3 to 1 Protestant, so when all names will be put in the ballot-box a fair jury may be obtained. This is what Fr O'Keeffe wants to avoid — if the trial had gone on now, twelve Orangemen of the worst type would have been selected to try the case. (K)

The Roman authorities certainly paid attention to what Cullen in his anxiety was telling them, for the implications of the Callan affair were enormous. Essentially what was being raised were all the old problems of *praemunire*, the offence of accepting the authority of the pope over that of the crown. In an open letter to MPs of both houses on 25 April 1872 O'Keeffe indicated what was at stake in the lawsuit:

> I am pronounced excommunicated by the papal legate in Ireland for having gone before a lay tribunal. . . . Cardinal Cullen is endeavouring to substitute in Ireland Roman for British legislation in temporal affairs and the Commissioners of the Poor Law of National Education have given him their active aid and have become instruments in his hands to oppress an unoffending British subject.
>
> (O'Keeffe, *PP Callan*, 52)

The *Daily Express* of 14 December 1872 editorialised on why O'Keeffe and his loyal parishioners were subject to such a

shower of interdicts, excommunications and what sounded
like 'curses', and enlarged on the implications of O'Keeffe's
open letter:

> The contest is not now between parish priest and cardinal.
> It is to decide whether the right of citizenship extends
> to Irish priests, or whether they are to be the merest
> slaves of the prelates, and without even the slave's privilege
> of complaining against injustice. The Rev. Mr O'Keeffe
> is, in fact, fighting the battle of every parish priest in
> Ireland . . . and of the laity whose interests are assailed
> when the hierarchy seeks to consolidate their despotism.
> . . . The gloomy ascetic who now rules the Roman Catholic
> Church in Ireland is too intensely papal to be favourite
> with the laity, and many of them are well pleased when he
> and his satellites are defeated in their efforts to rivet on
> Irish priests the chains of Ultramontanism.

When the trial finally took place in May 1873 Cullen's
defence was that in all he did he had acted only on the
authority of the pope. O'Keeffe's charge was the 'purely
Jansenistical one' that the pope had no legal authority
in Ireland. Much was made of a papal bull of 1741 which
excommunicated persons who brought Roman Catholic
ecclesiastics before lay tribunals. It was pointed out to the
court that both John MacHale and James Doyle in their
evidence before parliamentary committees had argued that
this bull was never accepted by Roman Catholic authorities
in Ireland. Cullen's testimony, corroborated by two canonists
brought from Rome, was that Pius IX had suspended this old
legislation, and that by a new enactment of 1869 the censure
of excommunication befell anyone bringing a prelate before a
lay judge.

The trial was a long and weary one, lasting some sixteen
days before Chief Justice C. J. Whiteside. Cullen kept Kirby
informed of its development day by day, and on 28 May
he summed up his ordeal:

> The judge (Whiteside) acted a most despotic part. He
> told the jury that it was their duty to give a verdict for
> O'Keeffe, that if they did not they would be trampling
> on the laws of the country and violating the constitution

of the Kingdom: he literally forced them to yield, and they gave a verdict for the plaintiff, adding that the damages were to be one farthing. So far this was not bad, but after the verdict Whiteside certified publicly in the tribunal and wrote on the verdict that my proceedings were wilfully malicious and decided that I was to pay all Fr O'Keeffe's legal cost. This decision obliges me to apply for a new trial, for if I acquiesced in the verdict Fr O'Keeffe would compel me in force of Whiteside's certificate to pay all his expenses immediately. (K)

Cullen rejoiced with Kirby that the new law on juries had resulted in the composition of this one being seven Catholics and only five Protestants, and said he had no doubt that if left alone it would not have given a verdict against him. Two years later, in February 1875, three judges decided that Whiteside's decision against Cullen was contrary to British law. A year later Cullen could tell Kirby that O'Keeffe had withdrawn all proceedings against him, but that his defence had cost him over £3000 in legal fees.

O'Keeffe still had cases pending against Moran, some of which he won with the award of small damages. Although a Protestant fund had been set up to help defray his expenses, his legal costs were enormous, and it was soon clear that the resources behind Cullen and Moran would enable them to outlast the old priest in a lengthy war of litigation. Still O'Keeffe held out, holding on to the presbytery, with several police required in the town to keep the peace, at considerable cost to local taxpayers. Meanwhile Moran kept up his pressure, bringing nuns to set up new schools and winning the people back to his authority. Protestant agitation had resulted in a parliamentary committee being set up to look into the educational question in Callan, but O'Keeffe's assault on a National Board inspector who had tried to enter his school did not help his credibility with the commissioners. The *Daily Express* on 9 June 1873 had now shifted its focus from the scene in Callan and was comparing the trial and the struggle as a whole with the *kulturkampf* in Germany, contrasting Bismarck's draconian laws with 'the lame and halting way in which we deal with the same question in this country'. On 27 September 1873 Cullen told Kirby that O'Keeffe, whose sanity he questioned, was now 'a sad man ... reduced to absolute beggary so I think his power of doing evil is entirely gone'. (K)

Although the old priest held out until 1876, by that time he was so broken that Cullen in compassion suggested to Kirby that he be given a pension to get him out of the way to live out his days in peace:

> It would be better that the unfortunate man should get enough to live on in peace. He is much broken down and not likely to live long. Indeed he appears also to be somewhat mad — at all events he talks about his own business as if he were crazy ... so it would be good to give him a pension to live without waging war on others.
>
> (NK: 7 June 1876)

Moran, however, told Kirby that he would not agree to any pension or other settlement until the 'wicked and obdurate' priest conformed: 'I am determined to do nothing whatsoever for him until he makes his submission.' (K: 7 July 1876) Finally O'Keeffe, totally worn out, did surrender and then retired to his native parish to die in peace.

The O'Keeffe episode was of great significance for Cullen, as it was for Rome, because it showed clearly the limits of his legatine authority in Ireland. As long as his efforts were directed towards an objective which was of concern to all Irish Catholics, such as the disestablishment of the Church of Ireland, there was little questioning of his mission. When he carried out his inquisition within the Church, however, putting the clergy and people on a war footing in support of the Ultramontane cause, he had to be very careful lest he upset well-established social accommodations and traditions at the local level. At the height of the Callan controversy both Cullen and Moran were desperately frightened that a serious schism might occur. If the Protestants had not been so traumatised by their recent Disestablishment defeat, or if John MacHale had been a younger man, then the victory of Cullen and his nephew might not have been assured. At times there were disquieting signs that the traditional and the new nationalist Gallicans might make peace long enough for them to support O'Keeffe and at least embarrass the mission of the cardinal. As it was, it was not a flagging of the spirit that made the doughty old Parish Priest of Callan give in. It was simply that he lacked reinforcement, and by himself he could not carry on a protracted struggle against his bishop, the cardinal legate and indeed the whole power of Rome. (CA, 1873/35) If Bismarck himself had finally to come to terms with the Ultramontane power of the papacy, could more be expected of Robert O'Keeffe?

VIII

The Catholic Nation

1. *Young Ireland and Independent Opposition*

The Irish Reform Act of 1850 trebled the county electorate, and this extension of the franchise encouraged the priests to use their religious authority to organise the people in the service of various political causes. By the time that Cullen arrived in Ireland he found the priests in many parts of the country busy agitating over matters like the Ecclesiastical Titles Bill, the Stockport riots against Catholics in England, and the newly founded Tenant League. Everywhere he looked he saw priests caught up in 'worldly cabals' and 'revolutionary designs', ready to make use of the altar, the pulpit and even the confessional for some political cause. The disturbed state of the country made him think of the *agitazione* he had witnessed in Rome in 1848, and he was in a quandary over how to handle the situation.

One of the important Catholic political figures at this time was Frederick Lucas, an English convert barrister and journalist, who was editor of the *Tablet*. In 1849 Lucas transferred the publication of the *Tablet* to Dublin. Cullen liked its policies, especially its opposition to the Queen's Colleges and the establishment of diplomatic relations between London and Rome. Shortly after Cullen arrived in Ireland he told Bernard Smith:

> Lucas is the only man that knows how to write a line in our defence. Our high Catholics do not know anything about our religion. The education they get leaves them completely ignorant, or what is worse hostile to every Catholic. (BS: 17 Jan. 1851)

Because of Cullen's friendship, when Lucas joined the Protestant nationalist Sir John Gray of the *Freeman's Journal* and Charles Gavan Duffy of the Young Ireland journal, the *Nation*, in support of the Tenant League's campaign for Irish land reform, he tried to induce Cullen to support this new social development.

Cullen, however, was very wary. He knew that the Tenant League had persuaded a group of Irish MPs to promise to withhold support from any government which did not try to advance the cause of Irish land reform. It was hoped that this 'independent opposition', supported by social agitation organised by priests on the parish level, would persuade the government to concede the reforms that were being demanded. Cullen had his own ideas about what agitation the priests should engage in, and in 1851 he had founded the Catholic Defence Association, with an English convert, H. W. Wilberforce, as its secretary. The object of this body was a purely ecclesiastical one, to organise resistance to the new 'penal laws' which Catholics were now to suffer under the Ecclesiastical Titles Act.

Cullen particularly disliked Duffy, the editor of the *Nation*, a paper which had once warmly praised the Carbonari. As a Young Irelander Duffy had also talked of the people of Ireland transcending sectarian differences for political reasons, and this to Cullen was anathema. As far as he was concerned, the Catholic Daniel O'Connell had been betrayed by Protestants like Thomas Davis, John Mitchel and Smith O'Brien. The kind of religious indifferentism that Duffy promoted would soon develop into the kind of anticlericalism that Cullen had experienced in Italy. In Cullen's view, as expressed to Bernard Smith, all Young Irelanders were Mazzinians, and the worst of them was Duffy:

> Lucas says Duffy is a saint. He may be so for all I know, but his past conduct was very bad and he never made any public retraction. When I hear of the sanctity of some of these gentlemen I always recollect . . . Rome in 1848.
>
> (BS: 18 Dec. 1852)

When an attempt was made to have Young Irelanders appointed to posts in the Catholic University, Cullen intervened, and it was probably his influence that denied Duffy the chair of Modern History.

Duffy and the other Young Irelanders then tried to establish co-operation with the Catholic Defence Association to promote the tenant-right cause. Cullen was furious. He was sure that what the Young Irelanders wanted was political revolution, and whatever use was made of the priests would certainly not benefit the Church. Ultimately Duffy and his associates were bound to turn on their religious allies and treat the Church in the way that Mazzini had treated it in Italy.

Cullen's greatest worry was how MacHale would act. Since his arrival in Ireland he was aware of MacHale's tendency to over-involve himself in nationalist politics, yet in 1848 he had dismissed some of the wilder charges against 'the Lion' as 'vile calumnies'. (C: 15 May 1848) In the 1852 general election, however, MacHale nominated and helped to have elected independent opposition candidates. He supported the Tenant League openly and showed his displeasure that an Englishman had been appointed as secretary of the Catholic Defence Association. At the same time Cullen was exhorting the bishops to keep secular politics out of the chapels, and the clergy not to engage in public political disputes. He forbade his Dublin clergy to attend political meetings and used his influence to help curb the activities of political curates in parishes like Callan and New Ross. Cullen made it very clear that unless priests served the spiritual mission of the Universal Church they would find themselves sent to 'bogs and morasses' to reflect upon their contumacy.

The difference of opinion between Cullen and MacHale over the proper role of priests in Ireland's highly politicised society was brought into the open when two of the MPs pledged to independent opposition, John Sadleir and William Keogh, broke ranks and accepted cabinet posts under Lord Aberdeen in 1853. MacHale was furious and poured his invective upon these 'traitors' who had abandoned the cause promoted by the Tenant League. When Cullen said nothing about this political development the worst suspicions of MacHale and the other nationalists were confirmed. By remaining silent the papal delegate was tacitly endorsing the defection of Sadleir and Keogh and was showing himself to be an enemy of all that MacHale and his followers were attempting.

There was some truth in this because from the end of 1851 Cullen had been urging Rome to use its influence to curb the activity of those priests in Connaught who neglected their spiritual duties to give their energies to political affairs. The result of Cullen's criticisms of MacHale over his inability to press his suffragans into a resistance of the Protestant proselytisers, who at this time were threatening to take over much of Connaught, was that 'the Lion's' credibility was greatly undermined in the Eternal City. Bernard Smith was soon reporting to Kirby that MacHale was very much out of favour: 'His whole history is now recalled to memory.' (K: 14 Feb. 1852) MacHale, of course, soon knew what was happening, and at the time that Cullen was deciding to turn against Duffy and the Young Irelanders, MacHale had declared war on Cullen. On sensing this, the papal delegate wrote to Smith rather ingenuously to say: 'It is reported here that the Lion will assail. I know not for what — but he is fond of roaring, and he must have someone to roar against.' (BS: 22 Sept. 1852) By the beginning of 1853 MacHale was indeed in full voice. Archbishop Carew had called on him to suggest a visit to Rome to defend himself against his detractors. MacHale now knew who was causing him so much trouble at the Holy See, and he lost little time in making a spirited attack against those who made accusations which 'if not destitute of foundation' were certainly 'grossly exaggerated'. (K: 25 Jan. 1853)

The *Nation* of 28 January 1854 contained an interesting discussion of the problem of the 'priest in politics' that had been given by John MacEvilly to an independent opposition audience which included MacHale and Lucas. It was not a speech directed to win nationalist approval, however, for it was made at about the time that MacEvilly had begun to transfer his allegiance from MacHale to Cullen. What MacEvilly said was meant to please the papal delegate, yet not offend his immediate audience, and it seems that he succeeded. He certainly kept the friendship of Cullen, and the argument propounded by MacEvilly also won the support of Duffy.

MacEvilly argued that Irish Catholicism had to be concerned about matters of natural as well as revealed religion. It had not only to defend the freedom of the Church, but also to protect the poor against legislation with a 'persecuting tendency' that might endanger the faith of the people. It was a 'duty of necessity' to oppose constitutionally everything that threatened the temporal as well as the spiritual well- being of the Catholic people of Ireland.

Where Cullen and MacHale differed was in the application of the theory which MacEvilly had sketched and which they both approved. Cullen was much more cautious in his interpretation of 'constitutional opposition' than was MacHale. Extreme political agitation by the priests was bound to evoke some penal legislative reaction by the government, which was just what the Orangemen wanted. Cullen was not surprised when the government passed the Corrupt Practices Act in 1854, which enabled elections to be set aside when clerical intimidation could be proved. As for the cause which 'constitutional opposition' was to oppose, Cullen's interpretation was much narrower and more directly religious than MacHale's. A matter like the ownership of land was secondary in Cullen's list of priorities for Catholics to consider, and much less important than 'godless education', proselytising by Protestants, or penal legislation like the Ecclesiastical Titles Act. When it came to resisting a heretical state in its promotion of these evils, Cullen was willing to use well-controlled agitation, so long as it was contained within constitutional limits.

At the beginning of 1854 Cullen knew that a major struggle with MacHale had started. The *Nation* was now patronised in Tuam; few of the clergy in MacHale's province expressed any intention of withdrawing from secular political agitation; and Cullen was not surprised when he heard that a Tuam memorial was being circulated calling for the abolition of the office of Apostolic Delegate in Ireland. 'The Lion' was also beginning to growl about Roman intervention in Ireland's affairs; and Cullen told Bernard Smith to alert Propaganda about the danger of any inopportune rescript or other statement: 'It would do mischief as the Young Irelanders would use it to influence the minds of the people.' (BS: 10 Jan. 1854)

It was in Rome, however, that the opposing Irish forces met when MacHale and Lucas and Cullen were there for the promulgation of the first great Ultramontane dogmatic decree of Pius IX – the doctrine of the Immaculate Conception.

When MacHale met Cardinal Barnabo of Propaganda he immediately voiced his strong disapproval of the plan to have the Catholic University governed by the four archbishops, with the Apostolic Delegate having a casting vote. Barnabo showed MacHale what Rome thought of him at this time by giving him a lecture on his failings which filled 'the Lion' with fury. Lucas told Duffy sadly that MacHale had made a great enemy of Barnabo by suggesting that 'the Church was a democracy and not a monarchy'. (NLI, 3738: 23 Dec. 1854) This falling out with Barnabo was to be of great consequence to MacHale, for very shortly afterwards the cardinal succeeded Fransoni as Prefect of Propaganda.

By the time Lucas arrived in Rome he had accepted that Cullen was an open enemy of the Tenant League, and he bore a memorial from priests who opposed Cullen's 'tyrannical' curbs on their freedom of speech and civil action. Lucas himself was intent upon persuading the Roman authorities that they were wrong in using Cullen as their authoritative guide to Irish affairs when he neither understood the needs of the country nor had that authority among the people which was needed if he was to manage affairs effectively. Lucas was granted an audience with Pius IX, who urged him to have moderation, especially in his role as editor of the *Tablet*. As for the division between Cullen and MacHale, the pope told Lucas that although MacHale was recognised as being 'a little strong' in what he said, the complaints about him came from the English, not from Cullen. The latter had long defended MacHale, and it was only since his translation to Dublin that he realised the dangerous situation in which the Church was placed when priests contributed to public disorder.

Lucas then met with Cullen, who was almost in a rage over the attack upon him which was being made in the centre of ecclesiastical power where his authority in Irish affairs had never been questioned. Lucas told Duffy: 'Dr Cullen in the course of that conversation said so many things that were untrue that I should have the greatest possible objection to have any further personal communication with him of any kind.' (NLI, 3738: 24 Jan. 1855) Cullen's separation from the nationalist bishops at this time was almost total. MacHale and Derry refused to attend a dinner at the Irish College, and

MacHale indicated to Barnabo that in future he wanted direct communication with Rome, not through the agency of Cullen's disciple Tobias Kirby. (NLI, 3738: 5 Mar. 1855)

Cullen survived this crisis because Rome recognised the dangerous development of *agitazione* in Ireland which the nationalists were unwilling to curb or apparently even to control. When Lucas had a second meeting with the pope he came away convinced that Rome had accepted Cullen's version of Irish affairs and that Cullen's policies were to be adopted. No longer was there to be Roman toleration of the now traditional agitating role of the 'priest in politics'.

What influenced Rome was the kind of report Bernard Smith received from Joseph Dixon early in 1855 about the 'violence and excitement' that he had witnessed in Louth during the recent general election. Most of it had been produced by clerical agitators from outside the diocese who came there deliberately to stir up the people. As a result, the people turned on their own priests when they did not support the agitators' cause: 'The people thought no language too gross to apply to their own clergy who presumed to differ from the views of the agitators.' This was the evil that Cullen opposed, said Dixon, and there was simply no truth in the Young Ireland charge that such opposition to irresponsible agitation made him a dupe of the Castle:

> Although he is a man of whom it is notorious that, whilst he has no fear of the English government, he is at the same time thoroughly and in every sense of the word independent of it . . . he yields to no bishop in the world in defending the liberties and rights of the Church against every temporal influence. . . . I said that he has no fear of the English government, but there is another fear to which he is also a stranger and that is the fear of what . . . priests may say or do in opposition to his efforts to carry out the wishes of the Holy See in giving new vigour to ecclesiastical discipline in Ireland. . . . As they despair of being able to frighten the apostolic delegate they have conceived the unreasonable hope of being able to induce the Holy See to withdraw its confidence from him that their discipline may quietly fall back into its former state in Ireland.
>
> (BS: 1 Jan. 1855)

The real significance of this battle in the curia was in the effect it had upon Cullen himself when he saw the attack upon him being pressed home at the very centre of the Roman world that meant so much to him. From this time forward he was completely at war with the MacHaleites, determined never to become, as he phrased it, 'vassal of a popular party'. When Paul Cullen considered the goals sought by the independent opposition supporters in the light of his Ultramontane mission, there was no doubt in his mind which cause served the higher morality. Rapidly he set about rallying support in his struggle with the Young Irelanders and MacHaleites. He warned Moriarty, the newly created Coadjutor Bishop of Kerry, about the dangers of listening to those who apologised for Charles Gavan Duffy:

> It matters not what he is himself while he is put forward and acts as the life and soul of a most dangerous party, the Young Ireland faction, the clerical members of which are likely to fall into the party of Father Gavazzi and the lay members to become disciples of Kossuth and Mazzini who have been so often idolised in the pages of the *Nation*. As long as Duffy is the leader of such a faction he ought to be looked on with great suspicion.
>
> (PM, II, 187: 20 Jan. 1855)

A letter to William Monsell indicated how much he had been helped by the Limerick MP, who had advised him how to present to the office of the papal Secretary of State his case against the independent opposition party:

> Cardinal Antonelli . . . highly approved of your views and remarked that the system of so called independent opposition would be likely to produce the evil occasioned in Italy by Mazzini's principles. Your statement of the case will have the effect of exploding the pretended appeal to Rome.

He assured Monsell that Rome had no intention of seeking to destroy the proper influence of the clergy in the land, but that it did oppose 'violence and imprudence'. As for Lucas, the pope wanted him merely 'to respect those in power and to be obedient to authority'. (NLI, 8317: 10 May 1855)

The MacHaleites in turn were becoming bolder in their open criticisms of Cullen. When he lingered in Rome, Cantwell of Meath grumbled that he ought to be at home minding his diocese. George Browne of Elphin told Kirby how difficult his position now was when he had been charged with being a 'Cullenite' at a meeting in Tuam. (K: 16 Nov. 1855) Cullen found that in any dealing with Connaught affairs he now had to work through intermediaries to avoid open conflict. He gloomily explained the situation to Kirby: 'Dr MacHale's opposition has done a great deal of mischief because it obliges me to leave everything in the hands of others in order not to provoke attacks from the Lion.' Furthermore, a rumour was assiduously being promoted that Cullen was in the pocket of the Castle, while even the Protestant *Dublin Evening Mail* was praising MacHale as the champion of the people against Roman encroachment. (NK: 21 Aug. 1856) In January 1857 Kirby was informed by a clerical correspondent that 'I fear Dr Cullen has become very unpopular, Dr MacHale is the great idol of the Irish people.' (K)

Cullen at this time was almost in despair over the situation in the west. George Browne of Elphin had assured Kirby and Cullen that he was now 'an out-and-out Roman in heart and feeling' (K: 14 Sept. 1853), but in fact his clergy in areas like Sligo were now virtually uncontrollable. Cullen told Kirby that 'it is the Lion who is getting up all the agitation in Elphin', but he himself was 'afraid to move lest anything disgraceful be done'. (NK: 17 Mar. 1854) As for Meath, in spite of the fact that John Cantwell continued to deny that the interference of the clergy in elections was any less cautious than previously, Cullen told Kirby in 1855 that he was afraid that there would be bloodshed in Navan, that there were 'sermons and furious personal invectives every Sunday from the altars', and that one priest had even been guilty of 'giving harangue and forgetting to finish the mass'. (NK: 2 Dec. 1855)

By 1857 Cullen was telling Kirby how the contagion was spreading uncontrollably throughout the country, particularly in dioceses where the bishop was as 'unvigilant' as was his aged friend Michael Slattery, the Archbishop of Cashel:

The Young Irelanders have acted with dreadful violence in Tipperary. Many old priests were well beaten or covered with filth. The young priests were all leaguered with the violent party. It was a sad illustration of the evil results of priestly interference. . . . Poor Dr Slattery never interfered to check the spirit then manifested . . . the young priests became regular leaders of the mob. (NK: 16 Mar. 1857)

In Enniscorthy the Young Irelanders were busy 'trying to return Orangemen wherever they can do no other mischief' (NK: 28 Mar. 1857), and Cullen also referred to the 'Mazzinian spirit' prevalent among the young clergy of Waterford as they responded to the agitation organised by MacHale:

In Waterford, Dr O'Brien is treated very badly indeed. Almost in every town the party had its adherents and though they are not strong they can do great mischief. Their great support is the Patriarch of the West. As long as he goes with them he is a divinity, but if he were to venture to dissent from them they would treat him as they have treated other priests and bishops. (NK: 26 Apr. 1857)

On the eve of the Fenian crisis Cullen indicated to Kirby how MacHaleite influence had induced a promising bishop like William Keane of Cloyne to publish a pastoral calling for agitation. The contagion had even reached into the Dublin archdiocese, where speeches in favour of agitation had been made at the consecration of an American bishop in 1861:

At Dr O'Connell's consecration Dr Cantwell made a . . . speech to the students on the necessity of wholesome agitation. Unfortunately the priests and other agitators who join will not agitate against any but Catholics and especially other priests and bishops – they have no intention of agitating against the abuses of government or the Protestant Church or bad education. (NK: 15 Feb. 1861)

Ideologically Cullen had no difficulty in identifying the elements of the agitation that appeared in the Young Ireland and then the Fenian movements. Ecclesiastically it was Gallican in its concern for Irish nationalist affairs rather than those of the Universal Church which were the papal delegate's prime concern. Religiously it promoted indifferentism, tolerating the faith of a Thomas Davis or a Charles Gavan Duffy, while it deplored the kind of sectarian division between

Catholic and Protestant which Cullen tried so assiduously to foster. Behind these movements, Cullen suspected, lay the sinister power of continental liberalism and Freemasonry; here was to be found the real cause of Irish *agitazione*. It is interesting to note Cullen's tendency to refer to the Fenians as Young Irelanders, and it is difficult to know where, if ever, he distinguished between the two movements. Both of them, whatever they were called, were enemies of the faith, and both owed much of their survival to the help given to them by John MacHale and his unlikely Protestant allies.

2. *Maynooth and the Irish College, Paris*

On numerous occasions in his letters to Kirby in Rome Cullen noted that the MacHaleite form of ecclesiastical nationalism had appeal to younger rather than older priests. This he attributed to the mutated form of Gallicanism which was nurtured in Maynooth and the Irish College, Paris. It was rare for the alumni of the Irish College in Rome to show much sympathy for *agitazione* or any other manifestation of liberal or revolutionary ideology. Cullen would have agreed with one of his secretaries who described the latter college as 'the nursery of piety and learning', the one seminary where an Irish student would be granted 'the opportunity of becoming a saint'. (NK: 14 Oct. 1850) Unfortunately for Cullen, most young seminarians went to Maynooth, some to the Irish College in Paris, and relatively few to Rome, where Kirby's reputation for rigorism was well known, the climate was unhealthy, and travelling expenses were heavy. When he arrived in Ireland and had a first look at the seminary situation, he told Kirby:

> This year we will not get many students. . . . Castleknock is going on well, Carlow has lost nearly half its numbers, Derry and Belfast seminaries are closing. Thurles also is nearly abandoned. Maynooth will be everything. God help Ireland when that will be the case. (NK: 19 Oct. 1859)

Cullen had much evidence to convince him that whether the Gallicanism of Maynooth was traditional in its subservience to the state, or new in its over-identification with Irish nationalism, it did exist, and it did little to inculcate among the young respect for the authority of Rome. In 1851 he told Bernard Smith of two Maynooth professors speaking vehemently against the Holy See while they were visiting Cornelius Denvir in Belfast. One of them was George Crolly, nephew and biographer of the late Primate, who had spoken in a manner that 'was really violent'. Cullen warned Smith: 'We shall have lots of Jansenists from such a school.' (BS: 7 Oct. 1851) But although he recognised the dangers in Maynooth, he was in no position to have any inquisition there owing to the generally depressed state of the Church and the consequent falling off of vocations. As he told Kirby, 'There is a great dearth of subjects here for the priesthood. I could not get boys to fill up the places in Maynooth, much less go to Rome.' (K: 3 Jan. 1853)

Another reason why Cullen hesitated to meddle directly in Maynooth concerns at this time was his knowledge that the government was about to have its own investigation of affairs there. Cullen was not the only one to conclude that Ireland's agitating curates were probably nurtured in their rebellious habits at Maynooth. Monsell kept Cullen posted on how the commission was preparing itself and did his best to reassure Cullen, who had revealed to him his fear that what the commissioners found would 'disgust and annoy the faithful who supported the college'. (BM, 43249, 285: 16 Mar. 1853) Cullen also told Kirby that he hoped the commission would lead to some dismissals: 'Unless Murray and Crolly be removed, the college will become a regular nuisance. They are eternally agitating Young Irelanders, enemies of the authority of superiors.' (NK: 4 Nov. 1853) Even though the college was in his diocese, he explained to Barnabo of Propaganda that he could do little about its deplorable state himself because 'there is a sort of republic established there which is almost independent of the ordinary'. (PM, III, 194)

When Cullen first saw the evidence gathered by the commissioners, which was leaked to him by one of the Catholic officials he was appalled by the Gallican spirit in the seminary:

I got a peep at the Maynooth examination yesterday. It is perfectly Gallican. Mr Crolly is little more than a Gallican. When a pope confirms a general council the council becomes infallible because it is to be supposed that the majority of the bishops agree with him. He is the man of the majority. Rescripts and bulls do not bind Crolly, and some others were determined to crush Ultramontanism. Crolly brought his answers ready written and read them. There was an immensity of intrigue in the whole business.

(NK: 24 Feb. 1854)

He had already sent some account of the deplorable state of Maynooth to Bernard Smith, explaining he would not try to withdraw the faculties of the offending professors to avoid being labelled as 'a great enemy of Maynooth'. (BS: 18 Dec. 1853) At the same time Propaganda was informed about what was happening. (PFS, XXXII, 42) Then, having received the backing of Rome to support him while he redressed the minor failings which the royal commission had revealed, he made his move against the offending college and its Gallican professors.

Some of the hierarchy showed disinclination to become excited by the Gallican statements made by the Maynooth professors, so Cullen precipitated a confrontation by persuading Joseph Dixon, the Primate, to offer his resignation as a trustee of Maynooth. George Crolly was then haled before a meeting of the bishops and obliged to sign a retraction of his opinions, which he did 'with the most admirable spirit of submission'. He also agreed to visit Rome soon, at the invitation of Propaganda. Kirby was told in detail of these proceedings in letters of 21 and 26 November 1855, and from Cullen's standpoint all went well, even without trouble from MacHale, who had arrived late at the meeting. At the special request of Cardinal Fransoni, Dixon then withdrew his resignation as a Maynooth trustee, and at least officially Gallicanism appeared to have been exorcised from Maynooth.

Nothing had really changed at all, however, though from this time the Maynooth Gallicans carefully conformed to Cullen's wishes in any public statement they made. He kept a watchful eye on them. When some of the Catholic commissioners on the Board of National Education expressed satisfaction with the system, Cullen immediately wrote to Kirby to blame this aberration on the encouragement they were given by the anti-Roman spoilt intellectuals in Maynooth:

What wonder is it that O'Hagan supports National Education, when he is encouraged to do so by Dr Russell, Dr
Murray and Dr Crolly of Maynooth. The salaries of the
professors in Maynooth amount to £6000 yearly. This
year they have contributed, I think, £8 to the Peter's
Pence in the diocese. How much is that per cent?

(K: 4 Sept. 1863)

C. W. Russell, protégé of William Crolly and friend of both
Newman and Wiseman, became President of Maynooth in
1857, and he was particularly watched by Cullen. Russell
was a good scholar and moved easily in society with friends
like Lord Dufferin, and although he tolerated the growth of
Roman devotions in the college, Cullen never forgot that he
had been an intimate of George Crolly. Another friend of
Crolly's from student days was Patrick Murray, who, although
in later years he became a vigorous supporter of papal infallibility, was regarded with great suspicion by Cullen because
he had not opposed the Queen's Colleges. Perhaps the common
quality these men shared was that they were all of Ulster
origin and had thought well of the much-maligned William
Crolly.

Another element in Cullen's attitude towards Maynooth
reflected his loyalty to the Irish College in Rome and his
jealousy of the popularity of the larger seminary. In 1865
he revealed to Kirby his concern that the men who had
received the best training available at Maynooth were becoming dominant in the Irish Church:

It would be desirable that those who have talent and wish
to study should be kept for some time after terminating
their course. The distinguished students of Maynooth are
kept three years. The students coming from Rome, unless
they get some extra time, cannot compete with them.
Hence all the offices of any moment are filled from Maynooth. Outside of Dublin scarcely any Roman student
occupies a high position. (K: 17 Mar. 1865)

When Disestablishment was being discussed, and it became
clear the bill would call for Maynooth to lose its government
subsidy, Cullen assured Kirby that even the closing of the
seminary would be no great loss to the Irish Church:

In Dublin we have Clonliffe which will soon suffice for this diocese. In others they have also large seminaries. The people are not now willing to pay because they hear so much of the large grant to Maynooth, but if they knew that we were receiving nothing from the government they would be ready to support their own children whilst studying for the Church. (K: 10 May 1868)

Cullen never lost this suspicion of Maynooth because to the end of his days he considered its essential spirit to be Gallican or Jansenist, influencing those priests who in their quest for Catholic ascendancy were more apt to ally themselves with non-sectarian nationalist movements like Young Ireland, Fenianism or Home Rule, rather than his Ultramontane mission. Cullen's problems with Maynooth's brand of Gallicanism were nothing, however, compared with the challenge to his authority presented by the intensely nationalistic Irish College in Paris. The college had been refounded, with substantial endowments, after the French Revolution, and its professors were well paid. It was an important institution, numbering among its early students and professors men like William Keane, Edward Maginn, Laurence Gillooly, David Moriarty and T. W. Croke.

From 1828 until his retirement in 1850 the rector was Patrick McSweeney. When he stepped down there was a reorganisation of the college under John MacHale, John Cantwell and Cornelius Denvir, who represented the Irish hierarchy. The French government also had a say in its organisation and direction, as did a council of professors who could hear appeals against the rector. The newly appointed rector when Cullen was making his way to Ireland was John Miley, a relative of Cullen and a friend of Daniel O'Connell who had accompanied the Liberator on his last tragic journey. Cullen thought highly of Miley, who had acted as one of his informants when he was on Daniel Murray's staff at Marlborough Street. Miley strongly opposed the Charitable Bequests Act and the Queen's Colleges and supported the Catholic University, and when a successor for Murray was being considered Cullen told Bernard Smith: 'Perhaps Dr Miley of Paris would be on the list. He would be the best of all.' (BS: 26 Feb. 1852) Unfortunately for Miley, however, he was destined to remain in Paris, and his ordeal there put an end to what had started out to be a promising ecclesiastical career.

The college had a bad reputation in Rome, where Cullen had been informed as early as 1833 that discipline within it was deplorable. (C: 27 May 1833) During his years as Irish agent in Rome he heard numerous stories of scandalous misbehaviour in the college, and on his way to Ireland he determined to stay there and see the state of affairs for himself. What he found was appalling. In subsequent letters to Kirby he revealed that McSweeney, who had retained authority as administrator of the college property, was showing signs of a breakdown ('the poor man is playing queer pranks') and would only meet him in the presence of lawyers. Cullen took the opportunity of lecturing the students, but he confessed that his strictures upon the need to show obedience to superiors were unlikely to have much effect: 'Altogether this college is in a bad way. Poor Ireland has much to fear from its future ministers — we must endeavour to keep up the Roman college . . . and keep a little better spirit among us.' (NK: 16, 20 Apr. 1850)

Part of the problem in the college was that the students were, according to Cullen, 'old rough fellows' with 'great pretensions' and ever ready to question authority. Laurence Forde had told him after a visit to the college that Patrick McSweeney had once been barricaded in his room by students who starved him into submission to their demands for an easier promotion to orders. As for the professors, Cullen told Bernard Smith that they were all badly infected with the rebellious Gallican spirit of Maynooth:

> The professors are nearly all young lads from Maynooth who bring the spirit of that college and propagate it there. If a few good professors from Rome were introduced there things might be much better. (BS: 28 Feb. 1852)

The complicated government of the college created a situation wide open for intrigue; the college was living beyond its means; and the probability of a scandal or an explosion seemed imminent.

The crisis came when MacHale, on a visit to Paris in 1852,

defended the college's use of the theology of Bailly, a French Gallican, on the grounds that his work was still studied at Maynooth. Miley protested that Rome did not like Bailly's theology, that it was soon to go on the Index, and that he did not want it used. However, he had to confess to Kirby that his counsel was ignored by a young professor, James Rice, who continued to use Bailly. (K: 28 Nov. 1852) Rice was supported by two other professors, one of whom was Thomas MacHale, a nephew of 'the Lion'. In 1854 Miley told Kirby that whenever a MacHaleite bishop stopped at the college on his way to Rome trouble inevitably followed among those who supported Rice and Thomas MacHale. In fact, at that time Miley was terrified that 'the Lion' himself would call on his way home from Rome 'to cause more trouble'. (K: 20 Sept. 1854) Trouble when it came, however, was even more threatening than Miley could have foreseen. After a brilliant course of study at Maynooth there came to the college 'to strengthen the Tuam faction' that most troublesome of agitating priests, Patrick Lavelle. He immediately established himself as a leader of the dissidents who were making Miley's life miserable, and stories soon began to be told in both Ireland and Rome about the unsettled state of affairs in Miley's institution. By the spring of 1856 Miley had to report to Kirby that stories about scandal in the Irish College were also appearing in the French press, and he believed some of them were written by Lavelle and his companions. (K: 6 Apr. 1856)

Matters became very bad during 1857 and 1858 as open warfare developed between Miley and the MacHaleites, with Rice and Lavelle alleging that Miley had ordered domestic servants to give them physical beatings. With the situation getting out of hand, Miley tried 'excluding' Rice and Lavelle from the college and turned to the Cardinal Archbishop of Paris for 'counsel and direction'. When the two professors were locked out they got a ladder, tried to climb the garden wall, and were arrested by the Paris police. This incident ensured that the college's internal disorders became a public scandal. Miley knew well how annoyed the Irish hierarchy would be about these developments, and he wrote to Cullen to deny that he had summoned the gendarmes and to describe his ordeal during the MacHaleite 'reign of terror' when the dissidents were getting up a petition against him:

> Students who refused to yield were afraid to go to their rooms after night prayer. The stairs were guarded by bands of the most violent armed with clubs; some had carried their knives from the refectory. Several times I was implored by the servants to have an armed force to protect them and others. Students took refuge under the greatest terror in my own apartment, where the servants arranged material for them to pass the night. . . . Other students feigned sickness and kept their beds in order to escape being forced to sign. (C: 31 Mar. 1858)

By the beginning of 1858 Miley was clearly breaking down under the strain of the never-ending agitating by the MacHaleites. He told Cullen how distressed he was that 'a venerable prelate member of the board' had called him a 'dangerous lunatic', and that this assault on his character had become common knowledge in the Irish Church. (C: 16 June 1858) Then in letter after letter he described the persecution he was enduring at the hands of Lavelle, Rice and others. His windows were broken, he was under continuous verbal assault, and an attempt was made to besiege him in his room. On one occasion he told Kirby how depressed and isolated he felt when bishops like Moriarty, Keane and Cantwell were all prejudiced against him, and when Derry was saying he 'was not fit for the mad house in Paris'. (K: 15 May 1858)

Propaganda's appointment of Joseph Dixon as visitor to the seminary in June 1858 was the last straw for Miley. He was convinced that Dixon was prejudiced against him, and his letters to Cullen and Kirby indicated that he was now on the verge of a total breakdown. In fact, Dixon recommended that Vincentians be brought in to reorganise the college while Miley continued as administrator, but the distracted rector so interfered with their work that they threatened to resign unless he was removed. Finally Miley was in August persuaded to vacate his post, and he returned to Ireland to accept the parish of Bray. Slowly under Vincentian guidance peace returned to the Irish College as Roman discipline was intro- duced and maintained. Miley died two years later in 1861.

3. *Patrick Lavelle and the Fenians*

One of the reasons why peace was restored to the Irish College in Paris was that John MacHale had recalled the pugnacious Patrick Lavelle to Ireland. There, after a short service as a curate in the Partry district of Co. Mayo, he became administrator and then parish priest in Cong. In his new area of influence he renewed a campaign initiated by his predecessor against Thomas Plunket, the Protestant Bishop of Tuam. By 1860 the *Mayo Constitution* was filled with reports of Lavelle's highly successful agitation and his lawsuits. He made enough noise in his 'war in Partry' for the affair to come to the notice of influential people far away from that remote and desolate area: the Bishop of Orléans preached against Plunket's 'inhumanity'; the *Times* took up the story; and the House of Commons set up a select committee to look into the wrongdoings of the Protestant prelate.

If Lavelle had confined his agitation to his attacks on the Protestant bishop, Cullen would in general have approved his campaign. In 1861, however, Lavelle became very much involved with the National Brotherhood of St Patrick, a front for the revolutionary Irish Republican Brotherhood. Cullen heard of this organisation and quickly passed on to Propaganda his assessment of it as a dangerous body, filled with Protestants who secretly served the government, one of its leaders being a Presbyterian called Underwood. The Catholics who supported it were dupes, led on by Protestants and Socinians intent upon promoting excesses which would bring back penal laws and the weakening of the Roman Catholic Church. (PFS, XXXIV, 208: 29 Nov. 1861) Writing to Monsell, he further developed this interpretation of the new brotherhood, which, like other Ribbon-type societies, was encouraged by the Orangemen because it 'fattened victims for the gallows and the convict ships'. (NLI, 7723: 7 Jan. 1862)

Lavelle brought himself to the attention of Cullen in a challenging way when he came to Dublin to deliver a panegyric and lead thousands of mourners in the *De Profundis* at the funeral of Terence Bellew McManus, the Young Irelander, whose body had been brought from America. Cullen had refused a lying in state in the Pro-Cathedral for the '48 rebel, and he was furious over the demonstration at Glasnevin.

He assured Propaganda that there had been no Catholics of any note in the procession, but he resented greatly a Tuam priest coming to conduct a service for McManus, who had never belonged to the Dublin archdiocese. As well as writing to Rome to defend the position he had assumed, he also expressed his concern to Monsell over what the new unrest signified:

> In Dublin some foolish people, following up the M'Manus manifestation are establishing clubs throughout the city. The persons engaged in this work call themselves Brothers of St Patrick. One of the rules of the brothers is to learn the use of firearms. They say that they have a great many of their society in Cork and Limerick. I suspect that these ... get the people into mischief and then inform on them. There are also some fellows here swearing poor dupes to fight for Ireland. I met some of them but they would not tell who was swearing them, or when or how they were to fight. I wish the leaders could be caught and prosecuted. All the clergy here are active in opposing the movement, so I hope it will not spread. (NLI, 8317: 8 Jan. 1862)

Cullen also reported to Rome the attacks being made on him by Lavelle which were reported in the newspapers, and how MacHale had replied to a request to call the agitator home by saying 'without courtesy and with insolence' that he would pass on to Lavelle a copy of Cullen's letter. He further urged Rome to order MacHale to curb Lavelle and to forbid his writing for men who served 'Mazzinianism and hatred of the Church'. MacHale's answer to Propaganda's request for information about what was happening suggested that when twenty or thirty thousand people could gather together in two cities against the wishes of both bishops, and when the bishops themselves were divided over how to control Irish nationalism, it would be wise to be prudent. As for Lavelle, MacHale continued, he had been reprimanded for leaving his parish, but the attempts to censure him for his alleged misdeeds smacked strongly of victimisation. In particular MacHale did not like the criticisms that were being made of Lavelle's past activities in the Irish College in Paris. There, said MacHale, John Miley had caused all the trouble, but never once had

Cullen criticised him. (PFS, XXXIV, 285: 19 Jan. 1862) Three months later MacHale made a further complaint about Cullen to Propaganda, saying that papal rescripts were not being passed on to him, and expressing the hope that for the sake of religion in Ireland all Roman affairs should not be handled through the agency of the Archbishop of Dublin. Cullen was a man of considerable ability, said MacHale, but the more his authority grew the more the esteem of the people for Rome declined. Unfortunately for Ireland, Archbishops of Dublin had always favoured the British government and put private interests before those of the Church. (PFS, XXXIV, 369-70: 14 Apr. 1862)

Rome had just had to deal with the nationalist crisis in Poland, and the papal states had recently been lost to the Italian nationalists. Not surprisingly, the curia decided to let MacHale and Lavelle alone if that was possible. When MacHale did receive a rather vague cautionary letter from the pope himself its emphasis was on MacHale's lack of support for the Catholic University rather than on the Lavelle affair. Even when Cullen visited Rome at this time for a canonisation ceremony, and talked to Pio Nono about the unrest in Ireland, it was clear that Rome was going to be 'prudent' as MacHale had suggested.

The papacy was wise to assume a 'wait and see' policy at this time. By 1863 Kirby was receiving letters from priests like John Crotty of Waterford, who told him that in his area the young men who were not emigrating because of the agricultural depression were becoming 'sworn members of one of the secret societies lately so common in Ireland'. (K: 12 Mar. 1863) In similar vein Archbishop Leahy of Cashel described to Kirby the kind of social conditions that had always spawned secret societies in Ireland: a great depression which diminished even the income of bishops and priests, and a 'wicked anti-Catholic, anti-Roman, anti-Irish, anti-everything dear to us government' which drove the people to despair. (K: 31 Mar. 1863) In this kind of situation all that Cullen could do was to try to control the people who were tempted to join secret societies which the government would assuredly try to persuade to engage in outrage so that penal laws would be brought back to Ireland.

Cullen could also, and did, keep Kirby and other Roman officials posted on the activities of the Brotherhood of St Patrick, to which Lavelle belonged. In June he told Kirby that MacHale had subscribed to the organisation's paper, the *Irishman*, and that Lavelle was in Dublin to promote membership in the society. The Brotherhood of St Patrick was condemned at a meeting of the bishops convened by Cullen in August, and all but MacHale and Derry joined in a criticism of Lavelle's writings. When he told Kirby of this Cullen said that MacHale had been very upset by the attitude of the other bishops, but in later letters he confessed that because of his stubborn nature he doubted that 'the Lion' would cease his covert support of Lavelle unless Propaganda forced him to do so.

During the autumn of 1863 he continued to pass on to Kirby what his agents were telling him about the activities of MacHale and Lavelle. The latter was reported to have received 'great sums' from the Fenians in America, and he was describing Cullen in the *Connaught Patriot* and the *Glasgow Free Press* as the Roman prelate who had crushed the Tenant League. Kirby was urged to have translated into Italian for Propaganda Lavelle's charge in the *Mayo Telegraph* that Cullen was gouging the poor of their subsistence for support of 'that West British, anti-Irish institution', the Catholic University. This, it was alleged, was part of Cullen's attempt to 'denationalise' Catholic youth. (K: 27 Nov. 1863) When he heard that MacHale had at last received a strongly worded letter of censure from the pope, telling him to suspend Lavelle, Cullen warned Kirby: 'Do not let him see the students or treat with them. If he gets among them he will upset everything as he did in Paris.' (K: 29 Dec. 1863)

At the beginning of 1864 Cullen informed Propaganda of his belief that there was a close connection between the Brotherhood of St Patrick and the American Fenians. He was convinced that the government was letting the Irish society flourish and expand, in the sure knowledge that it would eventually turn on the Catholic Church. (PFS, XXXIV, 1046-7: 15 Jan. 1864) He also deluged Propaganda with the writings of Lavelle and his supporters, pointing out that they were pro-Garibaldi and that they had openly attacked Cardinal

Barnabo and told the pope to mind his own business. He told Kirby that he was now satisfied that the connection between the Brotherhood of St Patrick and the Americans was so close that the Irish society with its new Dublin publication was in fact Fenian:

> Our Fenian brothers are doing all the mischief they can. They publish here a most wicked and insolent paper called the *Irish People*; it is more Protestant than Catholic, and it is very hard on priests, bishops and the Pope. It is supported by American money but I suppose it will not last long.
>
> (K: 4 Mar. 1864)

Much of Cullen's information came from lengthy correspondence with Archbishop Spalding of Baltimore. (DAA: 12 Nov. 1864) Turning to Lavelle himself, Cullen noted on 5 April that his sister had been sent to a good boarding school in England and was now well married, and it was clear to him that the ferocious little priest from Partry had wealthy patrons somewhere. Ten days later he recounted to Kirby a story about Lavelle beating up a poor man on the streets of Westport after a quarrel about money. (K)

Cullen was bothered by Lavelle's charge that the papal legate was extorting money out of the starving Irish peasantry to support the pope's war with the Italian nationalists, but he assured Kirby on 19 July that these attacks only stimulated the people to give more to His Holiness 'in these days of distress'. (K) On 6 August he reported that Lavelle was raising funds in heretical England:

> Fr Lavelle is working like a fallen spirit in England. He will do great mischief among the poor Irish. The whole of his lecture is directed against me, but he will damage the authority of all the bishops and the Pope. He preaches revolutionary doctrines openly. I think Dr MacHale is afraid of him. His Grace has probably written many letters of encouragement or sympathy to him, and he knows that Lavelle would publish them all and inflict great disgrace on his name were Dr MacHale to move in the matter. (K)

Not long afterwards Cullen discovered in the *Connaught Patriot* an article which he told Kirby was 'quite Jansenistical or Gallican. . . . The Pope's censures may be treated as waste-paper. . . . The councils are over and superior to the Pope.' (K: 9 Sept. 1864) He made sure that the offending piece was sent directly to the pontiff. In a subsequent letter he described the MacHale/Lavelle agitation as an amalgam of everything he hated ideologically:

> I fear our Fenians are spreading. I have no doubt they are encouraged by those who wish to keep up the Protestant Church. The *Irish People*, their organ, is as bad as a Mazzini paper. I have got the address of the clergy to Dr MacHale. It is drawn up in the name of all the clergy of the Province of Tuam. It extolls His Grace to the stars. At the end there is a paragraph expressing regret that the Pope has mis-understood his political opinions and compelled him to visit censures for undue interference in politics on a clergy-man who has certainly done good service in extirpating heresy and proselytism. (K: 9 Dec. 1864)

In what was popularly interpreted as a desperate attempt to regain political initiative once more Cullen organised the National Association at the end of 1864. Its stated purpose was the achievement of tenant rights, as well as the disestab-lishment of the Church of Ireland and reform in education. From the time of its initial meeting the organisation failed to catch the public imagination, and its critics pointed out that only the last two of its aims were of concern to Cullen. On 10 January 1865 the *Dublin Evening Mail* dismissed this ploy by the papal delegate:

> It will be generally regarded as only a fresh attempt to Ultramontanise the Irish people. . . . It is Ireland's mis-fortune that she can never find leaders who are able to rise superior to sectarianism.

Cullen's agents soon persuaded him that the National Associ-ation would never succeed. One of them, John O'Leary, an alumnus of the Irish College in Rome who was now on the staff of St Colman's College, Fermoy, wrote back to Kirby to report that the 'poor people . . . have not frequented the sacraments since the publication against the St Patrick's Brotherhood or the Fenians appeared'. As for Cullen's initiative: 'All people are downcast and hopeless, have lost their confidence in the bishops except in a few, and care not for the Association.' (K: 28 July 1865) Cullen was astute enough to recognise what was happening, and from this time little reference to the National Association appears in his letters.

As the events of 1865 unfolded, however, Cullen kept Kirby up to date on every development. He jubilantly reported news of the arrest of Martin Brennan, editor of the *Connaught Patriot*, explaining that the evidence brought against him showed how dangerous to the Church the Fenians were:

> In the statement ... of the Crown prosecutor it is asserted that the Fenians wished to establish an Irish Republic and that they proposed to confiscate all the property of the country and to massacre the gentry and the Catholic clergy. I have heard that Dr Leahy of Cashel and I were specially marked out. (K: 8 Oct. 1865)

At this time, in a pastoral of 10 October, he reminded the faithful that the Fenian movement was logically created by Orangemen. That was why those who persisted in supporting secret societies were excommunicated, whether they were Ribbonmen, Fenians or Freemasons, because they essentially served the real enemies of the faith, like the Protestants of England who were passionate supporters of Garibaldi. (*Letters*, II, 388-404) Cullen was delighted when James Stephens, 'an open infidel', was arrested, and when the Fenian Luby received his sentence Cullen reminded Kirby that he was the son of a parson and a nephew of a Fellow of Trinity College, and that the young man himself was probably an atheist. On 20 January 1866 he told Kirby that the events of the past year showed the Fenians to be 'nothing more than disciples of Mazzini', willing to take advantage of the 'foolish rage' of the people provoked by the Orangemen. Reporting that his house had been threatened by the Fenians, he was sure that any such undertaking had the blessings of the Orangemen. (K)

When the risings took place in the spring of 1867 Cullen described the rebels as 'reckless madmen who would rob us of the only treasure we have, our religion'. (K: 6 Mar. 1867) As for the soldiers who put down the rebels at Tallaght, he had nothing but praise for their actions:

The Captain Burke just mentioned is an excellent Catholic and he and his men all went to confession the day before the affray in order to prepare for the worst. . . . The unfortunate Fenians generally attempted to go to confession but they were always told that unless they gave up their insane projects they could not get absolution.

(K: 8 Mar. 1867)

One fact that gave Cullen particular satisfaction was the number of National School teachers arrested at the time: 'Lord Naas stated in the House of Commons that twenty-nine National School masters had joined. . . . This ought to convince our rulers that education without religious control is well calculated to promote revolution.' (K: 12 Mar. 1867)

His running account of the Fenian crisis in the spring of 1867 shows that Cullen interpreted the actual fighting in terms which strangely fused religion and politics: 'The police who scattered local Fenians are all good Catholics, Captain Burke a weekly communicant.' (K: 18 Mar. 1867) 'At the head of all in Ireland, General Massy has turned informer. . . . He is a Protestant.' (K: 12 Apr. 1867) Although he interceded with the Lord Lieutenant to save the lives of condemned Fenians, he told Kirby that this reflected 'great alarm here lest disturbances should occur if the Fenians were executed'. (K: 6 June 1867) When the 'Manchester Martyrs' were hanged his terse comment was merely: 'Three Fenians hanged yesterday. They were not half as bad as the Garibaldians.' (K: 24 Nov. 1867) He was greatly upset in December when Lavelle celebrated a high mass for the Manchester victims at Cong and another such mass was sung in Tuam cathedral, for Cullen believed 'it was a great mistake to canonise such men'. He told Kirby in disgust that the leader of the Dublin procession in honour of the martyrs was a Presbyterian called Martin, 'who cares little for prayers for the dead'. (K: 7 Feb. 1868)

Cullen's obsession with the religious element in the Fenian movement reflected his conviction that the whole unrest had its source in an Orange and government plot to 'disturb the people in order afterwards to curtail their rights'. After the editors of the *Nation* and the *Irishman* were arrested Cullen told Kirby cynically: 'They will be treated leniently as they were injuring Catholicity as much as the State.' (K: 20 Feb.

1868) When the government showed little inclination to curb Fenian demonstrations he remarked that it was a clever attempt to withstand the growing pressure for an end to the Established Church, for a major Fenian outrage would give the administration 'grounds for penal enactments and for resisting the suppression of the Establishment'. (K: 26 Oct. 1868) Above all, Cullen told Leahy, the people had to be kept quiet while negotiations with Gladstone continued. (CA, 1868/20)

The real danger for the Irish dissidents lay in their association with the infidel American Fenians who were open enemies of the faith. Commenting on the New York Fenian paper, the *Irish Republic*, Cullen pointed out to Kirby:

> The editors or correspondents state they care nothing for the religion of Ireland, their only object being to free the race. They attack the bishops and priests and contend that the parochial system is as bad for the country as if it had been devised by the devil. (NK: 3 Jan. 1869)

The tragedy for Ireland was that the government allowed such enemies of the Church to sow dissension among the Catholic people. When Gladstone approached Cullen in 1870, hoping to gain his support for the government's new Land Act, Cullen informed him of his dismay over the administration's toleration 'of a great number of adventurers from America who have plenty of money at their disposal'. Why did the government not drive them from the country? Why instead did it tolerate the publication of 'several Fenian and seditious papers in Dublin'? This was what was of importance to Cullen: 'the ravages of an infidel and revolutionary press subsidised and maintained to a great extent by foreign gold'. (BM, 44425: 12 Mar. 1870)

During 1869 Lavelle remained active, visiting Maynooth in Cullen's absence, and writing in the *Irishman* that the Fenians were not excommunicated by Rome and that Cullen was unjustified in using against them decrees aimed at organisations like the Carbonari or the Freemasons. Cullen was so exasperated that he told Kirby: 'Rome has something also to answer for on account of the way in which they let Fr Lavelle go on.' (NK: 2 Nov. 1869) Finally, however, the Holy

Office officially named the Fenian organisation as one of the forbidden and condemned societies whose members were subject to excommunication. When the Fenians then tended to go underground to carry on their campaign Cullen observed to Kirby that they were now finally showing the cause they served:

> The Fenians are coalescing with the ultra-Protestants. Their cry now is that we should give a share in all public Catholic institutions and in their government to Protestants. Here in Dublin they made an attempt to put in five Protestants as managers of a Catholic hospital. . . . They are also joining the Protestants in favour of mixed education.
>
> (K: 23 Jan. 1871)

If the Fenians, in Cullen's mind, were now 'coalesced' with the Protestants, he also had to admit that one of their staunchest supporters was still very much within the Catholic Church and ready to promote their nationalist ideals. By the time of Vatican Council I Cullen was furious when the Fenians boasted that the people of Dublin had no use for papal infallibility, and that the prelate the whole country looked to for leadership was not the cardinal but Archbishop John MacHale of Tuam. Cullen was not surprised when the nationalist movement metamorphosed again, or when MacHale once more identified himself with it.

4. *Home Rule and Cullen's Nationalism*

Cullen's falling out with Gladstone after Vatican Council I marked the end of his alliance with the Liberals, but before that he had become aware of a reappearance of a kind of constitutional nationalist movement that looked like a resurrection of the old demand for an independent opposition of the Tenant League days. In January 1868 some 1600 clergy had signed the Limerick Declaration which called for the repeal of the Union. On 9 August 1868 Nicholas Power, the Coadjutor Bishop of Killaloe, warned him that in the forthcoming general election there was no certainty that in some areas support would be given to Liberal candidates:

> The clergy of Killaloe will support the two Liberal candidates . . . but I fear we shall not have the unanimous

co-operation of Ardagh and Meath as they seem to entertain peculiar notions of independent opposition fostered
by the late Mr Lucas and they are likely to do now what
they have done before, oppose the Whigs at any hazard
and make way for a Tory. (DAA)

Cullen was certainly suspicious of Home Rule as it developed, and this suspicion deepened when MacHale and some
other bishops began to support what looked like a manoeuvre
by Protestants who were Orangemen and Tories to get into
parliament by playing the patriot game. Cullen had watched
carefully an election in Clogher in July 1871 where his
favoured candidate was a Liberal, Owen Lewis. Lewis lived in
London, but he and his wife were both converts, were great
friends of the London Jesuits, had a 'long purse', and supported
the demand for Catholic denominational education. Cullen
was upset, therefore, when Bishop James Donnelly of Clogher
wrote to him to say that Lewis was bound to be defeated by
the Home Rule candidate, John Madden, a vehement Orangeman whose supporters included a Dublin priest, Thaddeus
O'Malley, the erstwhile member of Daniel Murray's household who had annoyed Cullen greatly through the years.

O'Malley had written to Donnelly to urge that sectarian
rivalries be put aside for the sake of the nation. In his letter,
which was passed on to Cullen on 1 July 1871, he stated his
belief that only a 'federalism' like that suggested by Isaac
Butt, the leader of the Home Rule party, would be able to
bring to Irish society the reforms that were needed:

> Mr Butt, himself, has called me the father of federalism
> in Ireland. It is on that platform only we can ever rally all
> sections of the country in favour of Home Rule. . . . It
> would have an admirable effect to see the Catholic Bishop
> of Clogher and clergy sustaining so decided a Protestant
> from pure patriotism and it would greatly neutralise the
> Orange antagonism. (PRONI, DIO(RC) 1/11/10)

Cullen's reply to Donnelly on 15 July 1871 showed how
distressed he was that the Home Rule party, which was
enthusiastically supported by many Catholics, should consider
sponsoring an Orange candidate in Clogher. He was deeply
suspicious of Butt, whom he considered to be a Protestant

place-seeker of questionable morality. As for O'Malley, Cullen had long tolerated him because he was destitute, but in a private note added to his letter to Donnelly the cardinal promised: 'I will put Mr O'Malley out of the way of doing any more mischief.' (PRONI, DIO(RC) 1/11/32)

The support given by some Orangemen to the Home Rule movement was an aberration reflecting their wrath over Disestablishment, and it soon waned; but the kind of insight that Cullen received in Clogher was not to be forgotten. Whatever happened over Home Rule, he could not be easy over a party which welcomed ex-Tories, Protestants and even active Orangemen. These were not the men who could be relied upon to campaign for denominational education, close down the Queen's Colleges, obtain a charter for the Catholic University, or lend support to Pio Nono in the *kulturkampf* in Germany. Cullen never produced a comprehensive assessment of the new nationalist movement, but Moran did, and it is safe to assume that he was echoing his uncle's thoughts when he wrote to Kirby on 25 August 1871:

> The great political question now is Home Rule, but as usual this is only a mask for the real political views of the agitators. Some have taken it up in the hope to divide the people from the bishops and clergy, and hence the names of the most bitter Orangemen in Ireland will be found among the leaders of Home Rule; others have taken it up merely to save Trinity College, as they think by putting the people of Ireland on a false scent that attention will not be given to the Trinity College grievance, and hence some of the fellows of TCD have given in their names to the Home Rule ... others take it up in the cause of Fenianism, and hence all the Fenian newspapers and Fenian agents have adopted it as their cry. All the Tories are taking it up as a good party cry against Mr Gladstone, and, in fine, our agitators, who are only seeking to feather their own nests and to obtain a seat in Parliament, have adopted the same popular cry. . . . All the young priests have also taken the matter up in some dioceses to the annoyance of the peaceable parishioners. . . . At the same time no one wishes to attack the Home Rulers openly, thinking it better to let the bubble burst. (K)

Although some Protestants believed that 'Home Rule is auxiliary to the Ultramontane policy of the Church', and some Home Rule candidates pledged support for denominational education in return for Catholic votes, Cullen's Italian hand was in no way directing the new movement. He expected no aid from the victorious Tories of 1874 in issues that mattered to him, such as rendering assistance to the pope in his difficulties. Neither did he expect any help from the Home Rulers in the advancement of Ultramontane authority in the Irish Catholic Church. Fortunately for Cullen's peace of mind, he never lived to witness what he had feared might emerge from a non-sectarian political movement like Home Rule: the spectacle of Irish Catholics being led by a Protestant 'uncrowned king', and bishops so dominated by the passions of a rural land war that they would ignore even papal admonitions.

It is probable that the real basis for Cullen's lack of enthusiasm for Home Rule, or any other Irish political development, was that it would need to operate in an English context, and Paul Cullen was very much an Irish nationalist in the sense that he had no use for anything English. As far as he was concerned, England was an infidel country where, as he told Kirby, the unfortunate Protestants had 'never heard of Christ, and scarcely knew there was a God. . . . What happy effects of the Reformation!' (NK: 14 July 1840) Even the Catholics in this pagan land were influenced by this spiritual contagion, as was demonstrated by the fact that no more than one Catholic in ten ever attended mass. (K: 25 June 1842)

As for the English hierarchy, Cullen had warned Kirby never to trust Nicholas Wiseman if he called at the Irish College: 'He is very hostile to Irishmen.' (K: 25 Aug. 1842) Later he extended his suspicion of Wiseman to include all the English bishops, who 'may turn the tables on us some fine day and join the government against us'. (K: 10 Jan. 1851) Kirby later showed his own anti-English prejudice by refusing to join Wiseman in an audience with the pope. In 1860 Dominic O'Brien, Bishop of Waterford, wrote to him to indicate that most Irish bishops shared the feelings of Cullen and Kirby:

I congratulate you on the attitude you assumed in the

affair of the English address ... it has been my opinion
for many years that Cardinal Wiseman would like to have
the Irish Church at his feet. He would be glad to see our
ancient and independent hierarchy absorbed by England of
which he himself is the head. (K: 5 Mar. 1860)

When it came to the English Catholic clergy, Cullen pointed
out to Kirby that many of them wrote anonymously in support of Garibaldi and showed other signs of having no enthusiasm for Ultramontanism. As for the English converts to
Catholicism, Cullen never trusted them, especially in matters
relating to education. He particularly disliked the English professors brought to the Catholic University by Newman, and
he told Kirby: 'If they open a university in England, we ought
to send home every one of them.' (K: 12 Feb. 1864) In the
last year of his life he poured his scorn on one English
Catholic called Renouf, who had been made an assistant
commissioner of National Education in Ireland: 'Lately he
published a very wicked dissertation proving that Honorius
was a real heretic and condemned as such — he is now lent to
enlighten us all in Ireland!' (K: 7 July 1878)

Manning's appointment as editor of the *Dublin Review*
prompted a bitter comment to Moran: 'You can guess how
Irish it will be.' (PM, IV, 146) He had little enthusiasm for
Manning's idea of some kind of union of the English and
Irish clergy, asking Kirby: 'What do English Catholics who
support the Tories care for Ireland?' (K: 16 Feb. 1868) In
1876 he tried to find out from Kirby if Manning's visit to
Rome was for the purpose of establishing diplomatic relations between London and the Holy See. Only three months
before his death he again wrote to Kirby to inquire if a
deputation to Rome headed by the Duke of Norfolk was on
the same mission. (NK: 26 July 1878)

If Cullen believed that English Catholics were not to be
trusted when it came to Irish affairs, he became suspicious
to the point of paranoia when he considered the Protestant
British government which, he was convinced, was intent upon making the Irish Church a Gallican, Jansenist and anti-
Roman body. He refused to see the Whigs as other than 'pretended friends' of the Irish, and he told Bernard Smith that
when there was a Tory government Catholics, in the long run,

were better off: 'No one can be cajoled by our present ministers who are professed and open enemies.' (BS: 13 Mar.
1852) When the papacy was undergoing great stress during
the Italian unification crisis Cullen raged in his letter to
Kirby describing the attitude of the British government and
English society towards the struggle in Italy:

> All the Protestants are Garibaldians. They have got Garibaldi
> hats and cloaks. Even the ladies have got Garibaldi cloaks
> and a sort of Garibaldi hat with red feathers. The Tory and
> Orange papers are more revolutionary than the Whigs
> themselves. . . . The whole of England (even many Catholics)
> is for Garibaldi and Revolution. I dare say a change of gov-
> ernment will do no good — the only hope for the Pope is
> in heaven. (NK: 5 Nov. 1860)

During the early 1860s, when Sir Robert Peel, 'a most
determined enemy of every Catholic', was Chief Secretary for
Ireland, Cullen saw in almost every act of parliament 'a most
violent exhibition of bigotry', reporting to Kirby English remarks about Irish emigration being a blessing for all. In Cullen's
view, England's principal concern, next to oppressing the
Catholic Church, was to get as much money out of Ireland
as possible: 'I think all the money of Ireland goes to the Jews
of London. The landlords and bankers live in London and live
extravagantly. The Jews fatten on them, but Ireland is starving.' (K: 28 July 1864) He told Archbishop Spalding of
Baltimore that the government encouraged unrest in the
country and 'delighted' in the old maxim 'Divide and con-
quer'. (DAA: 12 Nov. 1864) In 1867 he indignantly complained to Kirby that such was the callousness of the English
that during an epidemic 'the old clothes of those who died in
London are freely sent over here and scarcely any effort is
made to prevent the spread of the contagion'. (K: 2 Jan. 1867)
In his last years he was sure that Protestantism was falling
before the onslaught of 'infidelity' which, he told Kirby, 'is
making terrible strides in England' (NK: 3 Nov. 1874) and
was obstructing any advance of Catholic culture in Ireland:

> Everything is quiet at present in Ireland, but Catholics
> are under a ban. No Catholic is promoted to any office of
> trust or emolument. Everything goes to Freemasons and

Orangemen. . . . In England infidelity is going ahead, a low revolutionary spirit is also at work. The whole world is more or less in a bad state. (NK: 3 Feb. 1875)

When Cullen was in a depressed state such as this it was because of his comprehensive theological outlook. He was convinced that there was a perennial battle being waged in this world between those who served infidelity and those who served the Roman Catholic Church. Promoting the cause of infidelity in every generation was the sinister power of Freemasonry, that great power in the fallen world which opposed the mission of the pontiff to gather all men into the fold of salvation. At times it seemed to him that the Freemasons were winning the battle, as when the pope was facing defeat in Italy, and when this happened Cullen became almost paranoiac in his denunciation of this occult and pernicious force. Commenting on his advent address of 1861, the *Packet* drew attention to the strange fact that his sharpest strictures were directed not at the government, nor at the rich who were oppressing the poor, but at 'Masonry, where he lists Robespierre, Danton, Marat, Kossuth, Mazzini and Garibaldi'. When Dublin Catholics attended a Freemasons' ball in 1863 he wrote to Propaganda to assure the authorities there that he had reminded the people often about the papal condemnation of Freemasonry, and that he had threatened with excommunication those who ignored the papal decrees. (PFS, XXXIV, 704-7: 12 May 1863)

Part of his anti-English prejudice came from this conviction that many of the ministers of state were Freemasons. He told Kirby that he avoided contact with the government, not because of criticism by the nationalists, but because 'The great people are so addicted to Freemasonry that I am afraid to have any close connexion with them. I would be looked upon as encouraging the craft if I associated with them too much.' (NK: 12 June 1872) Some Catholics were actually seduced by the Freemasons, especially those in the police forces, who had to take an oath not to belong to any political secret society, with the exception of Freemasonry. Some of the Fenians had also been identified as Freemasons; this came as no surprise to Cullen, who remarked to Kirby: 'What fine liberators for the island of saints!' (K: 23 Feb. 1866) Such inroads among the faithful prompted Cullen to be ever more vigilant in his protection of the people:

> Here the Freemasons are working very hard, like their master, seeking whom they may devour. Nearly all the respectable Protestants are members of the craft, and it is very hard for anyone to get a situation in any public office without being enrolled in it. . . . Very few Catholics join the Freemasons, but on that account scarcely any of them can get on in the public offices. . . . In the long run it throws great temptation on poor Catholics.
>
> (K: 25 May 1874)

At times Cullen's obsession with the occult force of evil to be found in Freemasonry appears almost pathological, but to someone nurtured in Ultramontane Rome in the early nineteenth century belief in the power of this sinister authority was commonplace. Pius VII in 1821, Leo XII in 1825, Pius VIII in 1829, Gregory XVI in 1832, and Pius IX no less than six times between 1846 and 1873 issued documents which specifically condemned Freemasonry and forbade Catholics under pain of excommunication to belong to the institution. Wherever the cult took root there was to be found naturalism, religious indifferentism, liberalism and revolution – all that threatened to oppose the mission of the Vicar of Christ upon earth. Cullen's obsession with Freemasonry underlines the difficulty of fitting him into a framework as simplistic as that of the Irish nationalist canon of history. Paul Cullen was in the deepest mystical sense a passionately religious man.

Scholars who try to exorcise this dimension in Cullen's life distort the essence of the man. Whether Cullen was a 'Castle Catholic' or an Irish nationalist remains a problem to some historians, but secular identifications such as this meant nothing to Ireland's first cardinal. He was the creature, as far as it was humanly possible, of the Vicar of Christ here upon earth, the universal ordinary of the Roman Catholic Church, the Supreme Pontiff. His mission was to bring the authority of the pope to the Irish Church, and to battle the power of the great adversary himself wherever he found it in Ireland. Sometimes it appeared in high places in government, and when Cullen opposed it there he was sometimes considered a champion of Irish Catholic culture, if not a nationalist. At other times he found evil which threatened the mission of the Church in those passions which led the Catholics of Ireland to develop their many nationalist movements. At the end of his life he remarked in a much-quoted statement:

> For thirty years I have studied the revolution on the continent; and for nearly thirty years I have watched the nationalist movement in Ireland. It is tainted at its sources with the revolutionary spirit. If ever an attempt is made to abridge the liberties of the Catholic Church in Ireland it will not be by the English government, nor by a 'No Popery' cry in England, but by the revolutionary and irreligious nationalists of Ireland. (Purcell, *Manning*, II, 610)

Some scholars have argued that Cullen as an Irishman, however, never lost a sense of 'deep if inarticulate patriotic feeling' (Edwards, *New History*, 178), and it may be that as the papal delegate successfully carried on his mission some of his opposition to Irish nationalism lessened. Dr Patrick Murray, who suffered Cullen's anti-Gallican inquisition at Maynooth in the early 1850s, which included suspicion of the intense nationalist feeling at that institution, believed that Cullen did mellow in his later years. When Cullen died Murray wrote in his diary:

> He came here as Archbishop of Armagh with very strong views which he often put forward in very strong forms. Very much to his credit, however, it must be said that for many years back those views had been greatly moderated, some of them entirely abandoned. (Corish, *Maynooth*, 180)

Yet few scholars could read into his attitude to the Fenians any nationalist sentiment, and even those who most strongly argue the case of his patriotism admit that he viewed the Home Rule movement with 'lingering uneasiness'. (Steele, *Cullen*, 260)

The overall evidence suggests that Cullen was always an uncompromising Ultramontanist, and, as such, his sense of universal papal mission gave him a deep and abiding suspicion of nationalism in every form. When it encouraged violence he tended to identify it immediately with the revolutionary ideology which had spawned Mazzini and Garibaldi. Whatever patriotism he had brought with him to Rome in his early years was vestigial by the time he began his Irish mission, long displaced by the values he had embraced during his years of Roman formation. Although Cullen may have instinctively distrusted English ways in church, state or society, it may be argued that if the British monarch had been a Catholic he would have supported a traditional union of throne and altar without any compunction. As a passionate defender of the universal mission of the Roman Catholic Church he was always on his guard against any secular authority which threatened to subvert the allegiance of the faithful to the cause of the Supreme Pontiff. His Irish experiences did nothing to dissuade him from his belief that 'later nineteenth-century nationalism showed definite signs of becoming a kind of religion in itself, in actual, if not always theoretical competition with supernatural Christianity'. (Corish, *MacHale*, 399)

IX
The 'Cullenisation' of Ireland

1. The End of an Era

In 1874 died Alessandro Barnabo, Cullen's old friend, who had been Prefect of Propaganda since 1858. Two years later the death took place of Cullen's advocate in the curia, Giacomo Antonelli, the papal Secretary of State who had helped him greatly during the O'Keeffe affair. The generation of ecclesiastics who had helped Pio Nono carry out his Ultramontane counter-revolution was passing away. By 5 May 1877 Cullen himself had grown so feeble that Moran was counselling the appointment of a coadjutor and was telling Kirby: 'He does not know at all how low his strength has decayed in the past year, but we all know it too well.' (K) In July of that year Edward McCabe was consecrated as Cullen's auxiliary bishop. Then came news of the death of Pius IX in February 1878, and Cullen went to Rome for the obsequies. When he returned he held a meeting of the bishops which all attended and where there was a rare spirit of unity. A few days later, on 24 October 1878, Paul Cullen died, working to the very end.

The obituaries in the various newspapers of Ireland and England reveal the respect held for Cullen, even by his severest critics. The *Dublin Evening Mail* on 25 October, as was to be expected, had little good to say about this 'Roman of the Romans' who had governed Catholic Ireland as despotically as any 'satrap of secular Rome in the days of the Caesars'. Cullen was a 'thoroughgoing champion of war to the knife against heretics', and in serving his 'external commission' he turned acquiescent Catholics against their Protestant neighbours. By doing so he destroyed among churchmen the traditional Irish instinct for independence which had characterised the church of Doyle, Crolly and Murray. The paper appreciated his zeal in erecting hospitals and other charitable centres, but it criticised the 'exclusive idea' which he insisted upon in their management and his 'narrow spirit' which required the 'separation of Roman Catholic society from all other, extending even to personal relationships'. It was noted that although Cullen had erected an 'impassable wall' between Ireland's Roman Catholics and Protestant peoples, yet many of his own people did not want such a sectarian division in the country, and with these he dealt as harshly as he had with the Fenians.

On the following day the *Mail* recorded what the English newspapers were saying about Cullen, including the final assessment of him by the *Times*:

> In him Rome was everything. . . . Fervently sincere, single-minded, devout, unflinching, distrustful of culture, a Catholic and nothing but a Catholic, domineering yet obedient, he represented the militant temper of his church.

The *Mail* agreed with the *Daily News*'s assessment of Cullen as one of the principal agents of the Ultramontane revolution which had in large measure changed Roman Catholicism:

> The papal monarchy has established itself. A sacerdotal Caesarism rules from the Vatican. The Gallican and similar liberties which gave variety and freedom within the limits of the unity of the Church have disappeared. Cardinal Cullen was a principal agent of this change in Ireland . . . wholly without that tincture of polite letters and that taste for . . . scholarly research which liberalised and humanised the sacerdotalism of Cardinal Wiseman. A narrow, rigid devotee . . . conscientious according to his lights and benevolent from a large sense of duty rather than from a genial human nature . . . Cullen won respect of men of all creeds in Ireland . . . but not strong affection.

The *Times* had more to say about Cullen's despotism than was recorded by the *Dublin Evening Mail*. On 25 October it contrasted his character with that of 'the mild and genial Archbishop Murray, whose liberal spirit conciliated . . . and attracted the cordial esteem and friendship of the Protestant gentry'. Zealous, devotional, narrow and illiberal, he was 'an Ultramontane of the most uncompromising type', an ascetic without social sympathies who 'looked if not with suspicion and distrust, at least with cold and gloomy reserve upon those of a heretical creed'. His great accomplishment in Ireland was the raising of 'the old barriers of sectarian isolation and exclusiveness'. Although many Catholics deplored his 'systematic policy' of division, few wished to suffer the fate of Father O'Keeffe. Gone forever now was the freedom of bishops, formerly elected by the clergy before appointment by the pope, and the 'independent parochial jurisdiction' of the parish priest. Ireland was now to a remarkable degree under the 'despotic control' of the Vatican, and the credit for that conquest belonged to Cardinal Cullen and his 'narrow circle' of votaries.

The Catholic press tried to play down the 'remorseless legate' image of Protestant papers like the *Dublin Evening Mail*, the *Times* or the *Standard*, which also had much to say about Cullen's attempt to prevent an 'amalgamation of races and creeds in Ireland' similar to that which had been taking place on the other side of the Irish Sea. The *Freeman's Journal* was bound in black on 25 October and argued that the Protestant press, with its talk of the 'hard Italian monk', the 'ungenial recluse', the 'implacable churchman', the 'unforgiving delegate' and the 'relentless prelate', failed to understand the essential charity of Cardinal Cullen:

> He taught his Protestant fellow countrymen how merciful is the spirit of the Catholic Church, and he made them feel that if ever there was a bishop who was disposed to interpret that merciful spirit according to its most merciful letter it was the man on whom they had so unsparingly poured out their indignation.

The *Freeman* also devoted considerable space to an apology for Cullen's politics, which it located within the O'Connellite tradition, and his belief that 'The man who would smite the altar for a political triumph would not be slow to betray the country if the way of betrayal led to selfish gain.' For Paul Cullen love of the faith and love of the nation had to go hand in hand.

The *Cork Daily Herald* of 25 October told a story of Cullen in humility and sanctity bringing the last sacrament to a dying Catholic domestic in a Protestant family. When he was accosted by the head of the household, and his identity revealed, the gentleman compared Cullen's exercise in consolation with that of his own Protestant bishop: 'You have done more than —— would do.' As for his politics, the Cork paper stressed his European style of conservatism. He served only one cause, that of bringing the people of Ireland to loyal support of the chair of St Peter, and he had done that magnificently.

The *Armagh Guardian* waited until 1 November 1878 to make a major assessment of Cullen's mission from the time he first came to Ireland 'fresh from the banks of the Tiber', laden with anathemas. When he encountered the freedom which then existed in the Irish Catholic Church, it 'must have appeared as licentious to a bureaucrat of the Vatican as the criticism of the House of Commons might seem to an official trained in the silent traditions of Russian obedience'. Fortunately his attempts to build sectarian walls between the Irish peoples, as in the case of education, had been resisted by many priests like Robert O'Keeffe who did not like being treated as 'ecclesiastical Janissaries' or 'mute servants of the Vatican'. In no way, said the *Guardian*, did he serve the Irish peoples. Although Isaac Butt and other important nationalists of both faiths had marched in his funeral procession, there was on that occasion not a single emblem exhibited 'to which the word national could in any sense be applied'. The *Times* was right in its comment that 'If he was not a great Irishman, he was at least a great Ultramontane.'

The Belfast *Northern Whig* of 26 October defended his keeping 'a somewhat high hand over his priests' by noting that in times of unrest this had made him a 'friend to the British government and to the British crown'. The *Londonderry Standard* of the same day confined itself to reproducing its assessment of Cullen as a very successful Catholic cultural imperialist:

The fruits of his zeal are to be seen in the fact that the religious element now enters not only into the question of education, but the ordinary concerns of life. We cannot but respect his sincerity while we deplore the narrowness of his views. At the same time we bear willing testimony to the fidelity and devotion with which . . . the vast power which he wielded was arranged on the side of law and order.

It is interesting to note how shrewd and generally balanced were the assessments made of Cullen's religious, political and cultural importance. It was appreciated that by his unflagging zeal in service of Ultramontanism he had done more to influence the development of life in Ireland than any person since Daniel O'Connell. It was Cullen who brought about the radical separation of the Catholic and Protestant peoples of the land, at the deepest possible level, as an abiding legacy of his creation of a strong, united and militant Ultramontane church in Ireland.

2. *The Man and his Mind*

Apart from trying to criticise or praise him from the viewpoint of their particular newspaper, the journalists did not attempt to consider the origins of Cullen's resolutely Ultramontanist way of thinking. They noted his inflexible antipathy to anything Protestant, and his vigorous anti-modernist spirit, but to consider the thought-processes of this most private of men was not a pursuit that appealed to his journalistic contemporaries. The historian, however, must attempt to deal with the complexities of his thought, if only to understand how easily and how often he could be misrepresented by so many people.

Within the Catholic Church of Cullen's age, as in any era, there were two general tendencies, mental outlooks, traditions, schools or parties of theology, one conservative and one liberal. Although the divisions between them only became clear in the decade of the Syllabus of Errors, when the pontiff's condemnation of liberal scientific thought was a direct challenge to many, the positions each side had assumed were to be found among every generation of churchmen. Generally the conservatives put great emphasis on transcendence and tradition, while the liberals were more open to ideas of God's immanent power in the world, bringing into being a new order. Cullen was a conservative by nature, an active ecclesiastic rather than a speculative theologian, and he found the traditional theology of the Counter-Reformation agreeable to his nature. Especially was the absoluteness of its principles of great value to him when he pragmatically tried to promote his mission of Ultramontane ecclesiastical and cultural imperialism.

Cullen was in every sense an intensely religious man, convinced of the ever-abiding presence of God's transcendent power operative in the affairs of man. In 1832, shortly after he had been appointed Rector of the Irish College, his friend John McCann wrote to him from Dublin, taking for granted that Cullen would understand him when he rejoiced that cholera was bringing a new spirit of penitence among Irish Catholics: 'One can hardly regret its long continuance among us.' (C: 17 Sept. 1832) Forty years later Cullen in a letter to Kirby revealed his continuing belief in the abiding and chastening concern of God during a smallpox epidemic in Dublin: 'The people who frequent the churches are not those who suffer. The drunkard and profligates are more exposed than the good and the virtuous.' (NK: 22 May 1872) God was with those who sought his grace through the mediation of the Catholic Church, but he was also the scourge of men like the Poor Law commissioner who was cut in two by a railway train near Dublin, his 'awfully sudden' death to Cullen being connected with his being 'very oppressive to the poor'. (NK: 10 Mar. 1865) In 1873 he told Kirby of the unfortunate Bishop Samuel Wilberforce of the Anglican diocese of Winchester, who had 'waited too long' before following his brothers' example by converting to Roman Catholicism; he suffered an 'awful death' when thrown from his horse while riding to meet Gladstone. Gloomily in the same letter Cullen told Kirby that he hoped the whole of Irish society did not face the same divine disciplining. The rich were 'never more intent upon amusement . . . newspapers filled with accounts of horse and dog races. . . . I hope things will not turn out as in the days of Noah.' (NK: 24 July 1873)

Cullen's view of the spiritual world which he shared with Kirby would have seemed superstitious, or at least reminiscent of the thought-processes of another age, to many of his contemporary liberal Catholics. In 1851 he described the conversion of a woman to the true faith after returning home from a mass celebrated by a married Italian priest in an Irvingite church ('they say mass validly') to find that wine spilt on her clothes had turned into blood. (NK: 21 July 1851) Another tale with a more sectarian flavour was related to Kirby in 1863:

> A curious thing occurred here lately at Enniskerry. A new church (Protestant) has been built here, and stained glass windows were put up, in one of which St Peter was represented with the keys. The low Protestants of the neighbourhood got indignant and broke off St Peter's legs. A few days afterwards there was a procession in the same town at the Catholic Church of the Blessed Sacrament. An old Protestant woman seeing the procession shouted out 'I suppose they are going to weld St Peter's legs' — on her way to her home some moments afterwards the woman herself fell and broke her own leg. (K: 3 July 1863)

When some priests refused to bless crosses put up in their fields by country people during a cattle plague, it soon became known that this could be done in Dublin because Cullen appreciated 'their great faith'. (K: 5 Feb. 1867)

Pius VI had invoked the protection of the Sacred Heart against the Jansenists, and when Pius IX had encouraged universal devotion to such intercession, Cullen attributed good weather and crops to prayers made through this divine agency in Ireland. At the height of his struggle with O'Keeffe he vowed, at Kirby's suggestion, to dedicate the Dublin archdiocese to the Sacred Heart if 'God turn the lawsuit into something good'. As the trial went on he told Kirby of some of the omens of special favour:

> Fr O'Keeffe fixed Friday, the feast of the Sacred Heart, for the beginning of his law proceedings. Some of the nuns, and especially the Redemptoristines, observed that circumstance and said that it was a bad omen for O'Keeffe. Thanks be to God the Sacred Heart regulated everything unfavourable and disposed the judges to act impartially.
> (NK: 20 June 1872)

By the eve of the last session of Cullen's legal battle with O'Keeffe, Cullen had decided to dedicate Ireland itself to the

Sacred Heart. Thus it was that Ireland from Passion Sunday 1873 was dedicated to a favourite Ultramontane devotion rather than to Patrick, the traditional saint of the Irish people. (K)

Cullen was not only convinced of the reality of religious powers influencing human affairs, but his concern for the supernatural resulted in his leading a singularly ascetic natural existence. His pleasures were almost non-existent apart from his work, and he could labour for long periods of time until exhaustion alone made him cease. His personal friendships, except for a few he had cultivated in his early days in Rome, were rare. The only person he confided in during his Dublin days was his nephew, Patrick Francis Moran. Occasionally he met with the seven Redemptoristine sisters that he had brought from Bruges in 1859, whose mother superior was a niece of Daniel O'Connell. His solitariness worried Laurence Forde, who told Kirby:

> His eminence is leading an eremetical life since Dr Moran left for Kilkenny. This is not good for him as his only recreation is the company of a person domestically intimate with him. (NK: 4 Apr. 1872)

His personal austerity led him to be critical of any self-indulgence on the part of the Irish clergy. When his relative James Maher the younger, who was Vice-Rector of the Irish College in Rome, wished to go to an American exhibition on 'a free ticket' Cullen told Kirby that he should resign if he was intent upon leaving 'the duties of the responsible post he has for the purpose of amusement'. (K: 11 June 1876) He was very critical of those priests who made large sums of money through agricultural commerce or some other worldly pursuit. He was equally upset by stories about the wealth of Cardinal Antonelli and other curial figures. (K: 10 Nov. 1876) As for drink, that other abiding vice of the country priests, even before he came to Ireland he had counselled that 'all ought to be a little mortified and to get settled habits of temperance'. (NK: 15 Aug. 1840) There is little doubt that if Cullen had had the power he would have established a society rather reminiscent of Savonarola's Florence or Calvin's Geneva. When he heard of the assassination of Lincoln he told Kirby:

What a fearful death, that of unfortunate Lincoln, and what a day, Good Friday, to be killed in a theatre. It is a disgrace in a Christian country to have theatrical exhibitions on such a day. (K: 2 May 1865)

This pietistic spirit was extended to intellectual concerns, and Cullen stoutly upheld observance of the Index of forbidden books. William Hutch, one of the brightest graduates of the Irish College in Rome, who was to become the head of St Colman's College, Fermoy, had to beg him for a special dispensation to read Protestant works during his studies. 'Father Prout' always referred to him as 'Anticopernicus' because of his opinions about science, and the title was not misplaced. When the Darwinian revolution began, for example, Cullen was scornful of the theories of the geologist Lyell and other scientists:

Man is only a development of the gorilla — Progress forever. All his arguments are founded on a jaw bone and one tooth of a human found among the fossils of antediluvian date. The *Home and Foreign Review* praises the work and says the sooner we get rid of our present chronology the better — such is the orthodoxy of a Catholic review.
(K: 29 May 1863)

In 1874 Cullen told Kirby what he thought of the inaugural speech given at the opening of the British Association meeting in Belfast by John Tyndall, 'son of a poor Orangeman' from Moran's home parish of Leighlinbridge. It was 'filled with all sorts of infidelity', representative of all that was wicked in the 'progress of science' way of thinking which Cullen was determined to keep out of Ireland. (K: 21 Aug. 1874) In the year of his death Cullen persuaded the Catholic bishops to publish a formal protest against the atheism promoted by men like Tyndall and Thomas Huxley.

Cullen was deeply satisfied with the Syllabus of Errors when it appeared, and he would have agreed with the evaluation of the document made by his protégé John Kilduff, to whom Cullen had acted as almost a father during a major illness when he was a Roman student. Kilduff wrote:

The Holy Father's encyclical has produced amongst the

turbulent spirits of the age a commotion. . . . They have set up a howl of madness, rage and despair which, calmly viewed and considered, constitutes the highest tribute that could be paid to the character of the illustrious Pio Nono. Verily, worldly wisdom and worldly power and worldly greatness and all upon which the presumption and annoyance and intoleration of the ages rest have received a shock under which they must stagger. How different with the faithful and docile children of the Church . . . when in the midst of the storm . . . the Pope rises to the dignity of his sublime offices and with uplifted vision indicates the truth that is eternal. (K: 19 Feb. 1865)

Cullen's support of the Syllabus was well known in Rome. When the Prussian ambassador to Italy sent a report to his Secretary of State in October 1875 regarding those cardinals who might succeed Pius IX as pope he spoke of the 'Syllabist and Infallibilist' Paul Cullen as 'the candidate of the reactionary cardinals'. (Walsh, *Vat. Council*, 59)

Cullen's uncompromisingly rigid outlook was partly responsible for his refusal to have anything to do with Protestants if he could avoid doing so. In 1868 he was forced to convalesce following a period of ill-health, and with Moran he moved into a Monkstown villa owned by a Protestant clergyman who, Moran told Kirby, 'gave up the church service for more congenial occupations'. (K: 5 Aug. 1868) Moran had to tell Kirby in other letters that he and Cullen were astonished to receive visits from Protestants calling to inquire about the cardinal's health, and to hear that prayers for his recovery were being said in Protestant churches. Fortunately for their peace of mind, however, Moran was able to discover that one of the callers, Vokes Mackey, a Tory and a prominent Freemason, was seeking election as Lord Mayor of Dublin. Satisfied that these Protestant overtures were insincere, Moran informed Kirby that he and Cullen intended to keep their callers at a distance. (K: 29 July 1868) There was, however, a certain softening in Cullen's attitude towards Protestants in his last days. His letters to Kirby, often in a very shaky handwriting, contain comments much less sharp than anything written in earlier times. When he told Kirby of the suicide of the Protestant Bishop of Meath in 1876 he said: 'I suppose he was mad — he had a large family and I believe he was very rich. It is a sad fate for the poor man.' (K: 31 July 1876) During his last illness he stayed in another Protestant villa, this time in Blackrock. It was rented from the daughter of the late Protestant Bishop of Tuam, Thomas Plunket, who had been a very active proselytiser. Cullen remarked on the kindness which was being shown to him by many Protestants, and even had a soft word for the Plunket family: 'Latterly they have got the name of souper, but probably Lavelle under whom they lived did not treat them kindly.' (K: 24 July 1878)

3. *Paul Cullen's Legacy*

Cullen's softening of attitude towards at least those Protestants who were personally kind to him without doubt reflects a mellowing that accompanied the decline in his physical powers. When he was in his prime he would have considered himself somehow disloyal to his mission if he had allowed, even on the personal level, any real degree of rapprochement with Protestants. Cullen's desire was to make Ireland as Catholic in a Roman way as it was possible for Ireland to become, and his chief intent was to establish Catholic ascendancy in his native land. By 1858, only eight years after his arrival as papal delegate, his secretary Laurence Forde was able to tell Bernard Smith what a 'total revolution' Cullen was carrying out in Ireland. Everywhere now Catholics were advancing socially, on the bench, in commerce, in railways, even among the landed gentry and nobility. No influential person would now dare to advocate interdenominational education in the Catholic world. A new Irish Catholic culture was being produced in the land, thanks to the incessant labour of the papal delegate with his 'unlimited devotion to the Holy See' which was directing him in his mission. (BS: 17 Feb. 1858) This was the 'Cullenisation' of Ireland that 'Father Prout' so often referred to, the development of a militant Ultramontane Catholic culture intent upon asserting its ascendancy over that of the heretical Protestants. (Mahony, *Works*, xxxiii)

In the days of Daniel Murray and William Crolly there had been among Irish Catholics at least a toleration of the concept of religious and social pluralism in the land. It was accepted that there were two ways of life, which were labelled Catholic and Protestant, and that if only a proper balance could be found between them in terms of ascendancy, then cultural conflict might be minimised. This was the era when in the case of mixed marriages custom often dictated the homely accommodation of the sons taking the faith of the father, and daughters the faith of the mother. The *Irish Catholic Directory* of 1837 in a gesture of ecclesiastical courtesy listed the Irish Protestant bishops from the time of the Reformation and recorded the dates of their consecrations. In the same directory appeared an advertisement for a Catholic college at Seafort, Williamstown, Dublin, run by D. W. Cahill 'for the special education of thirty young gentlemen preparatory to their entrance into Trinity College'.

Toleration of Protestantism in any form, religiously or culturally, became increasingly rare after the arrival of Cullen at mid-century. In a way that none of the bishops of the era of Doyle and Murray had done, he superimposed upon the traditional tribal tensions between Celt and Sassenach, between the oppressed and the ascendant people, between Catholic and Protestant, a spirit of religious absolutism that justified sectarianism in all its forms. Whereas liberal Catholic churchmen looked upon the papal delegate as a Roman ecclesiastical imperialist, Protestants saw him as a cultural imperialist, a promoter of Counter-Reformation Catholic triumphalism. In countless newspaper commentaries, as in the *Packet* on 13 November 1861 or the *Belfast Newsletter* of 18 November 1861, even before the crisis over Disestablishment, the anger of the Protestants over 'government by pastorals' is plainly evident. When a subservient, intimidated government gives in to Cullen's O'Connellite threat *not* to control the masses, it shows clearly that it will do anything 'to appease the anger of the pope's legate'. Ireland's Catholics now are demanding 'ascendancy and domination', and because of 'Ultramontane insatiability' the Protestants fear they face in the future 'universal serfdom'.

Cullen did want Catholic ascendancy in Ireland. Apart from his early years in a Catholic strong farmer's home, where the history of the family had long been one of striving for social ascendancy, his years in Ultramontane Rome had filled him with Counter-Reformation authoritarian zeal. 'Error has no rights', and as papal delegate and cardinal Cullen would have considered himself spiritually remiss if he had not used every possible worldly calculation to establish the spiritual domination of the Roman Catholic Church in the land of Catholic culture. When he battled with the Protestant proselytisers who 'perverted' the Catholic people, he sought to restore his church's numerical strength by using every possible enticement to persuade Protestants of privilege to 'convert'. A favourite tactic for Kirby to arrange a tour of the Eternal City which would, hopefully, fill them with Ultramontane zeal, so that on their return to Ireland they would be spiritually and culturally part of Cullen's crusade for ascendancy. In 1863 he sent Kirby a letter telling him that some influential Protestants who were potential Roman Catholics would be visiting Rome, and recommending also to his care a recent convert:

> I will give letters also to Sir Charles Domville, a late convert, and his wife, Lady Margaret Domville, daughter of Lord Howth, a Protestant. The lady is a most excellent Catholic. Sir Charles is a little strange, he has got into trouble with his tenants, but when he sees what Catholicity is he may become very good — he has great property, but as they have no children that property will go back to Protestants. (K: 20 Oct. 1863)

When Protestants reacted angrily to the continuing Catholic advance at their expense Cullen was delighted, for tactically he needed the growth of sectarianism to wrest ascendancy from the dominant minority people. In 1860 he told Kirby how he addressed an enthusiastic audience in support of the pope, deliberately including material which he knew would provoke the Protestants: 'I took the opportunity of making a very long speech into which I stuffed as much matter as possible, hoping that it would be published by the Protestant papers.' (NK: 12 Jan. 1860) Whatever the issue in Irish or international affairs, whether local educational concerns or the struggle of the great powers in Europe, Cullen thought in terms of Catholic/Protestant conflict. At the height of the Franco-Prussian War he told Kirby: 'All the Catholics are for

France — all the Protestants are Prussians.' (NK: 19 Aug. 1870)
Following the end of that war he praised France as a 'great
Catholic nation' which had long supported the papacy.
(Walsh, *Two Letters*, 90)

After the Disestablishment victory a moderate Catholic like
Bartholomew Woodlock, Rector of the Catholic University,
was willing to consider an armistice in Ireland's sectarian warfare, admitting to John Bright, the English Radical, that
there was then no real Catholic grievance in Ireland. Paul
Cullen never would have agreed with his co-religionists who
were willing to settle for a pluralist society. He was a man
who by nature was always at war, and he would settle for
nothing less than Catholic ascendancy throughout Ireland.
Almost his last words to his disciple Tobias Kirby gave advice
on how to continue the battle which Cullen knew was far
from won:

> There is no chance of getting anything from them through
> love of justice, so speak stoutly . . . yield nothing and
> threaten that you and all Catholics must join the enemies
> of the government if they refuse us justice.
>
> (NK: 27 Mar. 1878)

Although Cullen never came close to establishing Catholic
religious or cultural ascendancy in his lifetime, especially in
Ulster, he did put the Irish Catholic Church on a war footing
to carry on his sectarian mission. Within the Church the
triumphalist spirit of the Counter-Reformation became dominant, and ecclesiastical rewards came the way of those who
served the papal cause. A successful bishop like William Keane
of Cloyne made sure that Cullen and Kirby knew of the sentiments expressed at a dinner for Jesuit missionaries brought in
to win back those who had 'perverted' to Protestantism:

> Oh! Did not the name of Pio Nono sound sweetly on their
> ears!! And did they not with willing hearts and warm feel-
> ings toast his health and pray that he may live long, happy
> and triumphant!!! My dear Dr Kirby, you may be sure that,
> whatever they may have suffered for the faith, Pius the
> Ninth reigns sovereign in the hearts of the Irish priests
> and people. . . . In the synodal address the Peter's Pence
> is to be recommended. (K: 1 May 1861)

296 Paul Cardinal Cullen

A successful priest like Jeremiah Hally, Vicar-General of Waterford, could write to Kirby to seek approbation for his heroic work in service of Ultramontanism during forty-three years in Dungarvan, ridding the community of a National School, denying it a workhouse, building a church, two nunneries, one monastery, raising more Peter's Pence than any other parish priest, and always defending the pope's temporal power. (K: 10 May 1865)

In spite of Cullen's overall success in promoting his Ultramontane mission, he knew in the last years of his life that much still had to be done, particularly in Connaught, where John MacHale and his suffragans strongly resisted the inquisition of the papal delegate. In 1872 the reforming Coadjutor Bishop of Killala, Hugh Conway, who had just taken over from Thomas Feeny, described to Kirby the magnitude of the task before him as he tried to get the drunken and insubordinate priests of Killala back to their spiritual duties:

> The clergy have ... followed the example of the bishop, Dr Feeny, who during the last thirty years did not sit ten times in the confessional, and who during that time seldom celebrated mass, except on Sundays and holidays, and who never went through his diocese, except when he went sometimes to hold confirmation, and never looked after his clergy, except when formal complaints were made against them. (K: 26 Sept. 1872)

Conway even found one priest, 'perfectly imbecile in both mind and body', who had done no work for six years, and he had no difficulty in persuading Kirby and Cullen that the Church in Connaught was in need of religious revolution. He already knew from his informants what John MacEvilly was to finally confirm in 1881 when MacHale died, that the reforming decrees of Thurles had been totally ignored in most parts of the province of Tuam.

Because Cullen was so intent upon rectifying the religious malaise in the Irish Church, he showed little interest in the temporal needs of the people. His primary task was to use his legatine authority to revitalise the Church, and then to lead it out of its insularity to make it part of the *kulturkampf* of the Roman Catholic Church against evils like continental liberalism or British Protestantism. His zealousness in this mission was such that when, in the 1860s and 1870s, he had to deal with the massive emigration from Ireland, 'a furious exodus' in the words of Joseph Dixon, he told Propaganda that the blame for this tragedy lay with the Protestant government of Ireland and the Protestant landlords. (PFS, XXXIV, 1177-8, 1242-5) He showed little concern for the actual plight of the emigrants, whose flight was a reflection of the disastrous harvests of the time and the disturbance of trade by the American war rather than the injustices of the Protestant establishment. Where the government had in fact encouraged emigration was through the National System of Education, which made the young Irish restless. David Moriarty of Kerry, who was sick at heart over the suffering of the emigrants, explained to Lord Dufferin how important he considered this last factor:

> The National Schools have superseded the crowbar. Educated youths who have had the maps of the world before their eyes for years are not likely to sit down for life on a patch of potato garden.
>
> (PRONI, D 107/H/B/I: 23 Mar. 1868)

Moriarty's opinion was that education should prepare them even better for emigration, while the Church should develop its pastoral role to provide for the spiritual needs of the people. Joining him in this plea was Archbishop Joseph Lynch of Toronto, who described in detail to Cullen the kind of education needed by the Irish emigrant if he was to escape the bondage of the grog-shop and the slum in the New World. Cullen for ideological reasons showed little interest in new education to help the emigrants to survive amidst the challenges of a new society, or even in the provision of suitable spiritual guidance for those who were leaving. Such concern as he did exhibit for the plight of the people was concern in the abstract sense; his intention was to use it as an embarrassment to the government which he might refer to as he pressured the heretical administration about concessions in matters that really mattered to him, such as the obtaining of sectarian education, the ending of the Queen's Colleges, or the disestablishment of the Church of Ireland. Like any success-

ful general, Cullen never for a moment lost sight of his overall strategy. In 1851, in a long and thoughtful consideration
of emigration for Barnabo, Cullen indicated how even the
suffering of those who were leaving might ultimately contribute to the achieving of Catholic dominance in the land:

> Emigration is extraordinary; more than five thousand
> people leave every week for America and entire areas of
> the country are left abandoned. . . . Little by little all the
> great properties of the country are being broken up. In the
> end I believe the Catholics will gain — for up to the present
> time all land belonged to the Protestants, who had obtained
> it by way of confiscation, but at the public sales now being
> held the Catholics are buying a considerable part of the
> aforesaid land. (PM, III, 104: 10 Oct. 1851)

Probably Cullen's goal of a Catholic ascendancy religion
and culture dominant in all parts of Ireland will never be
achieved, and sectarian bitterness and warfare will pass only
when there is a return to the pluralist outlook characteristic
of the age of James Doyle and Daniel Murray. What will
impede this development is the real legacy of Paul Cullen, who,
as an 'agent of a great change', turned Ireland into 'an essentially Ultramontane country'. On the day following his death
the leading editorial in the *Times* showed that his Protestant
critics knew well what he had accomplished:

> Cullen was an interesting man precisely because he was the
> agent of a great change, and because he was admirably
> fitted to be the instrument of it. His ascetic temper cut
> him off from the cultivated, easy, tolerant ecclesiastics of
> a past generation. To him Rome was everything and he
> looked askance even at social pleasures which threatened
> to blur the line between her fold and that of heresy. To
> him obedience to . . . word of command was the first con-
> dition of order, and order the first necessity of a church.
> He was an ecclesiastical imperialist and he governed in a
> perpetual state of siege. Such a man could not have the
> play of mind or the broad sympathies which bring mental
> or moral influence, but the very narrowness of his view
> tended to give him fixity of aim, and to show him the
> shortest way to victory. . . . He will be chiefly remembered

as the prelate who made Ireland an essentially Ultramontane country.

Much of Ireland's tragic history of sectarian bitterness and warfare since Cullen's time has been a result of his striving for Catholic religious and cultural ascendancy in the land. Ireland's Protestants, confronted with the seemingly ever-expansionist Catholic confessional society which Cullen had so assiduously nurtured, resentfully withdrew into a ghetto of their own making, fearful of assimilation. They had no choice but to think in sectarian terms if they were to withstand a religious and cultural authority which, by Ultramontane definition, could never tolerate their harmonious existence because they were professors of spiritual error. After Paul Cullen any idea of a peaceful pluralistic Ireland, where there would be no threat of religious, cultural or (in our own day) political assimilation, was no longer looked for by Irish Protestants:

Once Ireland began to be regarded as a Catholic nation, there was built into this separate identity an element of puritanical exclusiveness very far from the vision of a Wolfe Tone, or a Thomas Davis, of an Ireland in which the different cultures would eventually be reconciled.

(Lyons, *Burden*, 17)

Select Bibliography

This work is almost completely based on the manuscripts referring to Paul Cullen which are to be found in Rome in the archives of the Irish College, St Paul's Without the Walls and Propaganda Fide. In Dublin use was made of the Dublin Archdiocesan Archives in Clonliffe College. Sources are referred to by the symbols indicated.

MANUSCRIPT SOURCES

AA	Armagh Archives: Curtis Papers
BM	British Museum, London (now British Library) Additional Manuscripts: Gladstone Papers
Bodl.	Bodleian Library, Oxford: Clarendon Papers
BS	St Paul's Basilica Without the Walls: Bernard Smith Papers
BV	Irish College, Rome: Cullen Papers (bound volume)
C	Irish College, Rome: Cullen Papers
CA	Cashel Archdiocesan Archives: Cullen Papers (NLI, microfilm)
DAA	Dublin Archdiocesan Archives: Cullen Papers
K	Irish College, Rome: Kirby Papers
NK	Irish College, Rome: New Kirby Papers
NLI	National Library of Ireland, Dublin, Lucas Papers, Larcom Papers, Monsell Papers
PFA	Propaganda Fide Archives, Rome: *Acta*
PFL	Propaganda Fide Archives, Rome: *Lettere e decreti*
PFS	Propaganda Fide Archives, Rome: *Scritture riferite nei congressi Irlanda*
PRONI	Public Record Office of Northern Ireland: Clogher Papers, Dufferin Papers
SPO	State Paper Office, Dublin Castle: Rebellion Papers

PRINTED MANUSCRIPT SOURCES

Letters	*Pastoral Letters and Other Writings of Cardinal Cullen, Archbishop of Dublin*, ed. P. F. Moran, 3 vols, Dublin 1882
PM	Peadar Mac Suibhne, *Paul Cullen and his Contemporaries, 1820-1902*, 5 vols, Naas 1961-77

SECONDARY PRINTED SOURCES

Akenson, D. H., *The Irish Education Experiment*, London 1970

The Anti-Protestantism of the Irish Executive Government Exposed, Dublin 1850

An Authentic Report of the Discussion which took place at Downpatrick 22-30 April, 1828, on Six of the Points of Controversy between the Church of England and the Church of Rome, Belfast 1829

Bane, Liam, 'The Life and Career of John MacEvilly, 1816-1902' (MA thesis, University College, Galway, 1979)

Bowen, Desmond, *The Protestant Crusade in Ireland, 1800-70*, Dublin 1978

Bowen, Desmond, *Souperism: Myth or Reality?*, Cork 1971

Broderick, J. F., 'The Holy See and the Irish Movement for the Repeal of the Union with England, 1829-1847', *Analecta Gregoriana* LV (Rome 1951)

Butler, Charles, *Historical Memoirs Respecting the English, Irish and Scottish Catholics from the Reformation to the Present Time*, 3rd ed., 4 vols, London 1822

Complete Catholic Directory, ed. W. J. Battersby (London 1836-66)

Corish, Patrick, 'Cardinal Cullen and Archbishop MacHale', *Irish Ecclesiastical Record* XCI (1959)

Corish, Patrick, 'Cardinal Cullen and the National Association of Ireland', *Reportorium Novum* III (1962)

Corish, Patrick, 'Gallicanism at Maynooth: Archbishop Cullen and the Royal Visitation of 1853' in *Studies in Irish History presented to R. Dudley Edwards*, Dublin 1979

Corish, Patrick, 'Political Problems, 1860-1878' in *History of Irish Catholicism*, V (II), Dublin 1967

Costigan, Richard F., *Rohrbacher and the Ecclesiology of Ultramontanism*, Rome 1980

Cullen, Louis, 'The Cultural Basis of Modern Irish Nationalism' (typescript, Board of Celtic Studies, University of Wales, 1979)

Cullen, Paul, *A Letter to the Catholic Clergy of the Archdiocese of Armagh*, Dublin 1850

Cullen, Paul, *Letter to the Clergy and Laity of the Diocese of Dublin on Some Recent Instances of Bigotry and Intolerance*, Dublin 1859

Cullen, Paul, *Publicam Disputationem de Theologia Universa et Historia Ecclesiastica*, Propaganda Fide, Rome 1828

Crolly, George, *Life of the Most Rev. Dr Crolly, Archbishop of Armagh*, Dublin 1851

D'Alton, E. A., *History of the Archdiocese of Tuam*, 2 vols, Dublin 1928

Derriana: A Collection of Papers Relative to the Siege of Derry and Illustrative of the Revolution of 1688, Derry 1794

de Vere, Aubrey, *The Church Establishment in Ireland, Illustrated Exclusively by Protestant Authorities*, London 1867; repr. in *Ireland's Church Question*, London 1868

Devoy, John, *Recollections of an Irish Rebel*, London 1929

Dixon, Joseph, *The Blessed Cornelius; or, Some Tidings of an Archbishop of Armagh who went to Rome . . . and did not return*, Dublin 1855

Downes, Charles, *The Constitution of Freemasonry; or, Ahiman Rezon*, Dublin 1807

Duffy, Charles Gavan, *My Life in Two Hemispheres*, 2 vols, London 1898

Edwards, R. D., *A New History of Ireland*, Dublin and Toronto 1972

Fitzpatrick, W. J., *Life of Bishop Doyle*, 2 vols, London 1888

Gladstone, W. E., *Vaticanism: An Answer to Replies and Reproofs*, London 1875

Godkin, James, *Ireland and her Churches*, London 1867

Healy, John, *Maynooth College, 1795-1895*, Dublin 1895

Knight, P., *Erris in the Irish Highlands and the Atlantic Railway*, Dublin 1836

Larkin, Emmet, 'The Devotional Revolution in Ireland, 1850-1875', *American Historical Review* LXXVII (1972)

Larkin, Emmet, *The Making of the Roman Catholic Church in Ireland, 1850-1860*, Chapel Hill 1980

Leadbeater, Mary, *The Leadbeater Papers*, 2 vols, London 1862

Leahy, Patrick, *Pastoral Letter*, Thurles [1862]

Leahy, Patrick, and Derry, John, *Statement on the University Question by the Archbishop of Cashel and the Bishop of Clonfert*, Dublin 1868

Lucas, Edward, *The Life of Frederick Lucas*, 2 vols, London 1886

Lyons, F. S. L., *The Burden of our History*, Belfast 1979

Lyons, F. S. L., *Ireland since the Famine*, London 1971

[MacCabe] 'A Catholic Clergyman', *A Memoir of Edward MacCabe, Archbishop of Dublin*, Dublin 1879

McCaffrey, L. J., 'Poets, Priests, Peasants, Politicians', *Victorian Studies* XXII (1979)

MacCormack, Henry, *Moral Secular Education for the Irish People versus Ultramontanist Instillment*, London 1879

McGhee, R.J., *Correspondence of R. J. McGhee with Most Rev. Dr Murray . . . on the Subject of Den's Theology*, London 1835

McGrath, Fergal, *Newman's University: Idea and Reality*, London 1951

MacNamee, J. J., *History of the Diocese of Ardagh*, Dublin 1954

McRoberts, David, *Modern Scottish Catholicism, 1878-1978*, Glasgow 1979

Mac Suibhne, Peadar, 'Ireland at the Vatican Council', *Irish Ecclesiastical Record* XCIII (1960)

Maher, James, *Observations on the Address Delivered by the President of Queen's College, Galway*, Dublin 1850

Mahony, F. S., *The Works of Father Prout*, ed. C. Kent, London 1881

Meagher, William, *Notices of the Life and Character of the Most Rev. Daniel Murray*, Dublin 1853

Molony, J. N., *The Roman Mould of the Australian Catholic Church*, Melbourne 1969

Moran, P. F., *The Catholics of Ireland under the Penal Laws of the Eighteenth Century*, London 1899

New Catholic Encyclopaedia

Newman, J. H., *Letter Addressed to His Grace the Duke of Norfolk on Occasion of Mr Gladstone's Recent Expostulation*, London 1875

Norman, E. R., *The Catholic Church and Ireland in the Age of Rebellion, 1859-1873*, London 1965

Nulty, Thomas, *Letter to Joseph Cowen, MP, on the State of Public Affairs in Ireland*, Dublin 1881

O'Connell, Daniel, *Correspondence with Rev. Dr Blake on Ecclesiastical Securities*, Dublin 1822

O'Connell, Philip, *The Diocese of Kilmore: Its History and Antiquities*, Dublin 1937

O'Farrell, Patrick, *The Catholic Church in Australia: A Short History, 1788-1967*, London 1969

[O'Keeffe] *Cardinal Cullen and the Parish Priest of Callan*, Kilkenny 1872

[O'Keeffe] Kirkpatrick, H. C., ed., *Report of the Action for Libel brought by Robert O'Keeffe against His Eminence Cardinal Cullen*, London 1874

O'Laverty, James, *An Historical Account of the Diocese of Down and Connor*, 5 vols. Dublin 1878-95

O'Malley, Thaddeus, *Home Rule on the Basis of Federalism*, London 1873

O'Malley, Thaddeus, *A Sketch of the State of Popular Education in Holland, Prussia, Belgium and France*, London 1840

O'Reilly, Bernard, *John MacHale: His Life, Times and Correspondence*, 2 vols, New York 1890

O'Sullivan, Mortimer, *Correspondence with Most Rev. Dr Murray connected with the subject of Den's Theology*, London 1835

Otway, Caesar, *Sketches in Erris and Tyrawly*, Dublin 1841

Otway, Caesar, *Tour in Connaught*, Dublin 1839

Parliamentary Papers, *Report of Select Committees of the House of Commons and the House of Lords on the State of Ireland*, 1825, VII-IX

Purcell, E. S., *Life of Cardinal Manning*, 2 vols, London 1895

Report of a Meeting of the Protestant Inhabitants of the County of Armagh Assembled in the Court House of Armagh, 24 January, 1827, Newry 1827

Rhodes, Anthony, 'Mission to Ireland: The Persico Papers', *Encounter* (Feb. 1980)

Scrutator, *The Home Rule and Ultramontane Alliance*, London 1875

Scrutator, *Ultramontanism versus Education in Ireland: The Case of Fr O'Keeffe, Parish Priest, Shortly Stated*, London 1875

Steele, E. D., 'Cardinal Cullen and Irish Nationality', *Irish Historical Studies* XIX (1975)

Turpin, John, 'John Hogan and the Catholic Religious Revival', *Maynooth Review* V (1979)

Ultramontane Intrigues Exposed: being a Report on the Irish Intermediate Education Act ... by a Committee of the United Presbyterian Presbytery of Ireland, Edinburgh 1879

Walsh, Katherine, 'The First Vatican Council, the Papal State and the Irish Hierarchy: Recent Researches on the Pontificate of Pope Pius IX', *Studies* LXXI (1982)

Walsh, Katherine, 'Two Letters of Cardinal Cullen, 1871 and 1873', *Collectanea Hibernica* XVI (1973)

Whyte, John, 'The Appointment of Catholic Bishops in Nineteenth-Century Ireland', *Catholic Historical Review* XLVIII (1962)

Whyte, John, *The Independent Irish Party, 1850-59*, Oxford 1958

Whyte, John, 'The Influence of the Catholic Clergy on Elections in Nineteenth-Century Ireland', *English Historical Review* LXXV (1960)

Whyte, John, 'Political Problems, 1850-1860' in *History of Irish Catholicism*, V (II-III), Dublin 1967

Wood-Martin, W. G., *History of Sligo, County and Town*, 3 vols, Dublin 1882-92

NEWSPAPERS
Armagh Guardian
Belfast Newsletter
Cork Daily Herald
Dublin Evening Mail
Dublin Evening Packet
Dublin Evening Post
Freeman's Journal
Irish Times
Londonderry Standard
Mayo Constitution
Newry Telegraph
Times
Tuam Herald

Index

Dorrian, Patrick, Bp Down & Connor (1865–85), 188–91, 211
Doyle, James, Bp Kildare & Leighlin (1819–34), 4–5, 8, 17, 48, 211, 241, 292, 298
Dublin city, 158–65
Dublin Castle (Irish government), 112, 138–9, 142–5, 160–3, 190
Dublin Evening Mail, Protestant viewpoint, 172; unfavourable view of Cullen and Ultramontanism, 120, 130, 137, 141, 195–6, 268–9; praises Cullen's opponents, 218–19, 239, 253; assessments of Cullen, 138, 282–4
Dublin Evening Post, 107, 116, 140, 194–5
Duffy, Charles Gavan, ix, 246–50, 252

Eardley, Sir Culling, 199
Ebrington, Lord, 51
Ecclesiastical Titles Act (1851), 118–19, 126, 129, 220, 246
education, primary, see National System, Model Schools; university, see Catholic University, Maynooth College, Queen's Colleges, Trinity College
Edward, Prince of Wales, 133, 139, 142–4
Egan, Cornelius, Bp Ardfert (1824–56), 104, 217
Emancipation, Catholic, 5, 8–11, 18, 75, 85, 112, 185–6
emigration, 277, 297–8
Ennis, John, 52, 110, 127
Evangelical missions, see proselytism
Exeter Hall, 104, 171–2

Feeny, Thomas, Adm./Bp Killala (1839–73), 78, 224, 296
Fenians, 168, 191, 219–20, 231–2, 238, 254–5, 266–72, 274
Fitzgerald, Andrew, 4, 5
Foran, Nicholas, Bp Waterford (1837–55), 39–40, 214
Forde, Laurence, ix, 18, 129, 289, 292; secretarial and administrative work, 31, 124, 158, 236, 240
Franchi, Alessandro, Cardinal, 147, 232
Franciscans, 38

Fransoni, Cardinal, 60, 89, 93, 94, 95, 96, 164, 169, 177, 257
Freeman's Journal, 107–8, 115, 140–1, 156, 284
Freemasonry, Cullen's obsession with, 13–14, 16, 142, 145, 239, 255, 269, 278–9
French, Edward, Bp Kilmacduagh (1824–52), 170
Furlong, Thomas, Bp Ferns (1856–75), 235

Gallicanism, ideology: papal view of, 13–14; in Irish College, Rome, 23, 25–6; in Irish College, Paris, 259–62; in Ireland, nature of, 30–43, 223; in Maynooth, 256–9, 280; Ultramontanist suspicions of and opposition to, 86, 90, 98, 205–8, 211, 213–14, 218, 221, 234–5, 276, 280
'traditional' Gallicanism: in Ireland, before 1850, 32–40, 42–3, 150, 177; Murray, 48–65, 109–10, 120–1; after 1850, 121, 129, 182–5, 188, 211, 220; O'Keeffe, 235–44; see also 'Castle bishops'
'new' Gallicanism: in Ireland, before 1850, 32, 36–43, 65–72; MacHale, 72–84; after 1850, 150, 181, 211, 255–62; see also nationalist bishops
Garibaldi, Giuseppe, 13, 90, 131, 190, 266, 269, 270, 276–7
George IV, 5
Gillooly, Laurence, Bp Elphin (1858–95), 199, 202, 225–8, 259
Gladstone, William E., 148, 155–7, 178, 195–7, 207–10, 271, 272
Godkin, James, 178
Grant, Bp Thomas, 152
Gray, Sir John, 246
Green, T., 43
Gregory XVI, 9, 11–15, 21, 24, 73, 90, 279

Hally, Jeremiah, 296
Hamilton, John, 50
Hickie, James, 221–3
Higgins, William, Bp Ardagh (1829–53), 22, 51, 63, 65–8, 83, 92–3, 170, 179, 224